The Working American Bulldog

The Working American Bulldog

Dave Putnam

Bulldog Press

Published by Bulldog Press, 1101 Canada Road, Woodside, California, 94062.
Bulldog Press web site address: http://www.americanbulldogger.com/

Printed in the United States of America on acid-free paper.

Author: Dave Putnam
Editor and Designer: Jerome Edwards
Front Cover Photograph: Rob Boyd's The Hammer taken by Martha Putnam
Back Cover Photographs: MGK Gator Red, Omar Van Mueller's Nikko, Joshua's Caleb

ISBN 0-9672710-0-2

Table of Contents

ABs are not for everyone

Most American Bulldogs are canine gladiators. Like many dogs, ABs can be trained for a variety of circumstances. However, we must never forget the awesome power of these dogs. ABs are products of hundreds of years of breeding with one goal in mind - to defeat man or animal. Whether they attack, pin, catch, or hold, ABs are ready and willing to fight. So before you purchase an AB, think about the following:

Owning an AB can be an awesome responsibility. To properly care for an AB the owner must be aware of the typical AB's desire to fight. Only when you accept the AB's desire to fight will you be able to properly care for it. A responsible owner learns to channel their AB's fight and prey drives. This can be done through play, protection training, or hunting. An irresponsible owner ignores them, or worse, tries to suppress them.

It is not uncommon for naïve owners and newcomers to ask, "Why does my Bulldog attack cats, raccoons, deer, or dogs?" However, the better question is why would he not. ABs have been bred to hunt, catch or bait animals not to herd. Never forget, in any situation, your AB can be lethal when a strange animal approaches.

Generally speaking, ABs can be very aggressive. They want to fight. Whether it is a tug rope, a Schutzhund sleeve, a wild boar, or a suspicious stranger knocking at the door, they want a piece of it. ABs are genetically programmed this way in much the same way as a good Retriever is genetically programmed to retrieve. They are gladiators by birthright. Training can control behavior within certain circumstances but it will never change the AB's basic nature.

ABs will behave like fighters when left to their own volition. It is your responsibility to control your AB. Don't believe you can teach him morally what is right or wrong. Whenever you are in doubt, keep your AB on his leash or chain or fenced in a yard.

While all dog breeds have some similarities they also have differences. ABs are not Labs or Pointers. They are not German or Belgian Shepherds. They are fighting dogs. They were not bred to point or retrieve. They were not bred to herd or to scent for drugs. Instead, they were bred for combat - to fight in the pits, and to hunt or catch animals.

It is true you can train an AB to retrieve and track. You can train them for police work and herding. But never forget, in the end, you will only have a fighting dog that can retrieve, track, or herd, not the other way around. So if you want a police dog, retriever or herding dog than buy a police dog, retriever or herding dog. If you want a fighter buy an AB.

Whether you decide to train for sport, hunting or protection, please be responsible. The last thing we need is for the AB to be banned like their closest cousins the American Pit Bull Terrier.

Lastly, if you decide to own one, be prepared. Know your dog's limitations and your own.

Good Luck and Good Bulldogging!

- The Editor

Acknowledgement

I would like to thank the American Bulldoggers who sent me photographs and spent countless hours on the phone and in person sharing their knowledge and expertise on the greatest American working breed. Without the help and support of my wife Martha this book could never have been written. Finally, I would like to acknowledge Bully, the dog who not only inspired this literary effort but serves as a constant source of inspiration for me in my primary career as an animal sculptor. When trying to capture the spirit of a courageous and cunning predator in stainless steel, I have only to look to her for guidance. Bully actually helped me make the sculptures below by digging roots out of the ground and finding objects in the woods. The objects she found I used for raw ingredients.

Nikko - Schutzhund III, AD, OFA

Why An American Bulldog?

The world of dog breeding has undergone a terrible change since the advent of dog shows 150-years ago, especially in the USA. At one time most domestic dogs were bred for a functional purpose, potential breeding candidates were given on the job performance tests and those that excelled were mated to each other and each generation got a little bit better. It was survival of the fittest and dogs evolved the way all animals did. Not only were dogs bred for hunting, herding and guarding, toy dogs were bred to be superior house pets. At one time little dogs were easy to housebreak, easy to train, had calm loving dispositions and lived long healthy lives. Show breeding fostered by organizations like the American Kennel Club (AKC) and its British equivalent have changed all that. Show breeders have focused primarily on coat color, coat texture, coat length and dubious confirmation characteristics known as breed type. Temperament, working qualities and physical soundness have been allowed to atrophy.

The original Bulldog resembled a performance AB or an ABPT, with long legs and a working length muzzle.

Breed type is any easily visible physical trait that makes one breed look different from another. A show breeder seeks to amplify these differences so that his dogs appear more 'purebred.' If the original Dachshund had legs that were half as long as most other dogs to make him a better underground hunter then a show breeder would want legs a tenth as long. It makes no difference that legs that short make the modern Dachshund ineffective at going under-

ground or simply walking a few yards: he looks different, he's 'typey.'

The complete and utter show version of the American Bulldog (AB) is the English Bulldog also known as the sour mug, the current state of this show dog illustrates my point perfectly. About two centuries ago both breeds of Bulldogs looked the same, they had long legs and strong healthy bodies. A modern performance bred AB or an American Pit Bull Terrier (APBT) still look this way. Their ancestors left England before the advent of show breeding and have since been bred by farmers in the American South who use ABs to catch cattle or wild hogs and people in all parts of the US that still fight APBTs in pits.

The original Bulldog had only a slightly shorter muzzle than today's ABPT.

True performance bred ABs and genuine fighting Pit Bulls are the modern equivalent to the working Bulldogs of medieval and renaissance Europe. If we eliminate Pit Bulls less than 45-pounds, ABs over 90, pendulous lips and coat color, these two breeds of dog are difficult or impossible to tell apart from outward appearance. Muzzle length averages four-inches but varies from individual to individual. The bite is either tight undershot, tight scissors or an even mesh. Small ears and eyes present as little surface area as possible to an enemy, loose skin is on the throat, everywhere else there is tight skin. This is what real Bulldogs looked like then and now, not the jowly monstrosity commonly called Bulldog. The only kernel of truth to the sour mug caricature is that the highly specialized, smaller, bull baiting dog was probably uniformly undershot since this would tilt his nose back for better breathing when pressed against a bovine cheek or snout. The specialized bull-baiter may have had a slightly shorter muzzle than the other types of Bulldog, but in period literature when that shortness is qualified, it is described as being short like a tiger not short like a monkey.

Performance ABs have working length muzzles and more importantly - Bulldog tenacity.

In early industrial England the unfortunate tightly built, medium muzzled, working Bulldogs were handed over to show breeders who, over the course of a little more than a century, transformed these dogs into something only remotely resembling the original bull-baiter. These changes have been (laughingly) justified in the functional terms of bull baiting, an ancient and bloody sport where bull and dog meet in combat.

The truth about these bizarre mutations is that at the turn of the 18th century English Bulldogs were crossed to Pugs and inbred for freakish traits. Ironically, the early stage of this transformation was probably the correct way to modify the performance Bulldog into a family pet and protector. Since the dogs were no longer used for baiting, modifications were in order. The early sour mug stage produced yard dogs that resembled whip tailed Boxers. These were healthy creatures that could live up to fifteen-years. They could out run normal dogs, leap high in the air to catch a ball, plunge into lakes and swim for hours. Early stage sour mugs could catch bulls or wild boar in cool weather just as a modern performance bred Boxer can catch large herbivores under similar circumstances. England has mostly cool weather. This was responsible dog breeding.

Irresponsible show breeders created the later stages of the sour mug mutation. They weren't even honest, explaining genetic butchery in terms of the ancient blood sport rather than the show ring. Legs got shorter and shorter, this

was supposed to allow the dog to withstand a fall from a great height if it were tossed in the air by a bull. The show breeders shortened the English Bulldog's muzzle until the nose resided somewhere south of the eyeballs, this was supposed to allow the dogs to breathe better while holding a bull. In reality it made it tough for the dogs to breathe period. The tail also disappeared, justification - a tail is excess weight not needed for bull baiting. The hind quarters were shrunk down in size until they became so spindly that today's sour mugs are not able to outrun a man and are 90% dysplastic, justification - more weight savings. The face and body were made so wrinkly sour mugs look like prunes. Supposedly bull's blood would be channeled away from the dogs eyes by all these wrinkles and he could see better in the frenzy of a bull bait, never mind that this was not a problem for real Bulldogs. If a little blood splattered in their eyes real Bulldogs simply blinked.

Early sour mugs were still functional.

Justifying these changes in functional terms is absurd. Consider the notion that short legs allow a dog to withstand a fall from a great height, then picture a Dachshund, a modern English Bulldog and a Greyhound perched on a high wall. Which dog could most easily jump down and land without being hurt?

Some of today's AKC sour mug breeders have this fantasy that their Bulldogs are actually more capable of chasing and catching a wild bull than the original working Bulldogs because of the 'improvements' they have bred in. These breeders act as though bull baits were performed in some weird dimension far removed from the real world.

If you go to an AKC show and watch the English Bulls you will notice some handlers placing oxygen masks around their dog's faces to give them enough strength to walk slowly around a show ring. Often they have to inject their dogs with cortisone to hold their limbs together to make this same short trip around the show ring. If one of these poor creatures were to fall more then a foot off the ground it risks shattering its leg bones. The list of genetic diseases that plague the AKC Bulldog is staggering. Today's sour mug can not breed without artificial insemination. It can not give birth without cesarean section. When I told our local veterinarian I was going to buy an American Bulldog he got very excited because he thought I meant the AKC breed. "Wow," he said, "maybe I can afford that trip to Hawaii after all."

Early sour mugs were only moderately wrinkled.

This doesn't mean that modern sour mugs aren't good pets if you can over look the health problems or get one from a non-traditional breeder. A friend of mine has two sour mugs and loves them as much as life itself. She says that just looking at their friendly wrinkled faces makes her feel warm inside. Her dogs require very little exercise and are easy to care for. I tried to talk her into switching to an AB but she balked when I said our dogs require a two-mile walk every day. Deep in his heart the sour mug is still a Bulldog and there is hope for this breed. A few years ago England changed the breed standard to allow for less exaggerated features. A new strain has arisen overseas called the altered structure English Bulldog. Intermediate sour mugs can be healthy and long-lived if kept under 60-pounds.

I trace four stages of decline in the physical capabilities of the English Bulldog:

1) The early sour mug or Philo-Kuon resembled a working Boxer. This Bulldog had no health problems to speak of, if bred properly. It could have baited bulls and performed other hardcore working tasks. This should be the goal of today's Johnson AB breeders, working ability should never be sacrificed for breed type.

2) The intermediate sour mug resembled an Olde Bulldogge or a small typey Johnson AB. This Bulldog would likely have had no health problems if bred properly and moderate health problems if not well bred. It could have lived a long healthy life.

3) The late sour mug resembled the Mack Truck Bulldog. This Bulldog would likely have had moderate health problems no matter how well bred and possibly major health problems if not well bred.

4) The modern sour mug is plagued with health problems and genetic defects, with an average life span of only 5-years. Structural limitations mean they are incapable of working tasks.

This is not to say that every American Bulldog is as capable as a 17th century performance type English Bulldog, less than 10% could make such a claim. A higher percentage of APBTs could be elevated to this status but the number would still be a minority for mental if not physical reasons. Most ABs are as show bred as an average AKC breed and roughly as functional as a typical AKC American Staffordshire Bullterrier. There are many shades of gray in working ability. If white represents zero working ability then a sour mug English Bulldog is spotlessly, bleached, snowy white. If black represents extreme working ability then fighting Pit Bulls, serious hog hunting American Bulldogs, Iditarod sled dogs and racing Greyhounds are glistening ebony. ABs as a whole include every shade of gray, a few black diamonds and a few pure white losers. Good home guardians don't have to be solid black but a nice dark gray is a must. There is a tiny minority of Doctor Frankenstein breeders who don't understand the concept of a Johnson type AB and are creating freakish creatures with bodies like bloated AKC Bullmastiffs and heads like giant English Bulldogs. On my gradation scale such a beast would be a dirty white nonfunctional mess, almost as bad as any canine on the planet, nearly tied with the modern English Bulldog in last place and sharing a five year expected life span.

Extreme Athletic   **Moderate Athletic**

Moderate Athletic   **Less Athletic**

In all fairness one must admit that it wouldn't be wise to be in the same yard with even a lame dysfunctional extreme Bulldoggy AB if he really wanted to bite. They can hobble pretty fast. A few modern English Bulldog sour mugs could put the hurt on anyone and are capable of guarding a small yard.

Most AKC breeds are not as bad off as the English Bulldog because there is a direct ratio between unsoundness and show breeding. The Chesapeake Bay Retriever may belong to the AKC but most people who breed them also hunt ducks and do little if any showing so their dogs are still functional. The popular breeds are all hurting though, once upon a time AKC St. Bernards, Newfoundlands and German Shepherds were all sturdy dogs, now they are over 50% dysplastic and bred for type.

Many of these AKC breeds are experiencing a renaissance due to the introduction of OFA hip testing (a technique that combats dysplasia), CERF testing for eye disorders and other scientific screening processes. Many American breeders are drifting away from pure show breeding by entering their dogs in obedience trials. The AKC should be given credit for sponsoring these trials. Recently the AKC has instituted hunting tests and field trials for Retrievers, Pointers and Spaniels. This apparent shift away from the show culture is still fumbling and tentative. AKC has had to provide experienced hunters as stand-ins for their field trials because many of the show owners have never fired a shotgun before.

Turbo's Penn-hip is .25 and he is OFA Good.

Some AKC breeders are even starting from scratch by abandoning their American bloodlines and importing dogs from Europe. If you look at the ads for German Shepherds in current dog magazines you will see these proud boasts: "Our dogs are straight out of Germany from working border patrol K-9s and Schutzhund sport dogs. Hips OFA certified." Sadly, you will also see ads that boast of pure show backgrounds.

ABs are as true as the Red, White and Blue. Photo - Michelle LeNoir

Most show standards contain phrases like, "A dog should have a look of courage in his eyes" or "His expression should denote intelligence and willingness to work hard." The pure show breeders have a fantasy where a judge can glance into a dog's eyes and tell if he will lay down his life for his master. Since their breeding stock is never tested in a real world situation where courage or intelligence is needed, there is no one to contradict them.

I know a lady who breeds show poodles, she insists that the breed's foo-foo image is undeserved and that her dogs could beat up Pit Bulls if called upon. She says this with a straight face. I hope she's kidding and not clinically insane. The problem with her dogs is not that they can't beat up Pit Bulls, it's that they are so barky, hyper and nervous they are useless as house pets.

I know another breeder of standard Poodles who wins obedience trials with her dogs, they can't beat up Pit Bulls either but they

13

have very steady nerves. They could be trained to do narcotics detection or a host of real world tasks. I would be proud to own one of her dogs and I'm sure they would be great watchdogs or alarm dogs.

What if you want more than just an alarm dog? There is no need to go into FBI statistics to realize that our country is still a dangerous place despite the lowering crime rate. Every now and then the media will report some new act of savagery that heightens our collective awareness of this problem. Several years ago in the San Francisco Bay Area (where we live) a psychopath broke into a little girl's slumber party and brutally murdered her. This incident received national attention and there is now a foundation named after her, yet this sort of thing happens every day without much media attention.

After you've read the section of this book that deals with breeders and specific ABs that have been protection trained for the street, try and imagine what would have happened to that psychopath if one of these dogs had been in that little girl's bedroom that night. I'm sure even the most fervent believer in non-violence would find satisfaction in what one of these Bulldogs would have done to that piece of human garbage.

Yet this is not an aggressive breed, it is (ideally) a courageous breed. A good AB will lick the milk moustache off your toddler's face one instant and fight to the death to protect him the next. This claim is not made because anyone can see a spark of courage in a Bulldog's face. It is based on 1600-years of history that I will present in the following section and what many ABs are like today.

There are other reasons to acquire a working AB besides personal protection, protection sport, weight pulling or catching cattle and hogs. Many people want one for the same reason they want a Border Collie, a working Bloodhound or a field-trials bred Labrador Retriever - any dog bred for a functional purpose makes a better pet than a show dog.

Unfortunately the show culture has made major inroads in the American Bulldog community and many, perhaps most ABs, are being bred for the show ring. There are also breeders selling puppies to pet shops, something the fancy was able to prevent for many years. This is called puppy milling, the mass production of inferior specimens, dogs bred only to turn

a profit. There are also careless backyard breeders who are breeding whatever is handy and has some sort of pedigree to indicate that it is an American Bulldog. This is called scatter breeding, an affliction especially dangerous when done to any guardian breed because man aggressive dogs can be bred to shy/high strung ones and fear biters can result.

Never buy a Bulldog from anyone other than a reputable breeder who can point to both parents on site, demonstrate calm temperaments, structural soundness, and excellent health, plus give you a lineage that shows ancestors of similar constitution. If a bitch is bred to another kennel's stud you should be able to verify that fact and like what you see at both kennels. After reading this book a potential AB owner will know enough to judge the working or domestic qualities of a given breeding pair or kennel. It is my fervent hope that the reader will then bypass puppy millers and show breeders who aren't producing even tempered working Bulldogs and help crush this inroad that threatens one of the last truly functional American breeds.

John D. & Mildred Johnson. Mr. Johnson is the primary architect of the American Bulldog. He actually coined the term "American Bulldog."

I would like to end this section by backtracking a little on show breeding. In Europe and parts of South America, show dogs are required to pass functional tests before they can receive a confirmation award. These tests include field and herding trials, running great distances, temperament tests, obstacle courses, hurtles, protection and obedience work. Breeders in these countries have proven that it is possible to produce dogs with beautiful colors and striking appearances that are still functional if the show ring is not the only criteria for selecting breeding stock.

Dog shows originated in England for the purpose of adding beauty to hunting dogs. The first show dogs were all used in the field by sportsmen. Experienced trainers can spot a working confirmation and to some degree see structural soundness. A race track Greyhound expert can look at a narrow chested, super skinny, delicate, show Greyhound and see that it will lose a race against its performance bred cousin. Such an expert can not look at a group of racing Greyhounds and predict the winner on the basis of confirmation.

The AKC should hire race track veterans and use them to judge show Greyhounds. The resulting dogs would still not win against the performance strain but they would leave any neighborhood dog in the dust and you wouldn't have any rabbits nearby. Not all American dog shows are distasteful.

American Bulldog shows often feature judges who are expert in protection sport, hog catching or weight pulling. AB shows usually include protection sport trials, obedience, weight pull, tug of war contests, timed foot races and often feature hog catching Bulldogs in the show ring that have earned formal catch dog titles. At AB shows most show champions also compete on a physical level. The current trend of Irondog triathlons that combine three grueling performance events into a single grand competition is especially tantalizing.

Many reputable AB breeders seek type as well as performance, knowing full well that they're giving up some raw ability. These breeders love extra wide massive heads, heavy bone and overdeveloped bulging muscles, as long as hips are X-rayed and declared dysplasia free, the dog has good structure, good speed and a working title. Some bodybuilders can win professional strongman competitions and others can't. Blocky confirmation champion American Bulldogs that are performance tested are the ones that can. Thank goodness there will always be a few diehard AB breeders that will not take type into consideration and produce a pure performance phenotype to breed back to when type becomes exaggerated and health problems start to emerge.

There's a big difference between bear hunting in America and bear baiting in Old England.

Bear baiting in Old England

Throughout the ages, Bulldogs have been used to eliminate pests.

History of the Bulldog

The story of the American Bulldog begins in the snowy mountains of Tibet, where the original Molossus or Mastiff type dogs appeared. They descended from the big, broad snouted, Tibetan wolf, which still exists in northern India and Tibet, where it is known as the Woolly Wolf. The Chinese were probably the first people to develop true Mastiffs. Their literature contains references to big, short muzzled and broad mouthed hunting dogs around 1121 BC. I believe Mastiffs had been in existence several thousand years before that time. These dogs were used to hunt dangerous animals like tigers, wild boar or bears, animals that were inevitably slower than traditional game and may be as likely to turn and fight as run. The hallmark of these canine monsters has always been their great size, relative slowness (compared to Greyhounds and the larger terriers) and exceptional ability to defend themselves.

Tibetan Mastiffs are the foundation for all Molossers.

The Chinese may also have used Mastiffs in staged fights between wild animals, other dogs and sometimes men. Even today the exaggerated features of the Chinese fighting dog or Shar-pei bears a strong resemblance to the excesses of its distant cousin the Neapolitan Mastiff, which also has a heritage of gladiatorial combat. The non-exaggerated functional ancestors of these widely separated Mastiff breeds probably looked even more alike.

When citing historical records and trying to guess how the real world Molosser looked it is important to remember the human tendency to embellish. The Mastiffs Marco Polo actually saw in China were not the size of donkeys, unless the donkeys were under a 100-pounds.

Rosa and Crib were considered the ideal English Bulldog through much of the 19th century. They were much closer to their ancient Molosser ancestors than modern sour mugs. Rosa and Crib could have baited bulls, worked as farm dogs or guarded British estates. It was a huge mistake for the British Bulldog breeders to abandon this ideal, and remove this painting from their standard.

The Asian Mastiff reached the Levant by way of India at the dawn of civilization. The Assyrians introduced them throughout the Mediterranean around 800 BC when their empire was at its peak. By this time Mastiffs may have been in the Mid-East for over two thousand years since archaeologists have found drawings of them on Egyptian monuments dating to 3000 BC. Stone carvings of the Assyrian variety show a brawny, shorthaired and tight skinned dog, not jowly and sloppy like modern Mastiffs. Some carvings show Mastiffs as large as lions. The carvers were taking artistic license. Compared to today's English Mastiff the ancient Molosser was less than half as big and built like a tight, heavy-boned, Pit Bull. No doubt these dogs were tight internally as well, limbs fitting tightly in sockets without the dysplasia of today's show Mastiffs.

Alexander the Great brought more Mastiffs into Greece from India around 333 BC. Greece remained the center of Mastiff breeding for 700-years until English dogs became predominant. In appearance and perhaps temperament the closest modern dog to the Assyrian\Greek Mastiff would be a Swinford Bandog, which is a ferocious combination of game Neapolitan Mastiff, the most athletic English Mastiff available and Pit Bull. Swinfords have large (but not huge) muscular bodies with tight medium sized Pit Bull type heads.

Stubby - an American Bull breed and a US Army war dog in WW I, serving in 18 battles, eventually promoted to sergeant.

No one knows when the English first developed Mastiffs, most historians think the original stock was brought over by Phoenician traders who got them from Greece or the Mid-East around the 6th century BC. Julius Caesar may have encountered English Mastiffs when he made his initial assault on England in 55 BC. Legend has it that he was so impressed with the ferocity of the brawny war dogs that were then being used by Celtic tribes that he took some back with him. These dogs may have presented a real hindrance to Caesar's full-scale invasion in 54 BC.

Purportedly the Celts had bred and trained them to bite the noses of cavalry horses. Ancient Celtic Bulldogs would hold on until the horse bucked and threw its rider. Even today if an AB attacks a horse he will usually bite its nose. Modern ABs and Pits capable of immobilizing a horse in this manner will weigh between 45 and 100-pounds. The ancient British dogs were probably the same size. Of course by the standards of the day these were huge dogs. Today we know them by their Latin name - Pugnaces. Because of its manner of attack we can say with confidence that the Pugnaces was a true Bulldog, perhaps the world's first.

The Pugnaces was either light brown with a black mask or dark brindle, colors similar to today's Bullmastiff. The Pugnaces was much tighter and leaner though. If we could bring one back in a time machine people would mistake it for a large Pit Bull or a small Bandog.

Some Celtic tribes also bred their Pugnaces to hunt wild boar, which was considered a magical animal in ancient Britain. A boar hunting Pugnaces would have been controllable enough to run with hounds. It was a catch dog, not a trailer. The hounds would have counted on the Pugnace for protection against bad boar or bear. The hunt was a mystical and religious experience for the ancient Celts. There is evidence that they intentionally bred wild (or semi-wild) hogs for aggressiveness and speed, perhaps to better test their dogs and provide more sport. I find this interesting because some modern AB and APBT breeders do the same thing.

By 300 AD the Romans had recognized the superiority of the British dogs for use in gladiatorial contests. The Emperor established a special officer called the Procurator Cynogie who operated out of Winchester. His job was to find the toughest and most belligerent fighting dogs in Britain and ship them off to Rome.

They shipped two Mastiff types: 1) A lighter dog (well under 100-pounds) for combat in the Coliseum against bulls, wolves and small cats. 2) A heavier dog (100-pounds or slightly less) to go against bears, big cats, and exotic challengers like hyenas. These dogs did not usually go directly against wild animals in pits the way they would later in England. Instead, they were teamed up with a special kind of human gladiator called a Bestiarri, who fought only against beasts. In effect the men and dogs hunted dangerous game in a confined space with spectators watching. Legend has it that the British dogs could beat all comers.

Bulldogs were fought against lions in the Roman coliseum.

There is evidence that the Romans actually referred to the lighter dog as a Bulldog. It is reported that they were able to break the neck of an ox and were transported in iron cages. The Romans so loved these dogs (both kinds) that they quit importing fighting dogs from Greece, which had been their main source for centuries. This must have been a blow to the Greek dog breeders because even the name Molossus is derived from a region in northern Greece called Molossia, which is named for a tribe called the Molossi.

Today there are still two kinds of Mastiffs in Italy. These are descendants of the ancient English Pugnaces: The 90 to 150-pound Neapolitan and the under 100-pound Cane Corso. The Cane Corso is still used by Italian farmers as a working Bulldog and must share genetic links with the English Bulldog, American Bulldog and Pit Bull.

Several centuries later a new Mastiff type reached British shores, brought to Europe by a nomadic people called the Alanis, who had been chased out of Asia by the Huns. The Alanis wandered around Europe and finally settled in what is now called Albania, a region not far from Molossia. Their dogs eventually became known as Alants or Alaunts in England around the Middle Ages. Alaunts have been described as having a short face, a large head, white in color (often with dark eye patches) and were excellent for hunting wild boar with bay hounds. This is the second type of Bulldog to be developed in Britain. The above description perfectly fits our modern AB. I believe the Alaunt is the most direct ancestor to the AB, APBT, sour mug, Spanish Bulldog and Dogo Argentino.

Spanish Bulldogs were descended from English Bulldogs and may be an ancestor of American Bulldogs.

There are direct descendants of the Alaunt alive today that are less well known. In the mountainous regions between Turkey and India there are big white Mastiffs that are still used to bait bears. I'm sure these dogs could be passed off as American Bulldogs or large white Pit Bulls. Harlequin Great Danes get their white color from Alaunt ancestors (crossed to sight hounds) and are still known as Alanos in Italy. In history books the ancient Alaunt is always described as being incredibly huge because we have references like Chaucer's in 1390 describing an English coat of arms:

Aboute his char ther wenten white Alaunts
Twenty and mo, as gret as any stere
To hunten at the leon or the dere.

A little common sense and comparison to modern working Bull breeds tells us that these ancient descriptions of Bulldogs the size of steers were exaggerations. There are songs from the old South (19th century) that also talk about ABs as big as cattle.

All regions of Western Europe had their own strain of light Mastiff by the medieval period. They were called butcher's dog or some variant of bull-biter. In England they were called

'Alaunt of the butchery' until the 17th century when the word bull-dog first appeared in print. Around the turn of the 16th century the words Alaunt, butcher's dog (boocher's dogge) and bull-dog were probably used interchangeably. These dogs were used to catch and hold live-stock, thus making the butcher's job safer and easier. It is possible that from this pragmatic function the sport of bull baiting evolved or the sport's roots may lie directly in classical Rome since the Romans occupied Britain for 400-years.

What seems even more likely to me is that the Celts had developed light Mastiffs that could catch horses and cattle (a.k.a. Bulldogs) many centuries before they had even heard of the Romans. The Celts were known for main-taining huge herds of domestic cattle as well as catching wild cattle from the forest. There is a Celtic object of art from the 1st century BC made from hammered metal that shows a dead bull, two dead Pugnaces, a live one and a man with a knife. Clearly this depicts a butcher and his Bulldogs.

If they had butchers with Bulldogs back then, they had bull baiting. This was probably how they perfected their technique of war dogs directly attacking a horse's most vulnerable spot. This tactic would have been a necessity for a primitive people. The more advanced Romans strapped complicated armored harnesses onto their war dogs. These harnesses were festooned with long sharp blades, which meant the dogs would only have to run under a horse's belly to slash him. The Romans even mounted heavy pots of burning resin onto the armored backs of their war Mastiffs. Obviously the Celtic Bulldogs had to be more nimble and athletic than their burly Mediterranean counterparts. In my opin-ion, this is the actual origin of bull baiting or bull running, a sport designed to sharpen a military tactic.

By the late Middle Ages bull baiting was pretty standardized in England. A bull would be tied to a sturdy post or ring with a long length of rope or chain that was attached to a large leather collar. Between the rope and post there was a swivel so the bull could easily make a complete circle. His horns were blunted with smooth metal balls or clumps of tallow and pitch. Men would goad the poor brute with sharp sticks and twist his tail till he was fighting mad. Up to three dogs would be held by the ears and either released one at a time or all at once. Once

released they would either creep on their bellies in a cunning effort to get underneath the bull's head unnoticed or (if young and inexperienced) make a bold rush straight at him. In either case they would at some point leap upward, bite his nose, ear or jowl and hang on for dear life.

A good Bulldog goes for the nose.

An inexperienced bull would throw his head up to its full height if he failed to stomp the dogs. Today a good AB can leap over six-feet and so could the old English dog, which made this tactic only marginally successful. If the bull had been baited before he might dig a hole in the turf with a hoof and bury his nose in the ground. A really experienced bull would make a full cir-cle before the bait began and dig several holes, picking one before the dogs got to him. This way his horns were right at ground level to meet the dogs and even if they got a hold it would be a less satisfactory grip on an ear or a jowl rather than the nose.

Once the dogs had their grip the bull would thrash madly and try to dislodge them. Once a dog was dislodged the bull would try to kill it with hoof, horn or rolling with his whole body. Often he would succeed in flinging a dog up to 40-feet in the air. Old English paintings show women breaking the dog's fall with out-stretched aprons. Sometimes the men would wear sturdier leather aprons or, if especially adroit, they would carry long smooth poles that would be used to expertly slide the falling dogs to a soft landing. Sand was often spread in a great circle around the bullring to provide fur-ther cushioning.

Doguin De Bordeaux, under 80-pounds

Usually the Bull would succumb to pain and exhaustion before his tormentors did and his head would fall to the ground. Once they hit earth, Bulldogs would immediately start backing up to keep the bull under control and to avoid a last minute stomping. When the bull had completely surrendered he was considered 'pinned,' which meant the dogs had won. At this point the dogs were either physically torn off the bull's face so the bovine could fight another day or the butcher would dispatch him easily with a knife. Sometimes if the bull gave up to early a fire would be lit underneath his belly to get him to fight again.

Bull running was an even bloodier sport, reminiscent of ancient Celts catching wild cattle in the black forests of Britain. Often the bull was locked in a dark shed overnight, upon release he might be slashed and liquor poured into his open wounds. After he was sufficiently enraged the bull was turned loose to run unencumbered in an open field. Once he got up to speed the Bulldogs were released. The best of these relatively large Bulldogs were capable of throwing a Bull cleanly to the ground.

Often the bulls could get into trees and try to scrape the Bulldogs off on branches or batter the canines against tree trunks. This sport was not only hard on the animals involved, it was also dangerous to the crowds of spectators lining the run, innocent bystanders could be trampled and gored. Towards the end of the blood sports era both events would be capped off with a boxing match.

Many historians claim that bull baiting and bull running were invented in the year 1209 by William Earl Warren, in the town of Stamford. The truth is that Warren created a special holiday six weeks before Christmas that was to be celebrated with a bull run. He formalized the sport and added religious overtones but in no way invented anything new. The actual origin of these blood sports was much earlier.

What I find interesting about Warren is not that he is the supposed father of bull baiting, but that he describes butcher's dogs as being both great and small. English Bulldog breeders were divided into two camps throughout the Middle Ages and right up to the industrial revolution. As we will see later, this size disparity is still with us and current AB breeders are divided into two camps, big and small, though even the biggest old English bull biters would be considered only medium sized today.

Belcher was an early 19th century English Bulldog. He won over 100 pit contests.

Some historians think that the Normans introduced the sport to England after their conquest in 1066. There are literary references to Norman jugglers who were trained in the many types of baiting. It is true that this is when all the references to bull baiting start to pop up in English literature. I think this is due to the general increase in culture and the written word that followed the Norman Conquest more than anything else. The fact that the Dogue De Bordeaux arose in coastal France about one hundred years later indicates that Normans took English dogs back and started their own Bulldogs. There is (or was) a sub strain of this ancient French breed called the Doguin that weighs 80-pounds and is the direct ancestor of the continental

Bullenbiesers, which are descended at least partly from English Bulldogs.

Who actually tied bulls to ropes and baited them with dogs first is unimportant. What is significant is who bred the best dogs for these activities. The English Bulldogs started making their way into the Bordeaux region of France in 1151 in much greater numbers because the English had gained formal control of this part of France in that year. They set up royal courts that were routinely charged with bull and bear baitings. The Bulldog they brought over caused a great deal of excitement with its ability to get a grip and hang on. The continental Europeans had been hunting wild boar with Mastiffs for ages but the 'lockjaw' grip was something new to them. Certainly the continental Mastiffs had tenacious grips but a true death grip is a defining characteristic between Bulldogs and Mastiffs and the English developed it first.

In England the act of bull baiting not only had religious overtones, it had a practical side as well. Baited beef was thought to be more tender and wholesome than non-baited beef. This may have been true since this was a brutal sport that tore up bull and dog alike, plus the carbonic and lactic acid that built up in the bull's muscles during combat may have accelerated the process of decay after slaughter. People knew this and were therefore forced to cook beef right away and not hang it to age like they normally would with fresh meat. When meat was immediately cooked it was indeed more wholesome.

I asked a friend of mine, a respected medical researcher, if this was physiologically correct. He wasn't sure and suggested I take two of my father's steers and bait one of them with my AB bitch and leave the other one alone, then slaughter both at the same time and hang them for a month or two. He would measure the rate of decay for me and we would have a definitive answer. I would like to have done that in the interest of historical research, but it just wasn't practical.

Whether baited beef was more wholesome or not one thing is incontrovertible, huge crowds would gather to watch the baiting, in fact people would come for miles. These spectators would then buy fresh beef when the affair was over, with such large crowds entire carcasses would be snapped up at once and no one had to worry that their meat had been hanging in a butcher shop for a long time. So in this era before refrigeration, bull baiting was a boon to public health.

The English have always been very conscious of public health. As it turned out this concern was fundamental in creating the ultimate canine gladiator. Bulldogs of England were superior to the dogs on the continent because bull baiting was a legally mandated practice through most of the island. Butchers had to bait bulls by law before they could sell beef. It was even believed that the thoroughly baited bull produced better beef than the imperfectly baited creature. Therefore the English dogs were subjected to greater performance breeding pressure than their cousins in Europe. Breed selection was not made directly by man as it is today with show dogs but by a gauntlet of hooves and horns that lasted for over 1450-years. Some breeders of today's American Bulldogs and APBT allow wild hogs to help make breeding selections, so the process has been going on for at least 1600-years and is still going on.

The Bulldog is the toughest animal on Earth.

Over this vast gulf of time a dog of unbelievable toughness has emerged. It was often reported that the Old English Bulldogs would hang onto the lip of a bull after their entrails had been ripped out. Sometimes butchers would subject Bulldogs to unimaginable levels of cruelty to prove gameness, cutting off feet while the dog was locked onto his adversary until only stumps were left and life blood drained away. A great Bulldog would hold his grip throughout the mutilation.

Some modern ABs and many Pit Bulls are just as tough and are capable of similar feats, though hopefully no one today would do anything like that deliberately. Genuine performance bred ABs and game Pit Bulls are the most courageous animals to have evolved on Earth. Before you protest and start talking about the courage of a lion, consider this: a lion won't normally attack an adult elephant. A game Bulldog would make such an attack if ordered to do so, he wouldn't survive, but he would die trying.

By the Elizabethan era some strains of Bulldog had became more specialized in bull baiting and were smaller and swifter, this is because as the population increased bull baiting became more popular than bull running, which required more space. A 90 to 60-pound dog could catch a loose running bull and use his weight to throw it. When the bull was tied to a rope a smaller dog could get under its horns and didn't need to use his own weight for a throw because the bull wasn't running. His only tool to force submission was the pain of the bite. A true bull-baiter probably couldn't weigh much more than 60-pounds and most were closer to 50, 40 or less.

People wonder why even the smaller performance bred American Bulldogs and catch weight Pit Bulls have grown larger than the English bull-baiters. They should remember that in the USA Bulldogs were and are used to catch loose cattle or wild boars in the wide-open spaces, which requires greater size. Sixty to 90-pounds is considered ideal for catch work if only one catch dog is to be used on a wild boar or a loose bull.

When bull baiting became more popular than bull running in England, Greyhound and terrier blood was likely added to the large Mastiff-like Bulldogs known as Alaunts to increase speed and reduce size. The Alaunt was often described as having a body like a Greyhound. White Greyhounds were common in medieval England and this color was reinforced in the already pale Alaunt. It is no wonder that today's AB is an overwhelmingly white dog.

The blood flowed both ways and the Greyhound was beefed up with a little Bulldog. One test for Bull blood in the old time Greyhound was to see if the hound would attack the head of a game animal, if he went aggressively after it then he may have had a healthy percentage of Bulldog blood.

An acquaintance of mine has a Pit Bull\Greyhound cross, this dog has a big brick shaped head and a muscular whippet body, it looks more like a very small AB than a Pit and

looks nothing like a Greyhound. When this acquaintance first saw our AB she thought we had made a similar cross.

The most important cross for reducing size and increasing quickness was some type of game terrier. This seems obvious from the erect ear carriage found in artist's renderings of the old bull baiting type. It is also possible that the Alaunt was reduced in size through natural selection and no out crosses were made. If terrier was used to reduce the Alaunt the infusions stopped around the early Middle Ages.

Old Bulldogs showed great variety of type, from heavy-boned to light-boned, from blocky to slender, whatever could get the job done.

English Greyhounds, Terriers, Bulldogs and Mastiffs became renown throughout Europe. This was especially true of the latter two. Even the English word 'dog' came to mean Mastiff in the continental languages. Dogue De Bordeaux means Mastiff of Bordeaux in French. Dogo Argentino means Argentine Mastiff in Spanish. Renaissance era Europe came to realize that English Mastiff/Bulldogs were better than their own just as the ancient Romans had.

One indication of the superiority of the old English Bulldog was their export to all parts of Europe even though these countries already had their own strains of light Mastiffs. Charles V of Spain imported 400 Alaunts from England in preparation for his war against France in 1518. These white Mastiffs destroyed the French war dogs at the siege of Valencia and became famous throughout Europe. Before he sent his Armada against England in 1588 King Phillip (Charles' son) imported dozens of pure English Bulldogs (at the time still called Alaunts). These dogs went not only to Spain but also to Cuba and Florida, where they were used for blood sports and were one of the first Bulldogs in America and possibly an ancestor of our current AB.

After Spain's war with England the importation of Bulldogs continued. They still existed in the early 1990's and have been kept functional. The Spanish Bulldog weighs 80 to 100-pounds and has long legs like the AB.

The organization of the Boxer registry at the turn of the 19th century was another example of English Bulldog superiority. The Germans were importing so many Philo-Kuon English Bulldogs and crossing them with their native Bullenbiesers (bull biters) that the German Bulldog was disappearing. So, in a fit of nationalism, they closed their registry to English blood and declared that their dogs were no longer Bullenbiesers but Boxers. Other than its super short muzzle, a good German Boxer is very close to a certain type of high performance English Bulldog.

This brings us to the discussion of different types within the original working English Bull breed. An examination of old prints and paintings of Elizabethan era Bulldogs shows a wide variety of animals, some have short muzzles and heavy bodies like our better Johnson ABs. Others are lighter (though still stocky compared to average dogs), have longer noses and resemble today's Scott type ABs or Pit Bulls. It is easy to believe that Scott type Bulldogs have more of a Greyhound heritage than the Mastiffy Johnsons. A third type was relatively light and springy, had a shorter muzzle and resembled a medium muzzled German Boxer or some modern Painter type ABs. Variety of type was greater than just body structure and size, some Bulldogs had medium length coats, others were short-haired. Colors also varied greatly as well.

There are two reasons for the type variety found within the old Bull breed: 1) The dogs were not all used as bull-baiters. I have already mentioned that bigger dogs were used in bull running. Though bulls were the most commonly baited animal, bears were also baited regularly through the centuries in old England. A heavier, harder hitting dog was needed to fight a bear, he didn't have to support his body weight with his jaws because the bear wasn't twirling him around to shake him off. In a bull bait a lighter dog could leap higher and hold on longer, he didn't usually use weight or leverage to overpower the giant bovine, instead the pain of his

bite on the tender nose would bring his opponent to its knees. 2) Uniformity in appearance is a modern phenomenon found in show dogs. One hundred and fifty years ago (before dog shows) all breeds showed great variety. Dogs were bred for performance and nobody cared about looks.

Bear gardens were a raucous place.

Within the old English Bull breed this variety was most pronounced in the 16th and 17th centuries because this was the heyday for bear baiting in England. What had been a rare amusement for royalty became as common and popular as bull baiting. Bear baiting was an expensive proposition since the bear had to be captured, caged and fed meat, all without producing anything useful beyond amusement. The renaissance era brought an increased standard of living and the ability on the part of the royal courts to provide this former luxury to the masses in the same way that the Roman government provided gladiatorial contests. Among historians there is more agreement that English bear baiting had its origins in Rome as opposed to bull baiting which is thought to be less ancient and home grown.

In the Elizabethan era bear gardens sprang up throughout the land and the demand for big heavy Bulldogs increased (60 to 100-pounds is considered a heavyweight). The two strains grew more distinct at this time. In 1609 an English playwright mentions both Bulldogs and Beardogs as though they were separate breeds.

The larger Beardogs were also called Bondogges or Bandogges in the 17th century because they were bound by a chain during daytime and released at night to guard estates. Bandogges were described as huge, ugly and fearful to behold. Besides bear baiting and guardian duty they were used in lion baiting as the English blood sport appetite grew more exotic. Sometimes they were pitted against a man armed with a pike, no doubt a good breed test for a guard dog. Modern dog experts would call Bandogges a kind of Mastiff, at that time the distinction between Bulldogs and Mastiffs was still fuzzy. Still, it is probably fair to say that the Bandogges were a kind of Bullmastiff as long as we don't confuse them with the non-functional modern AKC version.

Large APBTs bred to catch wild boars and run with hounds are true Bulldogs.

The 17th century is, of course, the beginning of permanent English settlement in America and the story of Bulldogs, Beardogs or Bandogges continues in the new land. Before we venture across the Atlantic let us chart the demise of the old bull-biter in his native land.

In 1835 bull baiting was made illegal in England, however the actual end of this ancient blood sport was closer to mid century. It had been declining rapidly for many decades prior to being outlawed. Despite propaganda about humanitarianism, this law (like most acts of Parliament) merely formalized changes that were already occurring in society at large. Dog fighting was replacing bull baiting. This change was part of England's shift from agriculture to industry. Dog fighting was the sport of coal miners and factory workers. Though the 1835 ban

was supposed to include dog fighting, this provision was not really enforced until the turn of the 19th century.

Bulldogs had been bred to fight animals larger than themselves, this required good speed but great strength. In the past when they had been put up against smaller animals like badgers or when speed was needed to catch herbivores it had been necessary to add terrier blood to improve quickness and reduce size. Supposedly in a dog fight the terrier blood was also needed to eliminate the Bulldog's tendency to get one good hold and keep it, which would make a fight boring to watch. This is doubtful, but smaller size increased endurance and made the fights last longer. As the law slowly roused itself to crack down on dog fighting small size was helpful in picking up dogs and fleeing the scene of the crime.

American Bulldog with a good jowl hold

Old timers knew all this and crossed terriers with Bulldogs to create a new dog fighting breed around 1800. However, pure Bulldogs had been selectively and intensively bred for dog fighting for at least 100-years before the introduction of terrier blood. Some diehards refused to make the cross. They would fight their pure Bulldogs against the crossbred ones, often with good results. Apparently, while the crossbred dogs may have been quicker and would usually get the first hold, the pure fighting Bulldog had more gameness and would more readily fight to the death. Because the two types were fought side by side and the distinction between them blurred with time, it seems evident that at most a quarter terrier blood was added to English fighting Bulldogs. The ancestors to the APBT must be at least 75% fighting English Bulldog.

The terrier used for the cross was the predecessor to today's Manchester, which looks like a miniature Doberman Pincer and was at the time called the Black and Tan. These dogs had been bred to kill rats. Some dog historians think Fox Terriers may also have been used because they were considered more game. Fighting a fox is obviously similar to fighting a dog. This new breed was originally called half 'n half dog or Bull 'n Terrier, later since the hub of dog fighting was the Staffordshire coal mining region, they were called Staffordshire Bull Terriers. In America they were fought in Pits and are now called American Pit Bull Terriers.

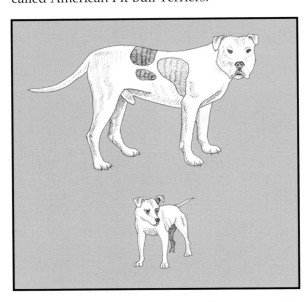

The 100-pound Colby APBT has no terrier traits, while the 25-pound APBT does. Large, blocky Colby Pit Bulls are physically identical to performance ABs. They could even be a wellspring for our breed.

In England, at about this time, a second type of Bull terrier was created - the White English Bull Terrier. It was originally used in competitive pit contests where each dog was given a hundred or two hundred rats to kill and they raced against a clock, the first dog that killed all his rats was the winner.

Unlike the butcher's dogs, a fighting Bulldog or Pit Bull is not a working canine - it is a sporting one. The butcher's Bulldog had to do other tasks besides bait bulls. Once in America the Bulldog was required to be even more multi-talented since he was used as a farm utility dog. The small game bred Pit Bull on the other hand has became very one dimensional, his heart is in dog or animal fighting and nothing else. They are pound for pound the toughest animal on Earth and have fewer genetic problems than any other breed except racing Greyhounds. Not all Pit Bulls are dog fighters. In America, large Pits that are bred to run with hounds and catch wild boar are well rounded, purebred, Bulldogs.

Many experienced Pit Bull men and a minority of dog historians disagree with the above, they don't think that there ever was any terrier crossed into the Staffordshire. They have several reasons for thinking this way. As mentioned, before the supposed terrier cross was made, at the turn of the 17th century, some of the smaller bull-baiters were trained and bred as dog fighters, this new strain was called the fighting Bulldog. There is no concrete documentation that fighting Bulldogs crossed with terriers produced more capable dog fighters. Many people feel that such a cross would only weaken the Bulldog who after all had been bred for animal combat for hundreds, maybe thousands of years, and for dog fighting at least a century before the putative cross was made. By this logic the Pit Bull or Staffordshire is simply the fighting Bulldog.

Another interesting point is that when the White English Bull Terrier (WEBT) was produced in 1850 the Bulldog that was crossed with the now extinct White English Terrier was called a Staffordshire. The early WEBT breeders introduced terrier blood because they thought the Staffordshire still looked like a Bulldog. The other Staffordshire breeders were strangely outraged by this introduction of White Terrier blood and claimed that the newly created WEBT would be a poor fighter. Despite a lot of anecdotes to the contrary the Staff breeders have been proven correct, that is, while the WEBT can easily beat any normal dog in a fight they are inferior to a Pit Bull or a fighting Bulldog.

Besides coal mining, the Staffordshire region had been long known for producing the world's best Bulldogs. Within that region there is a town called Tutbury that has held baiting contests for five centuries. The tradition was perhaps stronger there than anywhere else in Britain. Queen Elizabeth I attended the baitings in Tutbury. Even after the supposed initial Black and Tan Terrier crosses were made these 'half 'n half dogs' were still used to bait bulls and bears in Staffordshire.

It has been suggested that the name Staffordshire Bull Terrier came about because people either intentionally or accidentally confused the Staff with the WEBT. I say intentionally because the Bulldog had a very bad reputation in England at this time and people who kept them shared in this reputation. The English press vilified Bulldogs and their owners as monsters much as the Pit Bull is defamed today in America. The WEBT had a good reputation and was christened the White Cavalier by the upper classes. The Staffordshire breeders may have been doing some PR work by falsely adding the word terrier to their breed. To buttress this argument, old paintings and prints of the original Bulldog are compared to modern American Staffordshires and Pit Bulls. Large Pits are identical to some old bull biters.

A final argument for the word terrier being mistakenly added to the Staffordshire (Pit Bull) is that promoters of the short muzzled sour mugs had successfully convinced the public and dog historians that their cute little Pug/Bulldog crosses were the real McCoy. Supposedly Bulldogs always had squashed faces and short bowed legs. Mainstream dog culture came to believe that the long legged, long muzzled Staffordshire was part terrier, where else could that long muzzle come from? Incidentally, this is why you have to be careful with some books about English Bulldogs, the authors insist that their dogs haven't changed much since the days of yore so they are forced to distort history to make this fantasy work. Even the well researched and fairly accurate sour mug history books insist that the super short muzzle of the later type dogs was put there to help them breathe better during a bull bait, which is completely false.

When the written record is this tangled, I think the best way to cut the knot is to look at today's dogs. Some American Pits and most English Staffs weigh less than 25-pounds, have pointy noses and partially erect ears. Clearly these dogs have a great deal of terrier blood. There are strains of American Pit that are larger and look

more like Bulldogs, these APBTs have very little or no terrier blood. One explanation for this could be out crosses to American Bulldogs that occurred shortly after the Pit Bull Terriers hit American soil around 1860.

19th century show judges used line drawings of an 1877 English Bulldog.

However, if we are to accept the mainstream history of the Bulldog, then soon after the demise of bull baiting the pure Bulldog was becoming extinct in his native country. He was either being crossed with terriers to make Pit Bulls or crossed with Pugs to make sour mugs. Many were exported to Germany and America to make Boxers, ABs and catch weight APBTs. In an effort to save this symbol of English courage the first dog show for Bulldogs was held in 1860.

The Philo-Kuon show standard of 1865 was an honest attempt to preserve the heart of the old bull-biter and a physical form only slightly exaggerated from the original working dog, it included paintings of the famous Rosa and Crib, born around 1815. This foundation breeding pair probably baited bulls, had long legs and looked like short muzzled ABs or medium muzzled Boxers. Rosa and Crib probably had a drop or two of Pug blood or were selected for having muzzles shorter than average. This was the early sour mug type. It should have stopped there. If breeders had been satisfied with this slightly altered form, this small step toward breed type, this slight shortening of the muzzle and widening of the head and stopped breeding for type, then the English Bulldog would have retained its status as a working dog and enjoyed the consequent health benefits.

For decades - 19th century English breeders

adhered to the early sour mug standard and produced Philo-Kuon Bulldogs. This first standard described Bullies that were fantastic water dogs, able to leap off 15-foot tall cliffs, plunge into the ocean and haul a heavy plank onto a beach.

Philo-Kuon also said, "He is the boldest and most resolute of animals. There is nothing a good Bulldog will not attack, and ever brave and unapalled, with matchless courage he will give up only with life itself."

The difference between grandiose statements in modern breed standards and the lines from Philo-Kuon is that in those days the breeders took such words seriously and bred working dogs that were show dogs only as an afterthought.

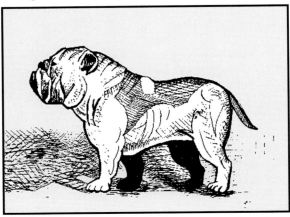

20th century show judges used line drawings of a 1950 English Bulldog.

Philo-Kuon implies that some of these early sour mugs were great watchdogs and others weren't so hot. The ones that weren't naturally man aggressive were reflecting the temperament of their pure performance ancestors. The original Bulldogs that had no Pug or Mastiff crossed in were animal aggressive and naturally friendly to any person. Today's animal oriented game bred Pit Bull or pure hog hunting AB not only physically resemble the 17th to late 18th century English Bulldogs, they have the same lack of desire to bite a man. Animal oriented Bulldogs can be trained to attack humans but left to their own devices a stranger can steal one easily. Early sour mug breeders were breeding away from animal gameness and toward man gameness, converting their bull-bear-badger dogs into man dogs.

By the 1870's the intermediate sour mug types started winning shows, dogs that clearly

didn't look like Rosa and Crib. From then on several strains of show Bulldogs became more and more exaggerated and less healthy while a minority of diehard breeders continued to produce Bulldogs that resembled Rosa and Crib. Tremendous pressure was applied to change the standard to allow for the extreme look. A fierce debate raged within the late 19th century English fancy that is almost identical to today's debate in the American Bulldog community. Today, in America, some breeders want only enough type to distinguish their ABs from Pit Bulls. Other breeders want really big, extreme, Johnson ABs or in effect giant sour mugs. The difference between the 20th century American Bulldog community and the 19th century English Bulldog fancy is that today, on this side of the Atlantic, there is a third camp that breeds pure performance ABs that resemble Pit Bulls. Don't be fooled by appearance, these purists often have dogs that are territorial and man oriented.

Nonfunctional AB confirmation

In late 19th century England Philo-Kuon Bulldog breeders told intermediate and late sour mug breeders to put their money where their mouth was and challenged them to long distance walking races. The point wasn't that the extreme sour mugs could beat the less extreme ones, it was that they wouldn't be able to even complete a 10-mile course. The first such challenge resulted in the extreme Bulldog collapsing after two-miles.

Such demonstrations of physical unsoundness failed to budge anyone from entrenched positions. Inbreeding for deformities became increasingly popular. The picture of Rosa and Crib was referred to less and less often at English dog shows. In the literature that chronicles this internecine debate the Philo-Kuon adherents didn't use my terminology: early, intermediate or late sour mug. They used the term cloddy, admitting that their own dogs were slightly more cloddy than the predecessor performance strain but insisting that any further movement in that direction will radically degenerate health and ability.

In 1898 the wrong crowd won the debate. The English standard deliberately eliminated the depiction of Rosa and Crib and made other changes which allowed show breeders to rapidly transform the rehabilitated gladiator into today's sad sour mug caricature. What a shame, he was fitting in so well.

This transformation was aided by a process biologist call neotony, which means genetic change driven by the acquisition of infant-like characteristics. This is a powerful and rapid way for a species to mutate. For example, Europeans developed blue eyes eons ago, yet babies of all races are born with blue eyes (that turn brown later). Blue eyes were a neotenous mutation.

The same thing happened to the new show type English Bulldogs, they were bred for juvenile characteristics, i.e. extra wrinkles, short bow legs, a stubby body and a shortened face. They look like overgrown AB puppies and are cute but a genetic nightmare. To transform their dogs even more quickly, Pug was introduced or reintroduced extensively around mid century. The Pug is really a toy Mastiff. At one time they were big guard dogs. They have been bred for juvenile characteristics like the sour mug but for centuries longer. This heavy infusion of Pug made the show Bulldogs too small for even the show breeders, some got down to 12-pounds. These toy Bulldogs were sent to France where a new breed was started of miniature French Bulldogs. Many people blame the sour mug's loss of athletic ability on the infusion of Pug blood. This is actually unfair to the Pug of 1840, who was still a fairly functional little dog. The first few generations of Pug/Bulldogs were tested in the rat pits and did very well. The modern Boston Terrier is similar to these tiny mid 19th century Bulldogs. In case you've never seen one in a scrap, I can assure you Boston Terriers can be pretty tough.

When the war in the English Bulldog world was at its height, from the 1840's to the 1870's, early sour mug or Philo-Kuon style

Spanish Bulldogs were imported to England to broaden the gene pool of the few functional Bulldogs left on the island. One Spanish dog used for this purpose was named Toro, he was an athletic 90-pounder that stood 21-inches tall and had a muzzle 2 ½-inches long. It is also reported that he had a good disposition. Functional English Bulldogs with lots of Spanish influence were still being bred at the beginning of the 20th century. Small English Mastiffs were also used at this time to back breed and recreate the slightly altered working estate Bulldog.

Small, athletic, English Mastiffs were crossed into English Bulldogs in the 19th century by Philo-Kuon breeders.

Unfortunately the show breeders shunned the functional Philo-Kuon breeders and developed more political clout by claiming Spanish out crosses were unpatriotic. Intermediate sour mug breeders used functional blood to get tiny Pug Bulldogs back up to 50-pounds, then Spanish out crosses were stopped and declared illegal. Dysfunctional, exaggerated and neotenous features were emphasized once more. With the revised standard a fait accompli, the hideous late sour mug type dominated and the last few kennels of functional Bulldogs were soon jettisoned from the British Isles.

By crossing to Mastiffs, the creation of the Bullmastiff was the final act of the few remaining Philo-Kuon Bulldogs left in the second half of the 19th century in England. From the 20th century on the sour mug type dominated and to a large degree most people think of this creature around the world when they hear the word Bulldog.

Most neotenous traits of the sour mug are highly recessive just as blue eyes are recessive. It's hard for English breeders to maintain the sour mug's exaggerated looks, if allowed to interbreed at random a taller, healthier dog would quickly emerge, his muzzle would still be short but not super short.

Old English Whites were super guard dogs.

Finally, we can jump to this side of the Atlantic. The following history is based on oral traditions passed down from generation to generation in the American South, as well as on conventional historical documents:

In the 17th and 18th century English settlers brought their performance Bulldogs and Beardogs with them to America for three reasons: to control livestock, hunt wild animals and personal protection. These early settlers didn't have the luxury of engaging in endless bull and bear baits like their cousins overseas so they bred Bulldogs to be less fierce and easier to train. The settlers also brought large White English Terriers on the same ships that carried Bulldogs, cattle and other livestock for rat control. It has been suggested that White Terriers were allowed to crossbreed with the Bulldogs to tone them down. This seems unlikely because the White English Terrier had an egg shaped head like today's

White English Bull Terrier, a feature rarely seen on an AB, though I do know of one AB with this head shape.

These dogs came to be known by many different names as regional varieties emerged. Most names were a combination or variation of these four words: Old, English, White and Bulldog. For example: Old English White, White English, White English Bulldog, Old English, or simply (and most commonly) Bulldog. Other regional names included: Old Family White, Old Country White, Old Time Bulldog, Whitey, Bully, Georgia Country Bulldog, Backwoods Bulldog, Mountain Bull, Alabama Hog Dog, English Pit Bulldog, Fighting Bulldog and many others. Some people in the backwoods of northern Florida (and other parts of the rural South) still use these names and raise dogs that are a type of American Bulldog. They are usually pure white and seldom have written pedigrees.

Some strains were not pure white or even predominantly white. These dogs were called Brindle Bulldogs or other less flattering names with racist overtones. In the old South the black community often kept Brindle Bulldogs. There is one black breeder today in Ohio who keeps this tradition alive and still breeds brindle and fawn Bulldogs. There are several reasons for the prejudice toward pure white dogs, mainly white farmers incorrectly thought white Bulldogs were smarter than the colored version. There are three valid reasons for breeding white Bulldogs: 1) White is a highly recessive color and would insure against cross breeding. 2) The White color may have also been more visible in the brush when the dogs wrestled with fast moving wild hogs, especially at night. 3) By breeding for white they were back breeding to the Alaunt. On the other hand, there are many health problems associated with white dogs and this is a bad color for a guard dog.

John D. Johnson of Summerville, Georgia coined the name American Bulldog. When Mr. Johnson was growing up in the 20's and 30's these dogs were known as Pit Bulldogs in Northern Georgia because they were sometimes used to fight dogs and large wild animals in Pits. He was the first person to sell them to the general public in the 50's, so the name he used, American Pit Bulldog, was the first name that became widely used outside the rural South. In 1985 Mr. Johnson realized that people were confusing this breed with the Pit Bull Terrier so he changed the name to American Bulldog. Mr. Johnson's friend, Joe Painter, was also instrumental in the name change.

The heart of Bulldog country was originally Georgia. The largest influx of Bulldogs came between 1732 and 1736 when English settlers first moved into this region. This colonization effort was unlike any other because the English government recruited the working poor of London, paid their passage and outfitted them. The first group came over on the English ship Anne. The livestock on board included hogs, sheep, ducks, geese and several dogs. No one bothered to record which breed of dog was chosen but they were taken from areas of London known for bear baiting.

This colony was set up in an unusually dangerous place even for the New World, bordered by hostile Spanish and French colonies as well as several war-like Indian tribes. The very reason for the creation of Georgia was strategic and these colonists knew it, they were all trained as soldiers and saw action almost right away. They soon found that the forces of nature were as hostile as mankind. In 1740 an eight-foot long cougar attacked a farmer who was working a field near Savannah. Luckily, he had one of these London Beardogs with him. The dog was able to fight the big cat off long enough for the man to shoot it.

Among later groups of settlers many were butchers who brought the smaller bull baiting type with them. The large Johnson type dogs became established as plantation guardians similar to the old Bandogges throughout the South. The smaller Scott type was used by farmers to catch semi-wild hogs and cattle that were allowed to forage for themselves unencumbered by fences. Ownership of hogs was established through ear notching. Notching smooth eared adults in the wild was a dangerous job for a southern mountaineer since he had to deal with several of these fearsome behemoths at once, any one of which could slice a man to ribbons in seconds. About the only thing between this lonely mountain man and the hog's slashing razor sharp tusks was his faithful Old English White. An interesting point was made to me by one of my old time southern experts, the small farmer was not hunting these hogs when he ear notched them and didn't want them unnecessarily damaged. The Bulldog caught and held a semi-wild pig, he didn't maul it.

This AB is mauling a dangerous wild pig.

These Mountain Bulldogs naturally had to do double duty as guard dogs against hostile Indians, other settlers and animal intruders, especially bears and wolves. They were frequently used to hunt big game and raccoons. In the early colonial era Eurasian wild hogs were released in the South to provide sport and meat, they have since spread to the West and Midwest but have really made a home for themselves in the deep South. The history of the American Bulldog has always been linked to the Eurasian wild boar, so it is important to remember that it is an entirely different animal than a farm pig. A common myth is that farm pigs will grow huge tusks and long black hair if they breed freely in the wild for a few generations, what is really happening is that they are interbreeding with Eurasian wild boars. The American wild pig is a hybrid of Eurasian and domestic stock. This cross breeding created a hybrid more dangerous to man than pure Eurasian (or Russian) wild boar because the introduction of domestic pig genes eliminated the natural fear of man that a Russian wild boar would normally have.

Another favorite prey animal was the southern black bear. Some of the information I've come across indicates that pure Bulldogs were considered a bad choice for hunting bear in America since they would attack too boldly and get mauled. While it is true that in England sportsmen would sometimes hunt bears in the woods with packs of hounds and Bulldogs, it was more common to stage bear baits, which usually entailed chaining and muzzling bears before they fought dogs. No dog or even combination of dogs is likely to beat an adult bear in the wild. A good bear dog may have been a cross between an Old English White and an Airedale or a hound. These dogs would bay a bear but not attack. On the other hand, there are people today that hunt bear with ABs.

Old fashioned bull and bear baiting was a frequent occurrence after the colonial era had passed in most parts of America. There were even bull baits held in Manhattan as late as 1850. At about this time, staged dogfights between English Bulldogs (a.k.a. American Bulldogs) were a common occurrence in San Francisco. Later in the 19th century, bull baits seemed to occur only in the Wild West. Sometimes soldiers stationed in frontier regions found that their Bulldogs were actually Buffalo dogs. In 1871 one such soldier wrote the following in west Texas:

As was the case on nearly all marches of troops changing station on the frontier, many dogs of all ages, sizes and degrees, had under protest, accompanied the column to the Colorado River; here many of the worthless curs were left or drowned while fording; but there were several remaining, and it was these that had turned the buffalo down the column. There was among them a large White English Bulldog belonging to the regimental band. He was a powerful brute, and had been trained to pull down beeves at the slaughter corral at Fort Concho. He was, withal, a prime favorite of the soldiers, not withstanding his ferocity. The pack of dogs were in full cry after the stampeding herds of bellowing beasts as they rushed and tore along the column with their peculiar rolling gate. But "King", the Bulldog, singled out the immense wounded leader, who had now slackened his speed and was faltering in his tracks. He sprang at his throat with great courage, fastened upon him, and the battle commenced, with the column as silent spectators.

It was a novel spectacle. The bronze troopers; the great shaggy beasts thundering by; the white-topped wagon train closed up and halted; the fleeting shadows, and the almost limitless stretch of surrounding prairie and vast solitude. The bull went down upon his knees, but so great was his strength that he quickly arose and whirled the dog in great circles over his head. "King" had been taught never to let go. The entire command now watched with breathless attention the apparently unequal struggle. Expecting every moment to see the dog crushed to death. Down went the bull again on his knees, this time not from any weakness, but to gore the dog; rising, he would stamp his feet in his rage, then shaking him awhile, he would resume swinging and snapping him like a whip cord through the air. The foam, now bloody, flecked the long, tawny beard of the Bison bull. His eyes,

nearly concealed in the long, matted hair that covered his shaggy head, flashed fire, and his rage knew no bounds. The dog, which had commenced the fight, a pure white, now turned a spotted crimson from blood which had flowed from the buffalo's wounds, and still his brute instincts, tenacious courage and training lead him to hold on. Had he let go for a moment, the crazed bull would have gored him to death before he could have retreated.

This story had a happy ending for King, one of the soldiers finally shot the mighty buffalo bull, after which the tenacious Bulldog at last relinquished his hold.

In 1879 a young girl named Jennie Marcy tried to stop a herd of 1000 stampeding Texas Long horns from destroying her family's farm in Kansas with a single American Bulldog. This event was recorded in her autobiography:

Suddenly, a queer, sonorous, rumbling sound reached the ear and in a jiffy I was out of doors and readily saw with my own two eyes that something was about to happen, for down the road not far from the little prairie home were a thousand cattle, more or less. Ugly strangers they were, with big heads, little eyes, long legs and crooked thighs, and horns a rod long from tip to tip.

Where was old Pete, the recognized 'holy terror' of a watch dog? Yes, there he was in the shade of the lean to kitchen. He was peacefully snoring, never dreaming of the excitement in store. With a loud snap of my fingers, I succeeded in arousing the two faced canine. It is true he looked that way, for his face was half black and half white, giving him a never-to-be-forgotten peculiar vicious and villainous expression, this big bulldog of ours. We together sneaked cautiously around the offside of the house, where I pointed out the strange intruders. Then I clapped my hands sharply and yelled, Sic 'em! Sic 'em!, he bounded off immediately for active duty. But instead of facing the enemy as I had planned, he reconnoitered a bit, then rushed directly around the moving mass to the rear, displaying his ivory teeth and the utter lack of one single grey matter in his huge cranium.

Pete's tactic didn't stop the stampede and the Marcy farm was trampled. Jennie was disgusted with her Bulldog and locked him in a shed that evening without any supper. I feel compelled to defend old Pete. If he had latched onto a single steer's nose in typical Bulldog fashion the remaining 999 long horns would have continued their stampede anyway. His only chance was to get behind the herd and try to turn it. Though he was unable to do that he at least had the right idea. Another incident was recorded in 1910 further north on a Dakota ranch where an American Bulldog existed that was truly not worth his feed:

The womenfolk insisted that a favorite of theirs, a big bulldog, be kept at the house. The boss, harassed by petticoats, gave in to coaxing. This unusual animal that had such fair pleaders was noted for his peculiar habit of sticking to only one steer and letting the other ranch dogs manage the rest of the fenced cattle. These others included a shepherd dog and a Newfoundland which successfully got the cattle out of nearby cornfields. One day, the pet bulldog grabbed by the nose his favorite antagonist, the three-year old steer, and an Olympian tussle followed. When the ranchmen rushed to the scene they found that the steer was 'swinging him around like a professional club swinger.' When peace reigned again, it was estimated that the steer, dog, and the cowboys had destroyed more corn than the animals could have eaten in a month!

These citations occurred after the Civil War and could therefore be referring to large blocky American Pit Bull Terriers that were bred to catch cattle and be relatively non-dog aggressive. In other words, the terrier was bred out and the Pit Bull was transformed back into a Bulldog. The distinction is almost a matter of semantics. In the South the larger and coarser 'Bull Terriers' were seen for what they were, declared Bulldogs and employed as hog/cattle catchers and farm utility dogs just like the Bulldogs that already existed in America for generations. To this day many rural southerners know the catch weight Pit Bull as Brindle Bulldog or simply Bulldog. The farm utility/hog hunting American Bulldog and the large catch weight Pit Bull (especially white ones) were essentially one breed at that time.

The 20th century was a perilous one for the Old English White. The smaller fighting Bulldog or classic APBT was never in any danger because he was a creature of the urban environment and a money making machine. The larger farm utility Bulldog was fast disappearing as small farms and free ranging hogs disappeared. At one point big American Bulldogs were wide spread throughout the entire country, after WW

II the breed had died out everywhere except the South. By the 60's the American Bulldog was dying out there as well. The fate of the AB seemed to be running parallel with his English ancestors. The AB was heading for extinction as surely as the working Bulldogs in Europe. The American dog's numbers never got as low as the English dog's because the Eurasian wild boars of the South never disappeared the way English bull baiting did. The big plantation Bulldogs however did experience a very drastic reduction in numbers and teetered on the brink of extinction. If it weren't for John D. Johnson they would have vanished.

By the late 60's and 70's several breeders were actively rebuilding the breed. Men whose names are found in AB pedigrees from these decades such as Scott, Williamson, Bailey, Tate and Johnson should be thanked for preserving the old English bull/bear biter and making sure he is still with us today.

White APBT may be a parent breed to the AB.

This historical version is far from being universally held by breeders and dog historians though. Actually, most proponents of the 17th century English origin theory would disagree with my version. They would say that ABs and Pit Bulls have seldom intermixed and our breed is the unmodified ancient Boocher dogge. Our disagreement revolves more on what is a catch weight Pit Bull than what is an AB. Other canine scholars completely disagree with the above and claim that the AB is only 30 or 40-years old. I call this the composite breed theory. Their argument is as follows:

It is unlikely that early settlers brought very many dogs with them because conditions were so rough then that people were barely able to feed themselves let alone big hungry Bulldogs. By the time any American could afford to import English Bulldogs the sour mug had taken over. The actual origin of the working southern Bulldog traces to a tradition in the South of crossing sour mugs and small fighting Pit Bulls in the 1950's and 60's.

The St. Bernard may be a parent breed to the AB.

These dogs in turn were crossed with another southern breed called the Catahoula Leopard dog. The origin of the Catahoula is more mysterious than the AB but most people think it originated with native Americans who acquired Spanish Mastiffs from De Sotto and crossed them with their own dogs and the French Beauceron (sometimes used on boar). The red wolf and some kind of white Bulldog are also in the mix. One thing is certain about the Catahoula; it is a world class cow dog and tough beyond belief. More recently, Bullmastiff or other large Mastiffs like St. Bernard have been added to increase the size of the Pit Bull/English Bull/Leopard dog crosses. The composite breed theory gives the AB a history stretching back to mid 20th century. Some composite theory proponents consider all the talk about 'Old English Whites' to be a kind of sales pitch. Others admit that there was an old English Bulldog in the South but its numbers were so depleted that these other breeds were introduced to recreate the original Bulldog. In this scenario the Old

English White is one of the parent breeds in a newly created composite.

Many of these composite theorists produce the finest ABs in the world and insist that a breed doesn't have to be ancient to be excellent. The most recommended breeder in America (by his fellow Bulldoggers) believes in the composite theory. He has trained many different breeds for Schutzhund competition and sees similarities between ABs and Colby APBTs in the way they attack and in how they mature. He has even trained an English sour mug for protection work and saw the same heart and tenacity there that an AB has, though without the athletic ability or endurance. He has noticed similarities in the sour mug's coat and the way it sheds to an AB's. Finally he sees a hound component in the AB because of the way they trail. I think what the composite viewpoint boils down to is that the AB is a modified version of the Colby Pit Bull; modified from a dog fighting dog to a guard dog or hog dog.

There are many different lines of Pit Bulls and the Colby line has produced some individuals with large size, heavy bone, white coat color and other Bulldog traits. The Colby line is descended from the old family reds or red nose Staffordshire Bull Terriers brought over from Ireland in the late 19th century. Red nose Pit Bulls share a color pattern with the Dogue de Bordeaux, not only do they both have red noses, coats and toe nails, they also have gold eyes. Pit Bull men are at a loss as to how these colors appeared in this strain but it seems obvious to me that somewhere a cross was made to the big red fighting Bullmastiff of France. Because of this cross, red nose Pits and Colby Pits sometimes have more Mastiff characteristics and fewer terrier traits than other strains of Pit Bull. Perhaps selective breeding has brought out these characteristics and transformed Colbys into ABs.

The most powerful argument for the AB being a 20th century Pit Bull composite are these two facts: 1) A strain of white Colby Pit Bulls existed in the twenties that produced 100-pound monsters that looked exactly like modern ABs. 2) If white Pit Bulls are bred to white Pit Bulls the progeny will get larger and larger. Again, the resulting Pits will resemble ABs.

There are only two or three fighting Pit Bulls actually documented in AB pedigrees. The most famous was Oso Negro, a large Pit that weighed 70-pounds. He was supposed to have had a huge head and a Bulldoggy appearance as well as an above average pit record. Oso Negro was a Carver, a line that produces even bigger dogs than the Colby line.

A variation of the composite breed theory holds that the Scott type ABs are true descendants of the Old English Bulldogs but the large Johnson dogs are a recent composite of Scott, some kind of Mastiff and sour mug. Of course, the Johnson breeders consider Scott dogs to be composites of Johnson and small fighting Pit Bull.

In defense of my 17th century origin theory I offer seven points:

1) There is a breed of dog from the Canary Islands that is descended from early Bulldogs and Mastiffs brought there by English settlers. This breed is called the Presa Canario and its origins are not in dispute because small fighting Pit Bulls were never introduced to the Canaries until just recently. The Presa's appearance clearly marks it as close cousin to the AB. In this instance the oral traditions of English settlers can be relied upon. I don't see why the oral traditions of the American South should be any different.

2) When Pit Bulls were introduced to America before the Civil War the larger and less dog aggressive ones (with no terrier) were interbred freely with American Bulldogs. Since both breeds are representatives of working English Bulldog stock, the 17th century theory is intact.

3) Dozens of old southern ballads and folk songs talk about Bulldogs, many predate the Civil War, others were composed just afterwards and some are from the 20th century. I will give you segments of a few of these ballads.

In 1880 Sam Houston (a notorious horse thief, not the famous statesman) wrote about guard type (not fighting) ABs in an Austin jail:

And here's to the cook, I wish he was dead, It's old boiled beef and old corn bread.
The chuck they give us is beef and corn bread, As old as Hell and heavy as lead.
We pop it down in us within our cells, Just like the pop from heaven to Hell.
The coffee is rough, and the yard is full of hogs. And we are guarded by two bulldogs.

An older folk song that speaks of guard ABs is the black spiritual called 'When The Good Lord Sets You Free'. One stanza goes like this:

Ain't no use for me workin' hard, I got a gal in the white folk's yard.
Sift the flour and reach at the lard, Wasn't for the bulldog I'd be in the yard
Chorus:
He might bite me, bad bulldog.
In the morning when the good Lord sets me free.

Another, more recent, song contains this line:

We gotta ol' bulldog hezzabouta five hundred poundah and when he barks it just rolls like thundah.

4) Bulldogs identical to the modern AB are depicted on canvas and ceramic from the old South, these pieces of art predate the introduction of the Pit Bull to America. The following ceramic plate is mid 19th century.

This plate depicts mid-19th century ABs.

5) To say that ABs have many traits that are similar to Pit Bulls and English Bulldogs is simply to say that these are related breeds. To say - "They have good noses so therefore they must have hound in them," ignores literature out of old England that tells us original Bulldogs were known for a keen sense of smell. Anyone who has tracked with hounds and Bulldogs will tell you their noses are good but not great.

6) The extinction of the Old English White never happened in the deep South. There are still hundreds of these dogs on small farms throughout the region. Some AB breeders like to visit these small farmers and use their Bulldogs to replenish bloodlines.

7) The white color of the AB foils all composite theories. None of the suggested com-

posite breeds would produce this color. Furthermore, in our breed white is a predominant color. In all dogs white is recessive. To remove the dominant brindle and black gene from the entire gene pool in this manner must have taken centuries.

Bulldogs and bulls have fought for eons.

When I say that the AB is descended from 17th century English Bulldogs, I don't mean that thousands of out crosses weren't tried over the centuries. People who kept these dogs weren't interested in purity of blood, they wanted performance. Most of the out crosses didn't work and didn't enter the gene pool because the original Bulldog was like a racing Greyhound, the best genetic combination for his assigned task as a catch dog and a guard dog, most crosses would only hurt. Conditions were different in America though and some of the out crosses helped. It is hotter in the South than in England and catch dogs needed to cover more ground with rougher terrain, they needed longer legs and longer muzzles. One old timer told me that a rare southern breed of mysterious origins called the Black Mouth Yellow Cur could be crossed into White Bulldog in small judicious doses without harming gameness or toughness but speed and endurance would be enhanced. The same thing has been said about the Catahoula Leopard dog, a cousin to the big Cur breeds. Cats and Curs have herding ability. This is why some American Bulldogs can herd livestock as well as catch. I have herded cattle with my ABs and seen other people do it with theirs.

With 300-years in America certainly some new blood was added to help adapt English Bulldogs to a different climate and conditions. This is how purebred dogs were bred before the AKC mentality took over, yes show

dogs are rigidly pure but they are also worthless for hardcore performance tasks. The biggest difference between the original bull biter and the AB is temperament, physically they are very similar but today we have a dog that is easy to train and gentle with animals when we want him to be.

There is a third origin theory that stands up to my seven points and the composite theory's contention that the first settlers were too poor to import dogs from England. It is called the 18th century Spanish origin theory:

In the late 18th and the early 19th century a series of laws were passed that outlawed the importation of foreign slaves to America. The effect of these laws was to create a black market for the easy to smuggle Caribbean and South American slaves. These slaves were thought to be more rebellious and prone to escape than others. Southern slaveholders traveling to Cuba, Brazil and other parts of South America not only bought slaves, they also bought dogs there that had been bred to capture these headstrong runaways. There are etchings of Bulldogs chasing runaway slaves in the American South.

The Spanish had imported big, highly functional, Bulldogs to their South American colonies and Florida, you will recall that these dogs were of largely English origin. The Spanish Bulldog was maintained there as a pure breed and used as a parent for composite breeds. Today there are two well-recognized hunting dogs from South America based on the Spanish Bulldog. The first is the huge Fila Brasileiro which looks like a giant AB crossed with a Bloodhound, it also has 18th century Mastiff blood which shows up in coloration like fawn, brindle or black, it was originally bred to chase runaway slaves. The second is the Argentine Dogo, which looks like a tall, lightly built Scott AB and is pure white, bred to hunt wild boar and puma.

American slaveholders brought back Bulldogs and Mastiff/hounds - the predecessors to the modern Fila. From the former our modern AB descended, from the latter we get the Mountain Cur, Black Mouth Yellow Cur, Old Florida Cur and Southern Black Mouth Cur. To avoid confusion I would like to emphasize that in the rural South the word Cur does not mean a mongrel or inferior dog, it refers to a group of purebred dogs used for hunting dangerous game and catch work. All these breeds are found only in the South. There are smaller Cur breeds that don't have as many Mastiff or Bulldog characteristics as the big Curs, which often come in Mastiff colors like brindle, are relatively square and heavy-boned. The black mouth is also a Mastiff trait. One of my southern friends described an Old Florida Cur that weighed 120-pounds and looked exactly like a Fila. Unlike most hunting dogs, Curs have the courage to catch wild pigs and tackle other big game head on. Small southern farmers still use Black Mouth Curs as catch dogs. When catching cattle, Curs go for the nose like a Bulldog.

Spanish Bulldog blood was just as effective at instilling courage as English.

Most breeders of Curs don't think their dogs came from South America, however, and they don't think they have any hound in them. Many of these breeders have maintained pedigrees for generations within their own families and have strong oral traditions regarding the origins of their Curs. They say that these dogs were brought here directly from continental Europe 300-years ago or more and are descended from the old European Butcher dogs. The continental Butcher dog was used to drive cattle not catch them. It was also a guard dog. Today in Denmark there is a breed called the Broholmer which is a direct descendant of the Slagterhunden or Butcher dog. They are yellow with black mouths and are identical to Black Mouth Yellow Curs in every respect, both of them look kind of like a yellow Lab on steroids. However, they don't resemble the other Cur breeds nearly as much, which do have a houndier look.

Some breeders think that Curs originated in colonial times when Bulldogs and hounds were crossed. These Cur breeders reluctantly admit there may also have been a Spanish connection later in the 19th century.

Even if you've never been to the rural South you probably know what a Cur looks like, this is the dog depicted in the Disney movie - 'Old Yeller'. You may recall that in this film the hero is a big blocky muscular dog that tangles with a bear, throws a semi-wild cow to the ground and catches wild pigs by the ear. These are all things that ABs and the big Curs do in real life. The Disney dog's real name was Spike. He weighed 115-pounds. Though the folks at Disney claim Spike was a mongrel, in reality he was a Black Mouth Yellow Cur and he can be found in the pedigree of many of the Curs around today.

Curs, ABs and sour mugs may have Spanish Bulldog blood in their veins.

Literature supports the theory that some southern hunting breeds are descended from Filas. Novels like Harriet Beecher Stowe's Uncle Tom's Cabin describe ferocious Bloodhounds running down and savaging runaway slaves. Pure Bloodhounds are not that man aggressive, those dogs were Filas and that is exactly what Filas were bred to do. The logical assumption here is that if Curs descended from Brazilian Filas then ABs must have descended from New World Spanish Bulldogs.

In American and Europe, Bulldogs were used as farm dogs.

Most historical references to southern Bulldogs seem to start around the same time period that the Bulldog/Hound/Mastiff (Fila or Cur) references are found, the late 18th and 19th century, not the seventeenth. Perhaps the oral traditions that subscribe a European origin to all southern breeds are partially motivated by a sense of cultural pride on the part of southerners, who are mainly from Europe themselves and think their dogs should be as well.

When discussing these three theories it is important to remember that they are not mutually exclusive. Our modern AB is probably descended from predominantly old time English, some old time Spanish (via South America) and a drop of miscellaneous. Even if you don't think 17th century settlers brought very many English Bulldogs over, they definitely came later, especially when bull baiting began to decline in the old country around 1800. This is when the historical references toward Bulldogs start to appear. The oldest reference I have found so far that is indisputably an AB is 1832. When these dogs appear in the historical record they are always called English Bulldogs, Brindle Bulldogs, White English Bulldogs or one of the regional names I mentioned earlier.

The fact that the AB has been called an English Bulldog so often in the historical record means that the sour mug has stolen our breed's history in the eyes of the general public. What kind of dog was the cartoon Bulldog that accompanied Buster Brown everywhere he went? Cartoon Bulldogs from the 1920's are usually depicted as tough athletic guard dogs. I think ABs, not sour mugs, inspired them. Any

American reference to an English Bulldog around mid 19th century or earlier is obviously an AB but after the turn of the century we can't be sure. For example, it is reported that an English Bulldog won five ribbons and a Bronze Star from the U.S. Marine corps in WW II. This dog must have been an AB because by the 1940's the sour mug was completely non-functional and probably couldn't have survived in the South Pacific, let alone performed as an active war dog.

There are a few academic references that are ambiguous. Immediately after the war, Leon F. Whitney, a veterinarian and animal researcher, conducted a study on pain tolerance in different breeds of dog. On one end of the scale were sensitive breeds like Cocker Spaniels. On the other end were the less sensitive breeds, including Bull Terriers, Staffordshire Terriers and Fighting Bulldogs. The latter being a regional name for our breed before the name American Bulldog was coined. It could also be that Whitney was differentiating between a Staff and a Pit Bull.

As late as the early 1980's our breed was still being advertised in national magazines as English Bulldogs. At least Hollywood is doing good research and using ABs when they show the indigenous Bulldogs of the South. In the movie - Forest Gump, an AB is shown tied up to a chain protecting a house in rural Alabama in the late 1950's.

Badger baiting was popular in Old England.

Old Spanish Bulldogs were used to catch horses.

Predator - Schutzhund III, IPO III, OFA

The American Bulldog Today

Today there are three main lines of the AB: Johnson, Scott and Painter:

1) The Johnson line is characterized by heavy bones and big bodies; their heads are big, blocky and as a general rule they have short muzzles, though some pure Johnson dogs like Rip'n Woody can have three or four-inch long snouts. A Johnson dog may have a half-inch to a full-inch of undershot lower jaw, which means the lower jaw protrudes beyond the upper jaw. In some extreme cases the lower fangs jut out and are visible through the lips. Other physical characteristics include facial wrinkles, elbows slightly turned out and very wide chests.

In some ways these dogs hearken back to the Philo-Kuon Bulldogs of the 19th century. They are furthest from the tight Pit Bull conformation because a dose of sour mug blood was added to increase type. The early English sour mug was a 30 or 60-pound dog and the Johnson Bulldog is twice that size. In that respect, Johnson ABs are reminiscent of the old Bandogges used in bear baiting and the big Bulldogs used in bull running.

Scruffy is a Farnetti bred Johnson AB.

Not surprisingly, they will sometimes try to throw a hog instead of catch it. Also, when going after a hog they may try to grab the nose instead of the ear. This is because they have not been bred as intensely on boar as some of the other lines that will instinctively go for the ear on a hog and the nose on a bull. Johnson type Bulldogs are partially descended from plantation guardians which means they have been bred to be yard dogs and have a strong sense of terri-

toriality. Another line of ABs from plantation guard stock was bred by a family in Georgia named Nations. This line was known for human aggression. There are few if any pure Nations Bulldogs left because this strain is being absorbed into the Johnson line and the Nations family no longer breeds dogs. Johnson and Nations Bulldogs were pretty much the same type to start with anyway. Johnson males weigh from 75 to 135-pounds. Johnson breeders have traditionally kept their dogs fat, so the weights stated above would be less if the dogs were fit. A lean Johnson Bulldog will seldom if ever weigh over 120-pounds.

Scott's Hero was a catch dog from the early 1970's.

2) The Scott line descended from farm utility dogs that have been catching wild hogs and cattle for either 40 or 300-years in the rural mountains of the South, depending on which theory you believe. These dogs have a slightly lighter build than the Johnsons, have longer muzzles and are closer to having an even bite with any undershot stopping at a scant ¼-inch. Males usually weigh between 95 and 60-pounds, though some will get up to 120-pounds. Bulldog people will refer to Williamson, Tate and Bailey as three lines distinct from Scott but the distinctions are minor, for example, Williamson dogs are known for a lighter build, narrower head, longer legs and a slightly longer muzzle. Some people say that Williamson dogs are easier to

train, which makes them good for sports like Schutzhund. Tate dogs are closely related to Williamson though they may have a medium build like a Scott and tend to have more color. We will consider these three as variations on the Scott theme.

Crusher was a Painter dog with a short muzzle.

3) The Painter line can be longer legged and occasionally shorter faced than the Scott but otherwise similar in size. Most Painter dogs are physically indistinguishable from the other performance line. There can be differences in dog aggression since Painter Bulldogs were developed as dog fighters; therefore they hearken back to the original Fighting Bulldog. The Leclerc/Koura strain started with inbred Painter dogs then added fresh out cross blood such as Bama Boy and is considered the modern version of this line. Koura dogs have medium to long muzzles, even bites and a tight performance build. Much the same can be said of the Screaming Eagle line from Alaska. The foundation dogs for the Painter line were all performance animals.

Indeed lumping all the non-Johnson lines under the catch-all term 'performance' is completely valid since all these strains can be traced from foundation dogs found in a 100 square-mile area of northern Alabama, so they are all obviously closely related. Most people think that the performance strains can be ultimately traced to one breeder in the Sand Mountain region of Alabama named W.C. Ashley. The Ashley strain of Bulldogs can be loosely traced back to the 19th century.

The performance strains were developed to catch wild hogs/cattle and destroy vermin/wild dogs, this means their focus was originally animal aggression. Serious modern breed-

ers are converting the performance dog's focus away from animal aggression and toward property protection/guardian duty, though I'm sure there will always be pure hog hunting strains and many Scott/Painter strains are good at both. There is limited dog fighting in the American Bulldog community today. I support anti-dog fighting laws and don't mean this as a justification, but ABs are typically fought in a different manner than Pit Bulls. The fights are shorter with few or no fatalities.

Sgt. Rock, foundation stud for the Painter line, had a longer muzzle.

Oathout's Dick the Bulldog was a short muzzled Painter dog.

One AB breeder told me that though he believes dog fighting is repugnant he has found that the only way to test the deep gameness of his breeding stock is to roll them with a large professional fighting Pit Bull just one time in the AB's life. A 'roll' is a fight with a short time limit. The dogs are separated after a few minutes, before any serious damage is done. They are then reintroduced or brought up to scratch to see if they will still fight. After a short time they are separated again and brought up to scratch again. This particular breeder has found that some of his dogs will probably fight to the death against a professional Pit Bull since the ones that pass his test are always willing to continue the fight no matter how many times they are brought up to scratch. No doubt Painter blood helps them to achieve this level of dog gameness.

Blackwell's Kemo was a 125-pound hill Bulldog with Johnson traits.

I asked him if protection work against a man or putting a dog in a pen with wild hogs would test deep gameness. He tests his Bulldogs in a modified Ring Sport technique plus stages home invasions where a decoy is dressed in street clothing and wearing a thin protective body suit underneath. For this individual such tests are unable to plumb the true depths of gameness. He is unsatisfied with boar hunting as well. As far as staging a fight with a boar, he believes that a big boar will do too much damage in a pen, killing the dog if the battle were to last any length of time.

There was a fourth strain called Old Time Johnson. This is a reference to the smaller, tightly built, performance type that Mr. Johnson bred for many years along with his big plantation Bulldogs. Since the 80's he has specialized exclusively on bigger, blockier, shorter muzzled dogs. Other breeders continue to use Old Time Johnson blood in their performance strains. Like Bailey, Williamson and Tate this blood should be lumped in with Scott or simply considered part of the over all performance family.

Much of the Old Time Johnson blood came from Scott's kennel and vice versa. Breeders producing extremely short-faced, wrinkly, squatty Johnson ABs claim that this is the Old Time Johnson type. This is a dishonest

and inaccurate assertion. The extreme Johnson type is a creation of the late 90's.

Another distinct blood line(s) is the unregistered hill Bulldogs of the rural South. All registered ABs are descended from hill Bulldogs originally and as of the late 1990's some breeders are still going back into the sticks and buying dogs that are pure American Bulldog even if they don't have formal pedigrees. Doing this requires expertise because you could easily wind up with a Pit Bull cross or a mongrel that looks like a Bulldog. Most hill Bulldogs have performance confirmations. There are a few big blocky ones that resemble Johnson/performance crosses, having at least medium length muzzles because no sour mug has been added.

Mitch Allison raises hill Bulldogs with Scott traits and champion catch dog credentials.

There are more than just physical differences between the Johnson type and the performance type. As we shall see, the Johnson line has to some degree been recently manufactured and should be considered more of a working Bullmastiff than a true Bulldog. This is not a bad thing. The original Bullmastiff was the finest guard dog ever, much better than an animal oriented Bulldog for man work.

The founders of our breed, Johnson and Scott, combed the South in concert to find likely breeding candidates, they also bought dogs from each other and bred dogs together. Painter got his dogs mainly from Johnson and Scott. Johnson started in the 30's, Scott in the 60's and Painter in the 70's. Today only John D. Johnson and Alan Scott are still breeding Bulldogs.

When examining a high performance but non-pedigreed hill Bulldog and trying to decide if he was a purebred Old English White or not, Johnson and Scott scrutinized the dog's conformation and gameness. If two dogs showed equal gameness on cattle, wild boar or wild dogs they would lean toward the one with a shorter muzzle, undershot jaw, white color, heavier bone and muscle. A preference was given to Bulldogs that had more aptitude at cattle catching than boar catching. Later Scott type breeders would select hill Bulldogs with longer muzzles and even bites because they wanted hog hunters.

Suregrip's Rattler is a combination of the Johnson and Scott/Painter type.

These efforts to save a breed from extinction by scouring remote swamps and mountains of the rural South did not occur in a vacuum. During the same time period other breeders covered the same territory and rescued other rare southern breeds, namely Curs, Catahoula Leopard dogs and several hounds. These southern breeders began formal registration and breed associations in the 50's, 60's and 70's. This does not mean that the various rare southern breeds are not ancient. The first historical reference to Leopard dogs is 1686. The same thing happened in the Midwest with the unregistered working farm collies which formed the foundation for today's registered English and Australian Shepherd, neither one of which is directly from England and neither has been anywhere near Australia.

To say there are three lines today is misleading since virtually every breeder has mixed the bloodlines and some have developed their own lines, having as many or more generations under their belts as Painter had before retiring.

Today there is a growing movement to create an intermediate type halfway between Johnson and Scott/Painter. Suregrip kennels has gone the farthest in creating a Johnson and performance blend. The AB community calls this intermediate type 'Hybrid,' an unfortunate mis-

nomer since a true hybrid occurs when different species are crossed, such as a wolf and a dog.

The Bulldog community has been a fractious and bellicose group for the past two decades. The breeders and fanciers are only now, at the turn of the 20th century, overcoming a horrible divide. Throughout the 80's to the late 90's there seemed to be almost two armed camps. On one side - Johnson breeders, on the other - Scott/Painter. This conflict seemed to start around '81 when Scott and Johnson, who were once friends, suddenly became less friendly. Apparently the flare up occurred because one of the breeder's dogs started beating the other's at NKC dog shows.

Slowly, ill will spread to the whole Bulldog community. Part of the problem was that unconsciously the modern breeders had adopted an erroneous AKC philosophy about dogs, namely that within a breed only one type is correct. Because of this rigid thinking the two camps were constantly accusing each other of all kinds of horrible things.

The performance crowd hurled these charges at the Johnson camp: "Your dogs are overweight, flat faced, non-athletic couch potatoes that would get cut to ribbons by a wild hog. If you're raising real bulldogs let's see you catch a bull or a hog. Furthermore, it looks like you've crossed in English Bulldog (sour mug), Bullmastiff, English Mastiff and St. Bernard, because of this you have a higher rate of hip dysplasia."

The Johnson crowd makes these counter-charges: "Don't talk to us about cross breeding, you guys have introduced Pit Bull and Catahoula to the point where we're ashamed to be registered in the same breed book as you. You're dogs are so thin boned and long snouted they don't even look like Bulldogs."

Performance crowd: "You're view of what a Bulldog looks like is colored by the English sour mug. If you look at old paintings our dogs are closer to the original. We should really split into two separate breeds."

Johnson crowd: "O.K. but we get to be called American Bulldog because the old paintings that we've seen look like Johnson dogs."

Performance crowd: "Oh no, we get to be called American Bulldog, you get to be called American Bullmastiff or Johnson Bulldog."

Johnson crowd: "Wait a minute, John D. Johnson invented the name American Bulldog."

Performance crowd: "No, Joe Painter did."

Throughout this period the two camps created different breed standards and brandished them as weapons as the Philo-Kuon and late sour mug breeders did a century earlier in England. Within the American Bulldog fancy many different standards have been popular at one time or another in the past 40-years. The first was a very short and inclusive description written by Johnson in the fifties that is on file with the Animal Research Foundation. The second was written by the American Bulldog Association (ABA) in the early 90's, it described a moderately blocky performance type or a Johnson/performance Hybrid, it went up to 120-pounds for males so most Johnson dogs could fit under its umbrella, at least in regards to size. The third standard was written by the American Bulldog Club of America (ABCA) and described a pure Johnson type with males going up to 135-pounds.

The last two organizations were engaged in a bitter turf battle over which standard would be adopted by the American Rare Breed Association and used in their shows as well as others. This battle raged through most of 1995. The champion for the ABA was Casey Couturier, for the ABCA - John Blackwell. The two camps lined up behind these two men and waged war through the pages of AB magazines, newsletters and the Internet. Some outsiders thought that this impasse was a blessing in disguise because it meant that ABs couldn't participate in many dog shows, which tends to eliminate show breeding. Mr. Johnson is of the opinion that standards are not really that important. One negative consequence of the battle was the vitriol and accusations that the two camps flung at each other confused tyros to the fancy.

In late 1995 Casey Couturier's magazine boldly announced that his side had won and the Rare Breed Association had adopted the ABA standard. Needless to say the Johnson camp felt crushed by this revelation.

A giant step toward reconciliation occurred when the ABA created a dual standard that allowed for a Hybrid performance type dog and a non-exaggerated Johnson type dog. The Johnson/performance Hybrid was dubbed the 'standard' type and the Johnson Bulldog was designated as the 'bully' type. ABA dog shows soon featured show rings with the two types

being judged separately. John Blackwell and his ABCA joined the ABA and non-extremist Johnson aficionados happily began showing their dogs and started earning ABA show points.

This didn't sit well with the Johnson extremists who formed small splinter groups, a fresh batch of standards that called for exaggerated features and started hosting their own dog shows. Meanwhile, the NKC created a new performance standard that allowed solid brindle and fawn ABs and continued holding shows. The ABA at first couldn't stomach the NKC's acceptance of solid brindle dogs but has since wisely liberalized its stance on colored Bulldogs. The NKC has since adopted the two standards within one breed idea.

Kevin White's Flo, OFA, is an example of a performance AB.

In the late 90's Al Joye created the American Bulldog National Alliance (ABNA) and began hosting large AB shows. The ABNA has a Johnson and Scott class that they call classic and standard. Like the ABA, the ABNA shows feature a plethora of working events such as tug of war, weight pull, protection, etc...etc...

My personal opinion in the Johnson vs. performance conflict is this: while the two types of AB may differ from each other substantially, neither one is more correct than the other. While it is true that the performance or standard type is older and closer to the original working Bulldog, neither type is more pure than the other. On the other hand, the two camps did zero in on some legitimate problems in their opponent's bloodlines.

To the charge that Johnson Bulldogs are all couch potatoes with bad hips I direct you to a later chapter in this book where I interview several breeders that are producing big (but not gigantic), short muzzled, athletic, dogs with hips of steel. Some of these breeders are even catching hogs with smaller Johnson Bulldogs, though admittedly pure performance dogs are much better in this arena. Big blocky Bulldogs have set world records in weight pulling and have excelled at personal protection. Large Johnson dogs are less successful at protection sports and hog catching because of the jumping and high-speed running involved. Many performance breeders consider 10% to 50% Johnson blood essential to their programs to increase a Bulldog's guardian capacity. There are no performance breeders with zero percentage Johnson blood because of the Old Time Johnson strain (which has no sour mug).

Machine Minnie of WAB is an example of a Johnson AB.

One legitimate gripe is that many Johnson breeders are not performance testing, weight pull testing or X-raying the hips of their breeding stock and are breeding just for size and exaggeration, this is the sort of thing that will turn Johnson ABs into giant sour mugs. Breeding for size and sour mug features will guarantee that the resulting progeny will have a serious problem with hip dysplasia since this disease is closely linked to rapid growth in the early life cycle of a dog as well as a cloddy build.

At an average price of $1000 an AB puppy is expensive. If a given breeder thoroughly tests his breeding stock this price is a bargain. If not, then you may as well save your money

and get a dog from the pound. A randomly bred mongrel will have better hips, and overall soundness, than a dog bred for size and a flat face.

Another kernel of truth is that Mr. Johnson has introduced AKC English Bulldog blood into his line. Anyone who has compared the Olympic athletic abilities of an AB to the slug-like capabilities of an AKC sour mug will recoil in horror at the thought of this blood polluting our gene pool. However, if one were to look at hundreds of AKC English Bulldogs once in a while an atavism or throwback to the original type appears. These throwbacks have longer legs, a big sturdy rear end, long tails, hard muscular bodies and smaller heads. Unfortunately they do not have very long muzzles and their jaws can be heavily undershot. One quality the atavisms have is the ability to deliver puppies naturally. Over 95% of AKC Bulldog bitches must have c-sections to deliver, so among the few naturally whelped litters a handful of true atavisms occur. The atavisms seem to always have long tails.

I personally know of one such dog here in San Francisco, a pure AKC Bulldog named Dudley who can run almost as fast as our ABs, leap like a kangaroo, has high prey drive, is only slightly undershot and actually has a muzzle. With the right training he could do catch work but the weather would have to be cool since his muzzle is still so short he can't dissipate heat efficiently. Dudley can leap high into the air, catch a rope and hang on while you twirl him around. When people see him they think he is a very muscular, extra wide, Boxer.

Mr. Johnson (through David Leavitt) also found an atavistic AKC Bulldog named West Champ's High Hopes, an athletic 80-pounder that use to run with a high school track team for his daily work out. This dog came from a special strain of English Bulldogs from Pennsylvania that sometimes produced dogs with long legs and long straight tails. High Hopes was a beautiful golden brindle with white flashing. He had an even and loving disposition but could take someone down if there was good cause. He was used in the 70's to create Johnson's Mean Machine and Sugar Doll strain. The Mean Machine strain has been widely used to produce superior guard dogs.

A charge often leveled against Johnson that is false is that he bred Olde Bulldogge into his line. Two dogs can be found in the Mean Machine and Sugar Doll strains that several people claim were Leavitt's Olde Bulldogges. These dogs were named Bullmead's Queen and Sugar Doll. These two females were not actually Olde Bulldogges but straight crosses between the English Bulldog - West Champ's High Hopes and pure Old Time Johnson stock.

Olde Bulldogge is the name of a recently created composite breed started by David Leavitt of Pennsylvania. The foundation breeds are: English Bulldog, Pit Bull, American Bulldog and Bullmastiff. Olde Bulldogges are fairly athletic, can be protective and they are true Bulldogs since by all indications some would be capable of bull baiting, in cool weather of course. Mr. Leavitt's breeding program is quite rigorous and includes X-raying for hip dysplasia as well as at least one foundation dog that was tested on wild hogs. Many Olde Bulldogges have dark masks and fawn or brindle coats because of Bullmastiff blood, this is an extremely dominant color pattern and shows up in any breed crossed to an English Mastiff or Bullmastiff. It is very rare to see a fawn AB with a black mask. As I mentioned, there is a strain of brindle Bulldogs bred in Cleveland, which still have white flashing. Ninety percent of American Bulldogs are white or piebald and less than 1% have black masks.

Bull Mead's Crib, an Olde Bulldogge

I don't think there is any English Mastiff or Bullmastiff in the Johnson line or any AB line because these rare black mask sightings could be caused by brindle Bulldog blood, which will once in a rare while produce a black mask.

How extensively the ½ English Bulldog and ½ American Bulldog females (Bullmead's Queen and Sugar Doll) have influenced the

Johnson line can be ascertained by looking at photographs of his dogs over the last 55-years. The only appreciable change has been a slight shortening of the snout, a more undershot jaw and an increase in the amount of color found on the formerly all white coats. The shorter snout does not even appear in the Collette strain which often produces three-inch muzzles or longer.

The performance crowd will say that Johnson's dogs have gotten much larger and other breeds like smooth coated St. Bernard are responsible. This perception is due more to the tendency to exaggerate weights on the part of Johnson breeders than anything else, for example, a famous recent Johnson stud, Elrod, was advertised as weighing 150-pounds. From videos that I have seen his actual weight was more like 120-pounds or less and much of this weight was fat. Johnson's first really big Bulldog was named Mau Mau, this dog was alive in the late 40's and weighed 120-pounds. There were no smooth coated St. Bernards in Georgia at that time.

After sharing a mouse, it's time for a nap.

His first big dog registered with an outside organization was King Kong in the 70's, weighing about 125. This dog's lineage has been absolutely verified by reliable non-Johnson breeders as pure Bulldog. Mr. Johnson keeps the collars from his biggest dogs of yesteryear. The collars are all about 28-inches around. Subtract for looseness and the dog's necks were roughly 27-inches, which translates to about 120-pounds of Bulldog. Any Johnson dog that weighs much over 120-pounds is probably carrying the extra weight as excess body fat.

I admit that some of the smaller, athletic, smooth coated St. Bernards do bear a striking resemblance to the larger Johnson Bulldogs.

Based on physical appearance and color this is the only big Mastiff blood that could be in the Johnson line. If you look at the history of the St. Bernard you will see a lot of Bulldog was crossed into this breed around 200 or 300-years ago. One theory on the origin of the Saint is that it was a cross between the Pyrenean Mastiff and the Bulldog 400-years ago. If St. Bernards are heavily inbred they become even more Bulldoggy in appearance, they are reverting back to a parent breed. This might be where the resemblance comes from.

Some St. Bernards also exhibit Bulldog traits when they fight. In 1970 the Ken-L-Ration dog hero of the year award went to a 170-pound Saint in Alaska who fought an eight-foot tall grizzly bear that was attacking his owner. This dog leaped into the air and locked his jaws on the bear's nose. When his grip was broken he attacked the eyes and face. He managed to get another lock on the nose, tore a piece off and finally drove the grizzly back into the forest. Only a dog with Bulldog blood would fight in this manner.

Mike Harlow works out APBT Rock. Large blocky white APBTs resemble performance ABs.

Of course you could also say these similarities would allow a Johnson breeder to introduce some small amount of St. Bernard without any noticeable difference other than size. Some people insist that smooth coated St. Bernard was used to get Johnson ABs back to their normal size after the introduction of atavistic English Bulldog shrunk them down. If this did occur then consider this: the Argentine Dogo also has a small amount of Smooth St. Bernard in it and they are one of the finest boar hunters in the world.

One must also bear in mind that originally Mr. Johnson bred the smaller performance Bulldogs along with the jumbo plantation dogs and mixed the two. More recently, he and other Johnson breeders have been selectively breeding for large size and have abandoned the performance type. There is only 30-pounds of extra weight to account for between the biggest old time bear-baiters of England and a modern jumbo Johnson Bulldog. The largest old time Bandogges probably weighed slightly over 100-pounds and most Johnson dogs today weigh less than 100-pounds. The first ABCA show champion weighed 88-pounds. Suffice it to say that anyone who has talked extensively with or knows Mr. Johnson well would realize that he would never cross anything into his dogs that he didn't consider true Bulldog.

Another contention from the performance breeders is that these out crosses have introduced a higher rate of hip dysplasia, a condition where the ball and socket of the hip fail to develop normally as the dog grows. In extreme cases there is no socket in the hip at all and the femur is held in place with leg muscles alone. This crippling genetic defect is on the rise in a breed once known for genetic soundness. Since hip dysplasia is linked to rapid growth and large size, the performance breeder's charge that Johnson Bulldogs have a higher rate of this defect may be true; on the other hand, just as many Johnson type American Bulldogs have passed OFA as the performance type. The cause of increased hip dysplasia (in my opinion) is not so much out crossing as indiscriminate breeding, puppy milling and breeding for size alone. If you intend to buy a Bulldog (Scott or Johnson) make sure both parents have had their hips certified by OFA or Penn-hip and have been performance tested or weight pull tested. To make sure the OFA rating is not faked get the dog's OFA number from the breeder and call OFA for verification or check OFA's web site.

For some reason even completely sound ABs rarely achieve an OFA rating of excellent, however they should at an absolute minimum test OFA borderline or better. A minimum acceptable Penn-hip rating would be lower than median on their numerical rating system with no degenerative joint disease. ABs with hips near the borderline should only be bred to dogs with superior hips. If all AB breeders would breed within these parameters our breed would soon

48

have no hip problems. The best breeders functionally test and X-ray the hips.

Penn-hip promises to be a very effective tool for conscientious breeders. Penn-hip uses more angles in their X-ray evaluation of a dog's hips than OFA. They compare the movement of the joint in the hip in these different positions and compute the amount of laxity, which is then expressed numerically. This number is called the Distraction Index. The lower the number the better. Penn-hip can be done on a young dog, it is not subjective and many breeders feel that it is the wave of the future.

The out crossing charge that has been leveled at the performance breeders revolves mainly around Pit Bull and to a much lesser degree Catahoula. This is a more difficult knot to untangle because large hog hunting strains of the American Pit Bull Terrier are true Bulldogs and these strains have shared many names over the years with ABs. Besides Brindle Bulldog at one time they were called Pit Bulldog as our breed was. An old southern strain of big bull-doggy Pits characterized by red noses, red coats, red toenails and green eyes were called 'Old Family Reds' which sounds a lot like 'Old Family White'. Hog hunting Pit Bulls probably have no terrier in them at all and may be a strain of American Bulldog or vice versa. There was a long established tradition of docking a brindle or white Bulldog's tail to differentiate between a fighting Pit Bull and a Bulldog.

Old timers from the South insist that though large hog hunting/bull catching Bulldogs have always been a separate breed from small fighting Pit Bulls, a dollop of fighting blood was sometimes added in the 50's to strains of performance Bulldogs when they needed more grit. The old timers were careful not to add too much because the Bulldogs had to hunt with other dogs and couldn't be dog aggressive. The addition of a small amount of fighting Pit blood made the AB a better catch dog. If you're wondering how the greatest catch dog in the world could be made better by a breed that is the greatest fighting dog, consider the American Quarter Horse and the Thoroughbred.

Until a few decades ago it was thought a pure Quarter Horse could run the quarter-mile much faster than any other horse, beating even a champion Thoroughbred race horse. We now know that when about 1/16 to 1/8 Thoroughbred blood (or hot blood) is added to the Quarter Horse it can beat a pure Quarter Horse and anything else in the quarter-mile. If too much Thoroughbred is added the advantage may be lost, certainly the ability to work cattle is lost. Today modern Quarter Horses have a drop of hot blood in them and are the better for it. I think the same thing can be said about the performance strain of American Bulldog in relation to the small fighting Pit Bull, a drop is good but any more is harmful.

Getting ready for the beach

A drop of game Pit Bull is a good thing to have in your AB even if you don't intend to catch hogs. I realized this myself the other day when one of our non-dog aggressive ABs (who certainly has at least a drop of Pit Bull) was minding her own business while we walked along a beach. Suddenly a big nasty Neapolitan bounded out of nowhere and attacked. Our dog performed what I can only describe as a judo flip and sent the Neo rolling down a sand dune. On another occasion she was running and playing on the beach with a friendly Pit Bull male when she was attacked by the male's mate, a tough Pit bitch. Our Bulldog used strategy by getting the smaller dog into heavy surf where she was able to fight it to a stand still until I (along with the surfers who owned the terrier) could tear the dogs apart.

Too much fighting APBT blood is certainly something to be avoided if, like most people, you are primarily interested in a guard dog. Fighting Pit Bulls are less territorial than ABs and less protective. Their natural enemies are other dogs. No home has ever been burglarized by a dog. There is probably some small amount

49

of fighting blood in any AB. The media hysteria against the APBT has created a false image of these dogs in the public's imagination. People have told me that Pit Bulls have swollen brains that make their craniums explode and drive them mad with a killing frenzy. Other people think they are part wolverine or the spawn of Satan.

Notice the clean whelping box. All breeders should take this much care of their dogs. In fact, Flo gets her teeth brushed twice a week with an enzymatic toothpaste.

Several years ago the media and Hollywood painted a similar picture of Doberman Pincers. Back then everyone loved to say Dobermans turn on their owners, which isn't true. The image of this breed is only now recovering from that onslaught. Sadly, Doberman breeders were forced to de-emphasize protective capabilities to improve their breed's acceptance. In my opinion the fighting Pit Bull Terrier has only one major draw back - an inborn tendency for animal aggression. The main difference between an AB and a fighting APBT is that a Bulldog will stop fighting once his adversary submits. ABs have been bred for centuries to make other animals and people cry uncle, not destroy them. If a strange dog is submissive right away the Bulldog won't do anything at all. If a small dog is aggressive most Bulldogs will ignore it. Our oldest AB has been attacked and bitten by Yorkies and toy Poodles and done nothing more than carefully hold the little dogs down with one paw until they submit. Some game Pit Bulls will attack any dog and not stop fighting until they have killed it. With proper training and socialization a skilled dog trainer can overcome this tendency. Every APBT that I have ever met was completely trustworthy

around children. Experienced Pit Bull men tell me that none of the horror stories about APBTs ever involve game bred dogs, that is dogs that actually fight and are bred to fight on a serious level by professionals. While I certainly don't condone dog fighting, whenever there has been an unfortunate incident it usually involves ignorant people and dogs that are scatter bred or crossbred. Often these novice dog people have insecurity problems and are encouraging their Pit Bulls (or crosses) to be overly aggressive in some misguided effort to appear macho. Of course people like that should never be allowed to own Pit Bulls or ABs. Luckily, the AB has not yet reached this crowd and still has a good reputation. This is partially due to the high price associated with our breed.

GWK's Landshark, 25-inches tall, 26-inch head, 110-pounds

If you want a performance AB that has does not have a recent infusion of fighting Pit familiarize yourself with the physical differences between the two breeds. The fighting Pit Bull has a wedge shaped head and tight lips. The AB's head is square or brick shaped and has more pendulous lips. ABs are more likely to have undershot jaws. Pits sometimes have short straight tails. AB tails are longer. Both breeds are muscular but ABs are heavier boned. The bodies are shaped differently, performance ABs have thicker, heavier rear ends that sometimes remind people of the rumps on Quarter Horses. ABs also have wider chests. When ABs run on a hard surface they even make a sound like a horse, small fighting Pit Bulls never give this impression. The reason for the AB's big rear end is that he is a catch dog and needs the driving power of these rear muscles to perform his job, so this is an important breed characteristic.

The predominant AB color is white. Most Pits are brindle, black or varying shades of brown. Sometimes white Pit Bulls have black spots, white ABs have brindle or brown patches, though dark brindle can look like black. ABs rarely have red noses or gold eyes. Pit Bull ears can stand more erect. ABs are usually taller, wider and heavier but if a Pit and an AB weigh the same the AB should be shorter. Pit Bulls have longer fangs than Bulldogs, ABs have thick fangs of medium length. Once again this is because the AB is a catch dog and fangs that are too long will penetrate too far into flesh, hit bone and break if the dog holds on for a long time. The AB has a thicker and softer coat than the Pit Bull. An AB is more likely to have a short muzzle than a Pit Bull.

The two breeds look more alike than different, which shouldn't surprise anyone since old time hog hunting strains of APBT are 100% Bulldog. Many Pit Bull breeders are producing big blocky dogs that weigh close to 100-pounds but are not using the old hog catching strains. Consequently, these big Pits can still have an insanely high level of dog aggression, a reflection of 200 or 300-years of selective breeding. Dog aggression doesn't come from any outward physical appearance, most ABs that resemble Pits are completely trustworthy around non-alpha dogs.

Physical Pit characteristics are healthy and functional. Tight lips allow a dog to avoid fanging himself when he bites. The Pit's almond shaped eyes are less likely to have entropia than the Bulldog's round eyes. Small Pitty ABs should (on average) be more physically sound than large sloppy Mastiffy ABs.

As far as Catahoula blood, the same advice applies, learn what these dogs look like and select parents that are Bulldoggy in appearance. There are no negative repercussions to a little Leopard dog blood. Catahoulas are less dog aggressive than Bulldogs, are super athletes and can be fine home guards. Our oldest bitch has some Catahoula characteristics and I'm sure this takes the edge out of the small amount of fighting Pit that's also in there.

It is ironic that performance breeders are charged with Leopard dog crosses when many pure Johnson dogs have eyes the color of glacier ice and blue spots on their bellies, which are Leopard dog colors. These big Bulldogs are usually very thick and wide so any Leopard blood

was introduced long ago and should be in there. The color to watch for is blue merle, a sign of a recent Catahoula out cross.

Any quest for ultimate purity is nonsense anyway since nobody really knows the origins of this breed. In old England, Mastiff, Greyhound and Terrier were judiciously introduced to the original Alaunt at one time or another to create the Bulldog and the Bandogge. Any doubts about the quality of an individual Bulldog's heritage back then was proven in the bear garden or bull run, not by pouring over a pedigree.

Tar Heel's Oscar

One important test for purity was observing where the dog got his grip while baiting a large animal. Pure Bulldogs always went after the head. When baiting a bull, going specifically after the nose was considered the best test for purity. I once owned a Pit Bull/Bullmastiff cross that would grab cattle by the tail when he got loose and wanted a joy ride. By physical appearance alone I could have passed him off as an AB since he was white and brindle, but his method of attack gave him away.

Every American Bulldog that I have ever seen catching a large animal has always gone for the nose or ear. By the standards of ancient England these are pure Bulldogs. Some Pit Bulls will grab a wild boar by the leg or tail, in old England they would not be considered true Bulldogs no matter what they looked like. Alan Scott would try the unregistered dogs he got from the hill country on cattle in this manner to test for purity. This was a much better test than some scrap of paper and is one of the reasons why today's AB is pure Bulldog.

All that one can be sure about is the performance and behavior of the immediate ancestors of a puppy. If the only thing wrong with fighting Pit blood is dog aggressiveness, then make sure your puppy's parents are not so inclined. If you feel Catahoula blood will make a Bulldog less heavy-boned or muscular, then look for these traits when you check out breeders. Anything in a dog's ancestry beyond three generations has almost no impact anyway. That's why we shouldn't worry if there is a dash of St. Bernard or fighting Pit Bull in a certain AB strain seven generations ago.

A typical Tomahawk pup

Karasek's Bear at 8-months, rag games are a good foundation for later protection work.

One final word on out crossing to other breeds, if you were to talk to fifty different AB breeders and ask them what breeds their competition has crossed into competing strains or lines you'll hear everything from Mexican Hairless to Alaskan Malamute. When you ask these same people if they themselves have ever out crossed the answer is always no. I tend to believe the latter and I think all the rumors about out crossing have been wildly exaggerated, mainly they are a device for one breeder to make another look bad, this may be a human flaw but it doesn't effect the quality of the dogs. Never try to learn about one breeder from another.

Buck - Chow Hound I

Bane - Ring Brevet, BST, Schutzhund Bh, OFA

Our First AB

When Martha (my wife) and I began our own search for a Bulldog puppy we wanted a large but not gigantic female that was non-animal aggressive yet could deal with a human intruder and do farm utility work. The horse ranch we live on is located in a sleepy little town 30-miles south of San Francisco. Our town had just experienced its first gang-related murder along with other big city problems, which we thought we were immune from. The horse ranch is surrounded by suburbia so a more realistic problem is neighbor dogs chasing cattle through fences, out of pastures and into street traffic. I wanted a dog that would chase away stray dogs but not kill them or go after cattle or horses.

Our living situation is unique because the two of us occupy only a tiny portion of the 21-acre horse ranch owned by my father. Besides my day job I have caretaker responsibilities. Our dog would have to be friendly towards chickens, cattle, horses and four other dogs. She would have to watch Australian cow dogs herd cattle and not join in. Though I would have to herd cattle with her in the event the cow dogs were out of town and a fence was down. Chasing stray dogs but not killing them was a must because these are not wild dogs; any strange canine actually belongs to our neighbors.

We began our search 70-miles to the north on a farm operated by John Martin, who raises rice and Bulldogs. He had two Scott stud dogs, five Scott bitches and one stud that was a Painter/Johnson Hybrid.

By way of demonstration the 85-pound Scott male, Askum, was turned loose in a huge flat field with several adult females. The dogs raced to the horizon and back, when they reached top speed they flattened out like Greyhounds, feet barely touching the ground. Occasionally they would hurtle over each other and engage in mock combat, all without losing a stride. Mr. Martin brought Askum back to his side and explained how raccoons can endanger a rice levy by burrowing. He told Askum to jump into a rice patty. The brindle and white Bulldog jumped into the water with a great splash and menaced an imaginary raccoon. He seemed fully capable of driving out if not actually killing an adult raccoon by himself. Apparently he has to do both as part of his duties as a working farm dog. Askum was hooked back onto his chain. All three males were kept on separate chains with lots of space in between.

In the course of his demonstration two females actually pulled a large muskrat out of an irrigation ditch. They tore it to bloody shreds. His prize bitch, Cindy, trotted up proudly to present us with this grisly trophy. Mr. Martin praised her for good varmint control. Martha's face turned pale.

Bully as a pup

We then looked at a six-week old litter. There were 8 pups, all white. As we approached the fence of their enclosure 3 pups stood up from a sleeping pile, ran over to where we stood and growled. Martha was shocked at the apparent ferocity of such young puppies. Watching the adult dogs had already unnerved her. Not because they weren't friendly after being properly introduced (we could pet them and play with them). No, it was simply their appearance that intimidated her. When they leaped in the air and snapped their jaws, huge white canines would flash like sabers. Martha had never heard of this breed before meeting me. Her last dog was a tri-color Collie.

Mr. Martin's dogs were the first ABs I had ever seen in person. I had been reading about them for years in Carl Semencic's books and in the ads of Dog World magazine. As I've mentioned, my last dog was a Pit Bull\Bullmastiff cross who was so irresponsibly aggressive toward cattle I had to sell him to some bikers who needed a guard for their clubhouse. Before that I had a Pit Bull\English Bulldog cross that was gentler but not exactly a Cockapoo. So I was prepared for my first

Bulldog encounter and thought I knew enough to recognize a good one.

Mr. Martin noticed Martha's trepidation. He brought out one of the puppies that hadn't growled. This pup ran in circles and wagged her tail. I noticed she had some pigmentation, three cream colored spots against a snow white body. I wanted to take her home but Martha wouldn't hear of it.

I asked Mr. Martin the difference between Scott and Johnson bloodlines and got my first taste of the deep disdain that performance breeders have for pure Johnson Bulldogs. He told me that his Scott dogs could run right over the bigger Bulldogs. He did show me his 116-pound stud, Spike, who is half Johnson, a Suregrip type breeding from Watchdog Kennels. Martha thought he looked a lot friendlier.

Matt Green's Bane, I could have purchased this dog as a pup. Photo - Michelle LeNoir

There was a litter on the ground out of Spike and a Bama Boy strain female. This breeding was ahead of its time, only now are Suregrip/Bama Boy crosses becoming popular. Martha was so upset that we didn't even look at this litter but hustled back to the Bay Area. In the years to come I would follow the career of the pick male from the Spike litter that we hadn't even considered. This dog's name is Matt Green's Dragon's Bane. Bane is a therapy dog, has a Schutzhund Bh, Canine Good Citizen, French Ring Sport title, BST, OFA, has foiled a real life car jacking and participated in police protection seminars. Bane took high in his Schutzhund and Ring Sport trials. If we'd been more thoughtful we could have had Bane or

Bane's sister. Of course many of Bane's accomplishments can be credited to Matt Green's training but he is clearly a great AB.

On the ride back Martha used words like fire-breathers to describe the dogs she had seen. In what seemed to me an example of feminine illogic, she was especially upset by the red color inside Askum's mouth. "It looks like fire or blood, how could a dog with a mouth like that be friendly?" There is no answer to a question like that so I grunted and stared straight ahead. She suggested that if our pup was to do farm work we should be looking at Collies next. With a sense of growing panic, I begged her to let us look at one more litter of ABs.

That next litter belonged to Mike Coffey of Oakdale, California. He had only one breeding pair: Roy - a pure white 90-pound Scott male and Smooch - a 95-pound brindle and white 1/4 Painter, 3/4 Johnson bitch from Suregrip. Smooch resembled Spike, heavy-boned and jowly but with a working length muzzle and a tight athletic build. There were 13 puppies on the ground, all fat and healthy. Smooch was able to nurse all these puppies because she was bagged up like a Holstein dairy cow. I had never seen such a canine milk machine.

Mr. Coffey had trained all these puppies to come to a whistle. He would stand on one side of his garage (which had been turned over entirely to puppy habitat) and whistle, the whole mass of squirming pups would leap toward him. The pup we would eventually pick reached the breeder first. I made a note of the fast pup's color pattern.

These dogs and puppies seemed more docile to Martha. What was important to me was that Roy appeared roughly equal to Askum in athletic ability, which isn't surprising since they are half brothers and came from the same kennel (Bill Hines' in Texas). Martha repeated the whistle and the puppy pack bounded toward her. The same pup that had won the first race was now in Martha's arms. This puppy immediately fell asleep. This was to be our first Bulldog.

When we came back in two weeks our pup was chasing her littermates around the garage like a brindle and white tornado. She seemed pretty aggressive. Mr. Coffey told us if we wanted a different selection, a pig hunter from Oregon had his eye on this one. Martha wasn't sure if her idea of acquiring a docile Bulldog was panning out, it was my turn to insist and we brought this pup home and named her Bully in honor of her attitude toward her littermates. Incidentally, Mr. Coffey was also disdainful of pure Johnson dogs, he told us about his visit to Mr. Johnson's farm in Georgia and his impression of Johnson's famous stud, Elrod. "All he did was sit around, I like my dogs to move." I should point out that he was visiting at the height of summer.

Both Martin and Coffey believed that the performance type could be effectively crossed to a larger, medium muzzled Johnson phenotype. The breeding that produced Bane was quite similar to the one that produced Bully.

Dave Putnam developing Bully's bite

The first thing Bully did was eat, she was so ravenous we assumed she was starving. We kept putting bowls of food before her. The food kept disappearing. We stopped feeding her when we lost count of the number of bowls she'd consumed and her round stomach was tight as a drum. This was the beginning of Bully's life long obsession with food, she has always been a glutton. Insanely high food drive is an AB trait and can cause problems such as eating foreign objects that can block the intestines. Another problem is obesity. On our veterinarian's advice we tried not to let her gain more than 1/3 pound a day by carefully monitoring her food intake. There are environmental causes of hip dysplasia as well as genetic, one is rapid weight gain, another is too much calcium in the diet because it makes the bony part of the hip grow faster than the tendons and muscles, which distorts the

shape of the hip socket. Professionals always make sure at least two or three ribs are showing on any Bulldog.

Bully was trained as a pup to be friendly with our cats.

My last dog could never be broken of his intense animal aggression. I had raised him from a puppy with a Persian cat, even with this early indoctrination he still tried to kill this cat and every other four-legged creature on Earth. I mentioned his favorite sport was to grab cattle by the tail and swing behind them like a water skier, the few times he did this the steer's tail would get torn off. So it was with great fear that I introduced Bully to the ranch cats, horses, cow dogs and cattle.

My fears proved groundless with cats, though I've had to reprimand her now and then, Bully has never hurt our cats and only chases a strange one. She loves the cats she knew as a puppy and will protect them from feral cats or other dogs. These cats love her and are always bringing her dead birds, which are immediately consumed with gusto. As a puppy she would corner a strange cat and just stare at it with her tail wagging and a goofy look on her face. As an adult she would kill a cornered cat that she did not know. No one can convince me that she has more than 1/16 Pit Bull in her, my 1\2 Pit Bull crosses would have broken through plate glass windows to kill any cat.

Even though as a puppy she was introduced to cattle, horses and chickens, all with great success, she did have a natural tendency to bite large herbivores on the nose. I was able to break her of this predilection and she never got to sink her teeth into any form of livestock except the ones ground up in her dog food with one exception and the fault was mine.

Bull, 111-pounds, Gator x Doozey

Bully's kennel runs adjacent to a corral that was being used to raise three young stallions. These four animals grew up together and became great friends. They would race around the corral joyfully at break neck speeds. At first when Bully got excited she would try to grab one of the horse's noses in true Bulldog fashion. Since I was able to break her of this bad habit (by using a long line and a pinch collar) I allowed her to continue to play with the stallions. She still made mock lunges for their noses and they would lash out with their hooves but they all knew it was a game and nobody was hurt.

One day it was decided that the stallions weren't going to be bred, they were gelded and moved to another corral. In their place two grouchy old mares appeared. At first I wasn't concerned because Bully had always ignored all horses except the three stallions. For some reason she decided that the old mares were replacement playmates for the friends she had lost. She started running and lunging at their noses. They didn't think it was a game and fought back. This raised the stakes for Bully and she became more aggressive. In old England and Spain horses were sometimes used in the blood sports when a suitable bull couldn't be found, history was quickly recreating itself in our backyard. I took very stern measures with Bully and with great difficulty eventually broke her of this new found sport of horse baiting. She became so enamored with the idea of not chasing horses that she will tackle any dog she sees chasing a horse. This has happened several times on a public beach that we frequent where horses and dogs are both present. The horse riders are very grateful to this public service we provide free of charge. If I had used a radio controlled shock collar I could have broken Bully of horse baiting much more quickly and easily.

Other than this one incident Bully's animal aggression has seldom been a problem but human aggression when she was young was a bit more taxing. Most puppies go through a domination stage where they vie for alpha status with their human parents. We all remember that month or so when needle sharp puppy teeth make us feel like human pincushions. Bully had a strong desire for alpha status and she challenged us constantly. Fortunately she learned quickly not to puncture human flesh and would instead go after pant legs or shoe laces, always at unexpected moments. It can be quite disconcerting to have a 40-pound ball of muscle suddenly grabbing your pant leg and begin pulling with the power of a mini-Mack truck.

Bam Bam, Bully's future mate

There are a few ways to correct this behavior. One way is to transfer this aggression to an accepted play toy like a knotted towel or old sock. Be careful not to use a broom or you will never be able to sweep again without driving your Bulldog insane. The other ways to correct the aggressive pup are with a squirt gun, noise from a shaker (a can half filled with coins) or by grabbing it by the scruff and gently holding upright the way a mellow mother dog would under similar circumstances. It is important that you don't hit a Bulldog as a form of punishment. The best way to check unwanted behavior in a young dog is with an obedience style correction, a snap against a choke collar with a leash or a direct snap on the collar. Most dominant AB pups can be dissuaded from attacking their owners by rolling a large hard plastic jungle ball in front of them and encouraging chase games. For most Bulldog pups aggressive energy should be channeled into play toys that don't involve tugging against a human.

I chose the more aggressive method because I thought I might need to have Bully protection trained some day. I wasn't interested in personal security so much as breeding her. Many reputable breeders consider successful Schutzhund or Ring Sport protection performance a vital breed test. I assumed that if I wanted to use one of these breeder's stud dogs he would want to evaluate my female's protection aptitude. If you want to protection train your Bulldog remember to always let him win at games of tug of war as a puppy. However, the vast majority of AB owners should not play tug of war with their dogs or attempt protection training.

During Bully's first year she attended a local obedience school and quickly zoomed to advanced level, leapfrogging over the intermediate classes. One of the reasons she did so well was that Martha began training her at three months, we should have started even earlier. One of the secrets to a well-adjusted Bulldog is to start obedience training very early, eight weeks is ideal.

I have been around dogs all my life and had never seen one as smart as Bully. I decided to try and quantify her intelligence. I chose a 12-step test developed by Stanley Coren called the Canine IQ test. It includes simple problem solving such as placing a food treat under a large towel and timing the dog with a stop watch to see how fast she can figure out a solution. Other parts of the test are more elaborate but to make a long story short, Bully easily mastered each step in the minimum possible time. For example, she grabbed the towel with her teeth and jerked it off the treat in seconds. According to Mr. Coren's scoring system Bully would be described as brilliant with fewer than 5% of all dogs scoring this high. For an American Bulldog her intelligence is only average.

Since Bully is a typical AB, physically and mentally, for the purposes of this book I decided to quantify as many of her capabilities as possible by having her compete with other dogs in various ways. I had her race against labs and other water dogs by throwing a ball into a lake and seeing which dog could retrieve it first.

All these dogs could swim so fast they threw out a wake. Bully beat every Lab I put her against until she met a big muscled English bred male who edged her out. I tried her against a Chesapeake Bay Retriever who barely won by a nose. I believe her swimming ability is in the upper one percentile for all dogs but only average for an AB. This should come as no surprise because while hog hunting in the South a Bulldog is as likely to catch his quarry in water as on dry land.

Bully and Martha Putnam graduate from obedience school.

I raced her against various breeds of dogs on land in a similar manner with more disappointing results. Almost any athletic dog that weighs 50-pounds or less can beat her. A physically sound German Shepherd at 90-pounds is about equal in the sprint but better at long distances. A Rottweiler of the same size she can usually beat. Bully has more of a Johnson build, which doesn't mean she's slow but somewhere around average for all dogs and slightly below average for all ABs, considerably slower than a 70-pound performance bred AB.

As far as strength goes I will devote a whole section to Bully's weight pulling career but suffice it to say that she ranks in a fraction of the upper one percentile in this category.

Also during her first year I showed an

amateur's ignorance by starting protection work without professional advice. We did rough games of tug of war that included rapping her rump with a stick. While she was still a puppy I foolishly tested her with a strange man (he trains horses and cow dogs) who acted as an agitator, running up to her, stamping his feet and shouting. At this tender age she would growl and lunge forward but break off her charge without a bite, circling the trainer stiff legged and bristling. The horse trainer backed off too because he didn't have protective clothing on and she would bite if pressed any harder. This meant Bully was slightly above average for an AB in protective instincts since the very best dogs will launch into a full fledged attack when agitated for the first time, even as a puppy. She had what it takes to be protection trained though. My next step would be to take her to a professional trainer.

Bully doing beginning cart work.

I would later regret my amateur efforts. I now believe that in protection training ABs should never have their defensive drives stoked. They should be encouraged to bite the protective gear out of a sense of fun and prey drive. Bully became a little too sharp because of the self-defense instincts I stoked in her as a young dog.

Before her first birthday I abandoned my plans for protection training. Bully had growled at a few strangers on her beach excursions, which made both Martha and I uncomfortable even though a quick correction curtailed this behavior. More importantly, I had seen an ad in Dog World magazine for Mountain Gator Kennels. A breeder in Colorado was training and breeding ABs for international weight pulling contests and his Bulldogs were apparently dominating this sport. This avenue seemed better suited to Bully's personality and physique. She's

only 24-inches tall yet weighs 90-pounds. Her musculature reminds me of a canine Arnold Schwarzenegger.

After reading some basic information on weight pulling I bought a cheap walking harness and padded it with fleece, then converted a sturdy garden wagon into a pull cart. Bully started weight training and found her true calling in life. She was quickly able to pull several hundred pounds a short distance with her cart. Every few weeks her strength would increase and I could add more weight to her wooden wagon. Later I would find out how inferior my equipment was and bought a professional harness and had a weight cart custom made that can hold 2500-pounds. I had done all this for only $350. My plan was to wait until she was two or three then compete in formal weight pulls with her. Our veterinarian recommended we not push her too hard in this sport until she was a little older. As you will see I didn't follow his advice, which was perhaps my second mistake.

Never let the cart hit the dog from behind

At the beginning of her weight pulling career Bully experienced an accidental agitation and I learned a valuable lesson. Some day laborers were being employed temporarily to haul away tree stumps near her kennel. She was locked up for two days while they worked. One of these men was a wise guy and he teased her for those two days. On the third day she got out and headed straight for this guy, he escaped by climbing a fence where she held him at bay. I couldn't call her off because she hadn't been formally protection trained and didn't know the out command. Her normal obedience commands were ineffective in this situation. The lesson is obvious, don't fool around with protection training unless you know what you're doing and have professional advice.

Some performance breeders are absolutely opposed to weight pulling as a breed test. I consider competitive pulling a good test for three reasons: 1) A successfully completed weight pulling regimen guarantees physical soundness. Rigorous pulling over many years is a good test for loose joints because every joint, muscle, tendon and bone is tested not just the hips. Of course catching wild hogs over a period of several years is a great test also. Some performance people I've talked with can't understand why I don't make the effort to pursue this avenue if I'm willing to put out the effort to weight pull. Actually Bully's breeding is 60% performance and 40% Johnson and I have a hog hunting friend who would help me train her. I would love to do it but Martha informs me that any steps in this direction will lead immediately to divorce. 2) It can also test for a stable temperament because at a formal weight pull other dogs, squealing kids and curious adults are milling around in a state of confusion. Loud speakers are blaring, schedules are changed, dogs are stressed by the competition mentally as well as physically. The first IWPA pull that I attended was held 100-feet from a railroad yard. The dogs had to compete while locomotives were being decoupled from trains, blasts from air brakes wafting in their faces as they pulled. 3) It demonstrates trainability and the spirit to win, also known as heart.

I decided to buy a male puppy to train and compete in weight pull with the ultimate goal of breeding to Bully and hopefully producing champion pullers. I thought (at the time) that we would need a male from a pure Johnson bloodline. Since then I have learned that pure performance as well as the Hybrid type have won IWPA gold and silver medals. I didn't know that then, so Martha and I took a road trip through the South, Southwest and Midwest where we visited only the prominent Johnson breeders. We made our first stop in Chaparral, New Mexico. At Ruffhaus kennels stood one of the biggest working ABs ever, Mullen's Bubba, a 120-pounds of muscle, sinew and bone. That summer a heat wave killed most of the breeding males in the South and Southwest that were Bubba's size. We had to cross off all the truly huge, short muzzled, Johnson studs from a list we were counting on seeing. We only got to see medium muzzled giant Bulldogs. It was 110 degrees in Chaparral during this heat wave and

big Bubba was unfazed. Heat prostration may have cut a deadly swath through jumbo Bulldogs with very short muzzles and lots of body fat but Bubba has a roughly three-inch muzzle and was trim as a fiddle.

Bubba, OFA Good, unfazed by heat wave

Mr. Mullens introduced us to his gargantuan pooch. He was far from a 'couch potato' or 'porch Bulldog,' nicknames that some performance breeders use automatically for any AB reaching the upper possible size for this breed. We watched a video of Bubba doing protection work. He seemed extremely agile for his great bulk. I brought up the performance breeder's arguments against dogs over 100-pounds and pointed out that any good 90-pound performance bred Bulldog would be about 30% faster than Bubba and could bite just as hard. While admitting this point, Mr. Mullens pointed out that Bubba was probably still twice as fast as the average man and that the dog's extra weight and strength was very punishing on the human agitator that we had just seen in the video. It was true, Bubba had streaked across an open field time and time again, hitting large men wearing body suits and hockey masks. The decoys needed all the extra protection available. Bubba leaped a good six- feet from his intended target and hit the men at chest level, biting and engulfing his victim with front legs then throwing the agitator to the ground with a hard thud and a bounce or two after impact. Bubba treated these men like rag dolls. Once he had the men down he tried to attack the few inches of exposed flesh that the bite suit and hockey mask didn't cover. He was very tough and Martha thought he had a mean streak. But when he was outed he let the agitator go. She thought he was a little reluctant to do this. Bubba was friendly to strangers if properly introduced, so he was not a complete psycho.

Blackwell's Rising Star, 100-pound daughter of Elrod and Suzie

Ironically Mr. Mullens wasn't at that time trying to breed really large dogs. While breedings before and after our visit have produced the wide, heavy, pull type dog I wanted at the time, the females that Bubba was being bred to at that point were smaller performance types with very high prey drive, which Bubba also has. The Mullens performance style bitch I liked best was named UFO. I played a game of tug of war with her and her intensity was beyond belief. She shook the rag I was holding so hard my teeth rattled. These dogs are very good for personal protection but in my misguided opinion only Bubba had the right build for weight pulling so we forged on.

We did learn that Bubba had a half brother named Deacon in Oklahoma, so this became our next stop. This brought us to John Blackwell near Tulsa, Oklahoma. His dogs are known to be of a very uniform type and quality, all the dogs we saw that day were Bulldoggy and beautiful. Some have also excelled at protection work. Mr. Blackwell bred Bubba. Another one of his breedings, Preacher, has proven to be a fine protection dog. Both of these dogs were out of a bitch named Black-eyed Susan. Descendants of Susan have also placed Best of Breed in conformation shows and have racked up Best in Shows. Apparently she throws working ability, another descendant is the first AB to become a certified Narcotics Detection dog.

The sturdiest breeding pair available then to my jaded eyes was Deacon (110-pounds)

and Honey Bear (100-pounds). Both these dogs were powerfully muscled with heavy bone and straight legs. They looked like they could pull up tree stumps. Unfortunately there wasn't a scheduled breeding of these dogs.

Mr. Blackwell is a recognized authority on this breed and was very helpful, imparting a great deal of information about Bulldogs in general. He showed us several old prints from England and compared them to modern dogs. He even studied our dog's pedigree and disqualified several of his breedings as a potential cross. His concern was with all the Scott and Painter in Bully's ancestry. Even though he is a Johnson breeder he uses performance blood and felt that for her to pass on her heavy musculature and other Bulldog characteristics she would need a pure Johnson male. The dog I liked, Deacon, was only half Johnson. Mr. Blackwell seemed very reluctant to sell us a male puppy out of his (in my opinion) best stud, he recommended that we visit John D. Johnson of Summerville, Georgia and Mark Landers. I had to admire Mr. Blackwell's conviction. He was willing to pass up a sale to do what he thought was right.

Purgavie's Penny, Blackwell's Deacon x Maggie

Which brought us to the father of the American Bulldog. While getting directions to Mr. Johnson's kennel we were reminded how different life is in the rural South compared to our yuppie existence in California. Mrs. Johnson warned us not to make any wrong turns and wind up in a neighbor's backyard or they would, "surely shoot you."

Kaser's Bulldozer Mack, MGK Gator Red x Blackwell's Georgia

Mr. Johnson is a wonderful and charming old southern gentleman. He talked with us for hours about his dogs and the breed's history. He showed us some massive leather collars that belonged to early monster dogs. Their necks must have looked like oak stumps.

He regaled us with stories of heroism performed by his dogs of yesteryear. One of the tasks that people in the 50's and 60's used Old Time Johnson dogs for was to clear out packs of wild dogs in the South and coyotes in the West. Mr. Johnson has raised purebred Angus for many years and he has used his own dogs to protect his cattle from these varmints for an equally long time. On at least one occasion feral dog removal abilities on the part of a Johnson dog saved a man's life. This incident involved Dick the Bruiser, who probably weighed 80-pounds.

In the late 1960's a neighbor of Johnson's was confronted by a pack of wild dogs. Luckily, Dick was nearby and able to come to this man's rescue by body slamming into the feral leader, temporarily disabling him. Then Dick engaged several wild dogs at once, holding the whole pack at bay. He noticed a sly loner was sneaking up on his human partner who had managed to shoot one dog before running out of ammo. Like lightning, Dick eliminated this sneaky threat and stayed to confront the massed fury of the remaining pack while his human partner went home to reload. Upon returning to the scene of the crime Johnson's neighbor found all the criminals (wild dogs) were dead except one, who was

breathing his last between the crushing grip of Dick's jaws.

Another interesting story involved a dog that couldn't be used in Mr. Johnson's breeding program because it was too man aggressive. This dog would tear through steel cyclone fences to get at intended victims. Finally, Mr. Johnson had to put it down by asking his neighbor to fire a large caliber round into its head. This dog lived for five minutes and was able to tear out of its enclosure one last time. He showed us a hole in a fence where this had only happened a week or so ago.

Johnson type, Harris Gypsy Girl, 100 lbs

As we listened to these stories I began to realize that Mr. Johnson, in his day, had performance tested his dogs in at least five different ways. He once used Bulldogs to catch wild cattle, domestic cattle and wild hogs. He once used them to wipe out packs of wild dogs and against human intruders.

Aware that Mr. Johnson was at the center of so much controversy within the fancy I abandoned my manners and baldly asked him if he'd ever crossed Saint Bernard into his line. His face grew red and he told me the name of a person who he thought had started that rumor. He stated flatly that it was false. I asked him, "what about English Bulldog?"

His face lost the angry red color and grew serene. A faint smile creased his lips and his eyes became misty as though looking into the distant past. Our visit to Georgia was before the admission of Johnson breeding to West Champ's High Hopes. I expected him to become even angrier by my near accusation. Instead, in a soft voice, he answered my question with a question. "Have you ever seen an English Bulldog born before the 40's, before World War II?"

I told him that I had spent endless hours studying old time Bulldogs. He grew excited and waxed poetic about the prettiest dogs he'd ever seen - pre World War II English Bulls, long-legged, sturdy, creatures with two-inch snouts. I nodded enthusiastically. He wasn't answering my question though, apparently changing the subject. Without explicitly saying anything I believed he was hinting that atavistic English Bulldog was used in his breeding program many decades ago.

Mr. Johnson gave us a second shock when we showed him Bully's pedigree. He told us it was false. A Johnson Bulldog named Aristocrat was supposed to be her great grandfather. He told us with certitude that it wasn't so. I got the feeling that his memory was pretty sharp and the information was accurate. Later research revealed that he was telling the truth and Bully actually has more Johnson blood in her than we thought, but out of Smith's Spot Bull, not Aristocrat.

Bam Bam is from the old Dick the Cruiser strain. Farnetti bred out of Dozer and Ruby.

We would have loved to purchase a puppy from Mr. Johnson but his best stud dog, Elrod, had just died that summer and his breeding program was in temporary disarray. He had three beautiful females that I thought would have produced good weight pullers if Elrod were still alive. Mr. Johnson told us if we were interested in pull dogs go straight to Mountain Gator kennels, so we packed up and headed west to Colorado.

We arrived early for our appointment with Mr. Landers so there was nobody around. We walked up to a cyclone fence that encompassed a ¼-acre enclosure. Bam Bam met us at

the fence; a wide and powerful Bulldog with a head like a trash can lid. He stared at me unmoving, unblinking and silent. There was a hard glitter in his eyes. I felt like a bird hypnotized by a snake. Slowly I touched the fence. His mouth opened fractionally and I felt more than heard a subterranean growl. Martha whispered, "let's get out of here."

Bam Bam showing perfect form

At that point Mr. Landers drove up the driveway and said, "oh, I see you've met Bam Bam. I'll let him out." Before we could protest a gate was opened and this behemoth was in our midst, wagging his tail and wiggling like a puppy, transformed from an evil Mr. Hyde to a kindly Dr. Jekyll because of his owner's acceptance of our presence. I was shocked to hear that he weighed only 95-pounds, due to his conditioning he looked much heavier.

We watched him dash from corner to corner of the large enclosure, leap in the air and cork screw twist his body out of sheer joy like a rodeo bull. His muzzle was as short as any dog we'd yet seen. His snout was broader, however, and he breathed as freely as Bully or any long muzzled Bulldog. Bam Bam is pure Johnson, out of the Farnetti strain, which is from Dick the Bruiser blood. Bam Bam is only a little larger than his forebear. At the time of our visit he was undefeated in his weight class in the IWPA (International Weight Pull Association) and showed no signs of ever being beat.

Like all breeders of ABs, Mr. Landers won't let adult males loose in the same yard. So Bam Bam was locked up and Gator was let loose. Gator is half Johnson, half Painter and weighs 115-pounds. As is the case with the other weight conditioned Bulldogs, he gave the impression of being even bigger. His rock hard body seemed to radiate power. At that time, Gator was the second strongest dog in the world. Not only did he routinely beat all dogs in the 120-pound and under weight class, he more often than not out pulled all the giant dogs found in the unlimited weight class. There was one 200-pound English Mastiff named Sly that consistently pulled heavier loads and was the strongest dog on Earth at the time of our visit.

MGK Gator Red winning a weight pull

Gator can literally run circles around this or any Mastiff. He is as swift and nimble as he is strong and proves it in 'tough dog' protection competitions. He leaped and sprinted around the ¼-acre enclosure in a convincing display of agility. When he finally came to a stop I stood in front of him, placed both hands on his shoulders and pushed, Gator pushed back. He was an unstoppable wall of living force. My feet skidded backwards. His face broke into a canine grin as if to say - 'don't even think about it buddy.'

Doozey having fun with her cart. Weight pull training has a practical side.

Then we looked at the females, they were all gorgeous, but the 103-pound Doozey impressed us the most. She is pure Johnson, Bam

Bam's sister and basically a larger version of her brother. She has as an IWPA weight pull record that is unbelievable, ranking her as one of the strongest dogs on Earth. A cross between her and Gator would hopefully produce the champion we wanted. Such a mating was being planned in the near future so we eagerly put a deposit down and reserved a male puppy. I would later learn that several dogs out of Gator and Doozey were OFA certified good. One of them (Tyson) weighs 139-pounds, making him the first jumbo Bulldog with certified hips of that caliber.

After this decision had been made Mr. Landers explained his program in general terms. He considers weight pulling a more realistic test than pig hunting since the vast majority of Bulldog owners and even breeders will never see a wild boar. Of the handful of people who catch pigs with dogs the majority use Pit Bulls anyway. The Bulldog men who do breed and use hog dogs may not consider weight pulling athletic but this feeling is not shared by the rest of the world. An article in Dog World magazine called weight pullers the ultimate canine athletes.

Bushwacker, 130-pounds, Gator x Doozey

The other test he uses is personal protection or man work, this recreates the Bulldog's original job of catching and holding large animals and is, of course, what everyone is looking for in a guard dog.

I asked specific questions about what would constitute the perfect dog in his program and a picture emerged. A weight of 110-pounds is ideal. The dog must be capable of dragging well over his own body weight a mile and a half over hilly terrain. He must be capable of a very high level of man work but should out (stop attacking) on command without the use of electric shock collars, even in the training phase.

Bushwacker showing his weight pulling heritage

Most breeders are very interested in muzzle length. Mr. Landers is more concerned with muzzle breadth and the length of the mouth from back molar to the canines. This is because his dogs have such wide heads and big foreheads that the muzzles are short if you measure from forehead to nose. Yet they have long, wide, mouths that are capable of engulfing a man's arm in a single bite or dissipating heat on a muggy day.

In his experience the smaller Scott dogs have broken down more frequently under his regimen than the larger heavy-boned Johnson dogs. He starts puppies pulling at 6-weeks old and in a few months they are pulling ten times their body weight. This stresses the dogs and magnifies any structural flaws they might have. Weak dogs literally fall apart and are put down. This may sound heartless until you seriously consider the alternative, breeding weak AKC type dogs that will develop dysplasia and live in agony.

After garnering all this detailed information I asked Mr. Landers if his family had a long history with the breed like Johnson and many other breeders. He showed me two telephone sized books that include his family history and family tree, which has roots in Georgia stretching back 270-years. It turns out that he is a direct ancestor of James Oglethorpe, the founder of the Georgia colony and the first man to bring English Bulldogs to America in 1733. Another branch of the Landers family tree includes the Nations family who bred their own line of Bulldogs in central Georgia for many years. His third stud dog, Half Acre, is a Nations/Johnson cross. It is clear that love for this breed is in Mr. Landers' blood.

We never purchased a Gator/Doozey puppy because I grew fearful of having a short muzzled dog that might weigh over 130-pounds. Instead, I converted my puppy order into a stud fee and bred Bully to Bam Bam. We kept the male pup from the Bully/Bam Bam breeding and named him Bear. He grew into 78-pounds of dense bone and striated muscle. Bear breathes freely from a broad, 2 ½-inch muzzle on a trash can lid head identical to his father's. He runs and jumps on OFA good hips connected to perfectly straight limbs and has fangs that jut from a moderately undershot lower jaw. Even experienced dog people guess his weight is over 100-pounds.

Action Jackson, 135-pounds, Gator x Doozey

Bear became Martha's cherished pet and she refused to let me protection train him or pull weights. When Martha's not watching us like a hawk, I have Bear drag heavy logging chains over a mile long course and guess that he could be a super star. I foiled her stricture against protection training once by staging a mock home invasion. Bear will launch into an attack on a genuinely threatening stranger yet is a pussy cat around invited guests and could be let loose in a kindergarten classroom and would roll over on his back to let little kids scratch his belly. The truth is that Bear is a much better watchdog than Bully, his hair trigger mother, because he has superior judgement. The other nice aspect of his personality is an utter lack of dog aggression, with non-alpha dogs.

After living with Bear for three years my view of the two-inch muzzled Johnson or Bulldoggy type American Bulldogs has radically changed. The maximum allowable size should be 95-pounds and the preferred weight under 80 for males, less for females. I can saddle a horse or climb on a mountain bike and go for a 20-mile run with Bear in moderate to warm weather. He can live through any heat wave if he has shade, fresh water and the mountain bike is left in the garage. He will hopefully live to be 12-years old or more. He is the modern equivalent to a Philo-Kuon Bulldog. I could bait bulls with him all day long if the temperature was below 75 degrees. I speak from a real world experience involving an encounter with a nasty wild steer that my Dad brought in from the Mexican desert. Bear will hit an aggressive charging steer on the nose and hang on like the grim reaper. A placid cow or steer he will ignore.

Gator - IWPA Gold Medalist, Runner-up in World's Toughest Dog

Bulldog Extravaganza

Our veterinarian advised us to go very slowly with weight pulling before Bully was two-years old. "Even then you should compete with her only once or twice." I winced when he made that pronouncement but Martha perked up. "Why is that Dr. Kennedy?" she asked.

"Your dog will go through the same amount of ligament stress that a veteran NFL lineman or running back will go through if she pulls competitively for any extended length of time."

As we drove away from the clinic Martha started quoting the vet and building a logical argument against Bully's weight pulling regimen, which was now four months old and just beginning to get intense with her first competition two and a half months away. Bully was only 17-months old. She shouldn't really be competing until she was a little older. Unfortunately the American Bulldog Club of America was holding its first Bulldog Extravaganza on June 10th 1995. I was so impressed with the content of this program that I accelerated Bully's training program to be able to compete in Tulsa, on that date. Part of the proceedings would include five canine competitions that would serve as informal breed tests for American Bulldogs: Weight Pulling, Protection, Temperament, Obedience and Conformation. A dog could be entered in as many categories as desired, each one of the five would be rated equally and an overall champion would be the dog with the most accumulated points from each event.

This was one of the early 'Irondog' competitions that would eventually become common at any AB show. At the time Irondog contests were rare. The coordinators of the ABCA were hinting that the performance events might be precursors to European style Breed Suitability Tests. If the ABCA included all these functional test in future dog shows and breeding selections were based on the results they would be creating a breed club almost as good as the protection sport organizations overseas. I wanted to support that effort.

We entered Bully in Weight Pulling, Obedience and Conformation. To get a certificate of merit we had to do well in at least three events. After we had already sent the check

away and confirmed our choices I found out that John D. Johnson was going to judge the confirmation competition and had second thoughts since Bully is a Scott type. After an internal wrestling match I decided not to switch from Confirmation to Temperament because this category had elements of protection work associated with it. In the temperament test a dog had to walk through a gauntlet of distractions and hazards and would have to show steadiness and good nerves throughout. One of the hazards was going to be a threatening stranger, the dog was supposed to react defensively and show willingness to attack. I had no doubt Bully would attack the agitator during this test, which would be the correct response and we would do well in scoring, but at the time we had decided never to agitate her again after we'd worked through her stranger aggression problem. This left Protection, which is real bite work or Confirmation.

OEA Trademark Pete, Penn-hip certified, champion weight puller

Martha pointed out that we had shown Mr. Johnson dozens of photos of Bully last summer and he had loved her. He did say that her muzzle was too long by just a whisker and that if he were to breed her, he would pick a male with a snout less than two-inches long, an opinion I might disagree with but had to respect.

With that decision under my belt, I had the task of competing with a Mark Landers' dog in Weight Pull. With only four months training completed, Bully had done almost no cart work but had advanced pretty well with her drag weight training. This latter technique consists of a dog drag pulling a percentage of his body weight over a gently rolling outdoor course about a mile to a mile and a half. Bully was up to 70% of her body weight for that distance. To compete seriously she should pull 100%. I had to forgo further drag training because in a very short time period I had to get her use to pulling a heavy cart a short distance in front of a large excited crowd filled with Bulldogs and boisterous Bulldog people.

Bully trains for the big pull

I called up friends and relatives and scheduled a single dog weight pull, three weeks before the competition. In the interim, Bully worked with a fully loaded cart. Her pulling surface was short shag carpet over a thick rubberized surface. This meant that when I put 500-pounds on the cart it would sink into the carpet and rubber, which made it difficult to pull. In the competition she would pull on a firm carpeted surface and the cart would have steel wheels on steel rails. The differences in surfaces meant that Bully could pull somewhere between three to four times the weight in the Tulsa competition that she could at home. She started her new training regimen able to pull 500-pounds her training distance of 25-feet, ten more than the competition length. After a few weeks she could pull 600-pounds.

I called Mark Landers for weight training tips and to find out what dogs he would bring. He claimed he wasn't going to compete in Weight Pulling with any of his world class dogs. He would show several dogs and Gator was going to compete in Protection. The only dog that was going to pull was an eight-month old puppy named Stumpy who would probably weigh about 80-pounds. Bully had lost a little weight under her increased pulling program and

weighed 85-pounds. She would have to compete with Stumpy. Mark's dog had been weight trained from birth and was one of his rising stars. Stumpy would probably pull over 3000-pounds in Tulsa. He informed me that the ABCA had decided to handicap his dog by 30%. So to win, Bully would have to pull about 2400-pounds on steel wheels. This meant that she would have to increase her maximum by 75-pounds a week and be pulling about 750-pounds on the rubberized carpeting before we left for Tulsa.

At the beginning of the third week she was ready for her mock pull competition. Bully reacted well to the small crowd I had assembled. I decided to allow some clowning. Bully warmed up by pulling several little kids piled onto her 16 square-foot cart.

After this we got down to business and I put real weights onto the cart. She pulled harder than ever when the crowd cheered. I piled more weight onto the cart and urged my audience to applaud even more enthusiastically. A change came over the crowd though when she was struggling with a load near her failure point. My kinfolk saw Bully's muscles quivering and her eyes popping out as the cart inched forward with agonizing slowness. They stopped cheering and started begging me to reduce the load. I told them that Bully had to pull this weight at least two more times to get a good work out. "No way," one of them said while Bully was still pulling, "can't you see she is exhausted?" They mutinied on me and surged forward and started petting Bully, declaring that she had won the contest. Naturally my Bulldog stopped her pull and started licking everybody's face. I unhooked her harness and pulled it off. She romped with the children to celebrate her victory. I'm sure in Colorado her nemesis Stumpy was still harnessed up and pulling in her traces.

A week and a half before the competition Bully was right on schedule, able to pull 700-pounds, only 50-pounds from her goal when disaster struck. She sprained a shoulder muscle during a running session on the beach. I stopped pulling with her and watched the limp subside over a two-day period. I hesitated starting the regimen again though. Just because she had stopped limping doesn't mean there wasn't an injury. I called our vet and set up an appointment.

The first thing Dr. Kennedy did was have me trot Bully around in circles. "Yep she's lame," he said. "She's pulled her right front shoulder muscles. I can see the swelling from here." He was standing about five-feet away. "Let's get her up on my examining table for a closer look." To get to his office we had to walk past his stable of Polo ponies. Dr. Kennedy said, "it looks like she got this injury from running, not from pulling. It happens all the time with my Polo horses." I told him that he was correct, the first sign of limping came after she had run in soft sand. He then asked me to give him the details of our entire work out program. I told him it includes running nine-miles a week in three-mile segments, swimming a couple hours a week and heavy cart pulling every other day. Before that she had done the same thing except instead of cart work she had pulled drag weights for a mile every other day.

Capt. Crunch, Bam Bam x Mary, both parents IWPA gold medallists

"O.K." he said, "if you want to have any chance at pulling with her in Tulsa her new program has to be swimming every day, no running, no weight pulling. I want you to swim the bejesus out of her so she's tired and doesn't want to run. Give her these supplements twice a day." He pulled out two large plastic bottles filled with pills. "Here, smell this one." He pulled out a green pill and crushed it. The whole room was filled with the smell of raw seafood. He showed me another pill that contained glycosaminoglycans, a nutrient for the connective tissue between muscle and bone. He went on to further explain the effects the supplements would hopefully

have on her recovery. He would look at her the day before all three of us took off for Tulsa, in eleven days. He would advise me then if she could compete or not.

I took her straight to a small fresh water lake nearby and had her swimming five minutes after I had finished talking to Dr. Kennedy. She seemed strong in the water, powering across the 100-yard lake like a motor boat. She reached the other side and raced up the bank. I winced with every step and threw a stick in the water on my side of the lake. She swam all the way back to retrieve the stick. I made her retrieve for a half-hour of hard swimming.

When my pickup came to a stop in our driveway I ran around to the back and told Bully to stay. Normally she would jump out of the bed herself, this time I hefted the sopping wet Bulldog and set her down gently. I toweled her dry and made her walk on heel up into our house. She wasn't supposed to run even in her usual routines. Bully had to stay quietly indoors all day and all night.

The next morning I blearily opened the front door to let her out without noticing the feral cat sitting next to our garbage can. Bully did notice and remembered it was her duty to chance a wild cat off the property. We were then living in a converted hayloft above a large working barn and stables. Bully tore down two flights of stairs. The feral cat zoomed ahead of her but not so fast that our Bulldog was far behind. The pair tore through corrals and pastures, soon disappearing from sight. Bully came back a few minutes later having successfully taught this particular cat to never return. I winced when I saw her limp was more pronounced.

I called my mentor Mark Landers for some further consultation on her pulled muscle. His questions were exactly the same as Dr. Kennedy's. I explained the whole exercise program that Bully had gone through. "Hey buddy," he said, "too much running on loose sand. You should be doing exactly what you're doing but without the running. I just injured Gator the same way, on loose sand. Catching friggin' frisbees on loose sand."

He was right - that part was my addition to the regimen he had suggested. I thought that very heavy weight training might reduce her flexibility so I wanted her to stretch out in a full run every other day. I made her run on the softest part of the beach so her toenails wouldn't wear down. Pull dogs need long toenails to dig into carpet. "Yeah, but Dave, not right before a competition when she's going gonzo with the heavy cart work. A weight pull dog isn't built to go on a four hour hog hunt in a boiling hot Louisiana swamp and you shouldn't train one like he's going to. Look at Bam Bam, he has the perfect build for this sport. He has okay endurance and speed but that's not the main focus of his training."

After her weight pulling career ended, Bully focused her efforts on bite work and obedience.

"I gotcha, what do I do now for recuperation?" He asked me to repeat the veterinary advice I had received so far. Mark agreed with everything that Dr. Kennedy had recommended, but added two things: routine massage for the torn shoulder and I should make her do some light pulling with the drag weights on the day of the vet inspection. If her injury reappeared or was exacerbated with this small amount of stress then there's no way she could compete in Tulsa in her strongest event. I would be forced to enter her in the temperament test. Maybe the injury would prove to be a blessing in disguise. I knew she had ability in weight pulling and would compete in this arena at a different time when her shoulder healed. When would I get a chance to go through a formal temperament competition? Fortunately the temperament test was one I didn't have to train for since the only part that would benefit from training, the encounter with an agitator, we had decided to forgo completely with this dog. This one last agitation would be made begrudgingly on our part but we figured that she'd been foolishly agitated several times already, once more wouldn't make any difference. At that time we thought none of our dogs

should be protection trained at all, they would work in weight pulling and obedience, period.

I wasn't giving up completely on weight pulling in Tulsa. I woke up June second and thought, "I have seven days to heal Bully." I swilled a cup of coffee and looked out my front window for evidence of wild animals or other mischief. It was a good thing I did because I saw my brother's athletic 45-pound Boxer bitch, Fritzie, was running loose just outside. Apparently this city dog was here to visit her country cousin. Fate seemed to be conspiring against me. I grabbed Bully's heavy steel prong collar, which has steel tines that dig into a dog's neck when you pull on the leash. With the prong collar, I could control Bully even if she lunged in full attack mode. These two dogs have known each other since puppyhood. They are very rough playmates. Their normal routine when turned loose in a yard is to stage a huge mock combat ending with Bully slamming Fritzie into the ground, triumphant once more.

Once outside, I held the Bulldog on a tight leash and braced myself as the canine guided missile named Fritzie headed straight at us. Boxer slammed into Bulldog and Bully reared up on hind legs. I grabbed Fritzie's collar and held her down. I couldn't stop Bully from smashing into Fritzie's back with two front paws. She held Fritzie with her right paw. I helped. "Come on Fritzie," I admonished in a stern voice, "you know Bully can kick your butt so don't tempt her." The Boxer looked up at me and wagged her stump tail tentatively. I petted her and calmed her down then let her loose.

I walked over to my shop with Bully on an even tighter leash while Fritzie circled us at top speed. Bully whined to be let loose to play. I told her, "no" and tied her in the back of the shop, out of range of any sparks that would result from my welding. I also wanted her near a window to avoid noxious gasses from my work. Occasionally I glanced at her from the corner of my goggles while welding and twisting hot metal bars that morning. She tried to look mournfully or even reproachfully at me for denying her exercise. This would be a tough day for the poor Bulldog. Bully's only exercise would be a swim.

Later that evening I thought about her weight loss during the heavy pulling and decided the commercial dog food that we were using wasn't giving her enough nutrients. She should have been getting heavier with muscle build up, not lighter. I asked Martha her opinion on our beleaguered canine athlete's nutrition program.

Her reply was to open the freezer and begin thawing a huge chunk of ground sirloin. She said, "in their last book the Monk's of New Skete recommended raw beef as a dietary supplement, besides it will help me feed her all these pills." She swept her hand out in a grand gesture to indicate eight pills lined up on the table. She noticed my frown and interpreted it correctly. "Don't be so cheap, open your wallet and let the moths out."

For the next few days I tried to keep Bully quiet and swam her so much she almost sprouted fins. On the ninth of June I loaded dog, harness and drag weights into my pickup and headed off to the vet. I had a pretty good idea what he was going to say since she had a slight limp though her swelling had gone down. And I was right, he said she was still lame after just seconds of observation. I confessed my failure to keep her from running since our last visit. I blamed feral cats and other forces of nature that seemed lined up against me. He wanted me to harness her up and have her pull anyway to see if the limp became more pronounced.

Bully was excited when I pulled out her harness and hooked her up to the drag weights. She hadn't been allowed to pull for awhile and missed it. She had looked wistfully at her harness as it hung on the wall many times in the last few days. Now she stood still, waiting eagerly for the command "pull," only her tail moved with vigorous gyrations. I hesitated, trying to think of a way to get her to pull gently but her training was to tear forward with all her strength. Finally I just said the word quietly. She surged forward, the concrete weights fish-tailing wildly behind her. I trotted in front, leading her around a dirt field. Dr. Kennedy watched studiously. When she was done, I unhooked her and we walked around again. Then Dr. Kennedy walked her and I watched the left front leg. The slight limp was still there, neither better nor worse.

"What's interesting," he said, "is that she doesn't seem to be in any pain when she pulls those weights. On the other hand, she clearly has a muscle pull that will take at least eight weeks to heal completely. If she was an old dog at the end of her career as a weight puller and this was to be her one last competition, I would say go

ahead, do it. But she's not even two-years old." He made a gesture that said the conclusion is obvious, there will be plenty of other opportunities for her to compete.

OEA Miss Piggy, future weight puller

My shoulders sagged with defeat. I knew that much of my motivation for rushing her recuperation as well as rushing her initial conditioning was because of this book. My chapter on the Bulldog Extravaganza would be much more satisfying if I could write about Bully's triumph over Mark Landers' superstar, Stumpy.

Dr. Kennedy asked me about my mentor's advice and I recounted his warning against a regimen of long distance running while doing heavy cart work. Kennedy agreed with this sentiment. "Bully isn't really built for long distance running anyway. If you're afraid the weight work out will reduce her flexibility I recommend cross training her with swimming. This will stretch out her muscles but won't stress her joints. It seems to me that she gets plenty of running no matter what you do."

The lake that we go to is about three-miles from the vet's office. I drove there slowly and trudged dismally down the trail that led to the small body of water, Kennedy's words about her running too much no mater what I did ringing in my ears. Bully pounced on a lizard, literally jerking me out of my lethargy since she was on lead. She emerged from a bush with the squirming reptile in her mouth and gulped it down happily. I laughed, at least the pressure was off for some kind of super recovery, she could heal at a normal pace now and a little running wouldn't hurt. I unhooked her collar and Bully dashed into the water with a cascade of spray etching rainbows into the afternoon sky.

Our flight landed in Tulsa at three the next day. We rushed to the special baggage claims area to get Bully out of her crate. We were relieved to find her in great shape. As I walked her outside the airport the first person we met exclaimed, "wow, is that an American Bulldog?" Almost no one in California will recognize our breed, invariably they say, "wow, that sure is a big Pit Bull." I guess that while not actually in the South, Oklahoma is close enough for a heightened degree of Bulldog awareness.

Mike Bell's Rosie, working hard pulling a heavy load

That evening we took Bully out for a walk in a big field behind our hotel. About ten other breeders were walking ABs. Bully had never seen a Bulldog after she left her littermates as a puppy. She reacted very strongly and positively. At first she just stood there transfixed then she whined eagerly to be let loose. We let her run around with one of the big Johnson males. She had a blast.

The American Bulldog Club of America could just as easily have been called the Johnson breeders group. Almost every dog out in that field was anywhere from 80% to 100% Johnson. They all had very short snouts. Some of the breeders started teasing me and called Bully "Pinocchio" because of her relatively long muzzle. About this time Mr. Johnson came out. I asked him if he thought her beak was too long. His reply was that a dog should be looked at as a whole and it made no sense to focus on just one thing. I probably shouldn't have been pressuring him on this point because he was going to judge her in confirmation soon anyway.

Mark Landers showed up about then with Gator on a tight leash. He checked out our dog and thought she looked nice. I asked him to examine her sprained shoulder. After a thorough inspection he told me she should pull tomorrow. I was elated on one hand but mad at myself on the other, I hadn't brought her harness. Mark said, "that's too bad because everything I brought is either too big or too small. Don't worry though, we'll come up with something." I asked him where Stumpy was and he told me she was in his hotel room listening to a Yanni tape, which always psyched her up before a pull.

The first event the next morning was the pull off. A crew of very experienced weight pull men were setting up steel rails and a rail road type cart in the middle of a parking lot, between the rails there was a carpeted surface where the dogs would be harnessed. When they were done the weight pull experts looked at Bully's shoulder, they all agreed with Landers, she could compete.

MGK Stumpy pulls slow and steady to pace herself for the heavy loads to come.

The competition arrived, Mike Bell from Wyoming had his bitch Rosie and of course, Mark Landers had Stumpy. Both of these dogs were from Mountain Gator Kennel's bloodlines. They were smaller than Bully by one or two weight classes, but were more highly trained in this sport. We would all be competing as though we were in the same weight class. Mike Bell was a protegee of Landers and had been at this sport for years. Naturally these two dogs were bulging with muscles.

The handlers loaded 1000-pounds on the cart and we all did a trial pull. This pull actually seemed to take the knot out of Bully's shoulder somehow because her slight limp disappeared. I knew the sprain was still there but there was no outward manifestation of it now. Perhaps the adrenaline and endorphins unleashed by the pull were masking the injury. The harness I had borrowed was too big, so I cinched it up with a towel, which was hardly ideal but would have to do.

Bully shows good technique by keeping her nose down.

The competition was on. All three of our dogs blew through the starting weights in the low teens. As we took our turns with the heavier weights in the high teens Bully and Rosie showed signs of strain. Stumpy, however, seemed to get her body lower and pulled slow and steady without strain. Each pull was timed and the two less experienced dogs were racking up quicker pulls but seemed to be burning out. I was a hopeless rookie and didn't understand many of the ABCA rules. Such as the option of passing at a given weight providing you pulled the next one, or the fact that you were allowed three fouls, which meant if your dog couldn't pull a certain weight in 40 seconds you would be given two other chances at it. Because of my lack of knowledge I had Bully pulling every time she came up to bat. Which burnt her out early. I didn't understand why the other two dogs were skipping turns until it was too late.

Mark Landers could see how bummed I was once I'd figured out my tactical mistake. He told the judge to let Bully and Rosie wear leashes on their next pulls as a further handicap against Stumpy, the ringer.

At 2000-pounds all three dogs were struggling. At 2200 Rosie had maxed out and had to stop. Bully took her first foul at 2350-pounds. She strained and strained but couldn't pull it, finally getting tangled in the too large

harness. I steadied her, tightened up the harness and gave the command to pull once more. Her whole body leaned into the harness, toenails digging into the carpet, her nose went down until it was only inches above the carpet. Her muscles swelled with effort, slowly the cart crept forward, picked up speed and thundered across the finish line, the crowd cheered. On her next pull Bully maxed out at 2500-pounds. The gallant Stumpy finished the event with a pull of 3000-pounds. She could have pulled about 500-pounds more but Mark didn't want to stress her anymore. The crowd gave all three dogs a huge round of applause. We were each given a first place medal because we had each won our separate weight divisions and had pulled 70% of the maximum amount pulled that day.

Keep that nose down

Mark Landers critiqued my training style after we'd put our dogs away. "You've been training her with obedience techniques," he said. "You have her sit perfectly still and straight until you say a single command then expect her to pull without another command. You even have her sit still afterwards." He could see that I didn't get his point. "Its not that controlled and precise. She doesn't need to learn to stay. She needs to explode. When you say 'work' or 'pull' get down on your knees and pound the ground with your hand. Keep saying it over and over in a rhythm that matches the dog's effort. Get excited. Get worked up." A light went on in my head. I could see exactly what I'd been doing wrong. Then a wave of disappointment washed over me. Bully was strong enough to have pulled much more than she did. As if reading my mind he said, "your dog pulled much faster than Rosie or Stumpy. If we'd stopped before she balked she would have won. She should have pulled 4000-pounds today." Bully should certainly have been stronger than the other two dogs since she weighed 20-pounds more than Rosie.

The next event was Temperament. In this event dogs were subjected to sudden bursts of deafening rap music (most Bulldogs have only heard country-western), a blast from a horn, an umbrella was opened suddenly in the dog's face, pieces of metal were clanged together unexpectedly and finally an assailant came at the dog and handler with a cracking whip. Not only did the dog being tested show evidence of going after this agitator but every Bulldog in the crowd growled and strained at its leash.

Dave Putnam gives Gator a bite.

I was congratulating myself on avoiding an agitation with Bully by participating in Weight Pull and foregoing Temperament when I was pressed into service for Protection. They needed another agitator to take a bite from a real protection trained dog, in this case Gator. I was fitted with a leather and jute sleeve that seemed heavily reinforced. Following instructions I menaced the dog with a short bamboo pole and held the sleeve in front of my body. The 115-pound bruiser came at me like a freight train, hit the sleeve and knocked me off my feet. His power was greater than I had expected. It felt like the sleeve was being gripped by a bear not a dog.

Martha was watching all this about 50-yards away with Bully sitting at her side on leash. When the big dog hit me Bully went berserk and lunged toward him, pulling Martha off her feet and dragging her along the wet grass for several feet. After a brief struggle and several shouted commands she regained control of her animal. The fact that Gator had stopped his attack probably helped Martha re-establish authority over our protective pup. Bully wound up with a sort of agitation anyway.

After this adventure we were ready when John Blackwell announced a break for lunch. We scarfed chicken fried steaks and turned Bully loose in an empty baseball diamond with Mike Bell's Rosie. The two bitches ran and cavorted like puppies. I was somewhat surprised because I was under the impression that same sex adult Bulldogs would automatically fight. Throughout the entire weekend there was not one incident of dog aggression, unless you count the time Bully tried to attack Gator. Since then, at other AB shows, I have noticed more animal aggressive dogs. I partially attribute this lack of dog aggression to the pure Johnson breeding of most of these Bulldogs.

Dailey's Tug O' War, OFA, muscular rear

When lunch was over the obedience competition began. Perhaps because everyone was getting ready for the conformation show Bully was the only dog entered in this event. I thought she would probably have taken first place even if there were some serious challengers. Bully went through her obedience routines like a soldier on a drill field, albeit a tired soldier. The crowd was milling around her during the long stays off leash, kids were dropping cans of soda and running like crazed banshees. Her head didn't even swivel at these distractions. She remained frozen in the stay command like a statue, then on the recall command she trotted slowly toward Martha and sat at her feet. Martha said, "heel" and Bully wheeled to her side and remained glued there while Martha walked past and around two men that Bully had never seen before. When this was all over the crowd clapped politely. Obedience is not nearly as exciting to watch as weight pulling or protection but actually a lot more important in day to

76

day life. We had another first place ribbon to add to our collection. Later some experienced obedience people that had been observing this event told me that Bully probably wouldn't have done very well in an AKC competition because she only walked toward Martha instead of running and wasn't moving that fast in the other commands either. People are always defensive about their own dog, perhaps unreasonably so, my indignant reply was that in an AKC competition the contestants wouldn't have just finished pulling a combined weight of over 15,000-pounds. There's no denying that for all her drive Bully has a lazy streak.

Tug O' War, show winner, Farnetti bred

Next came the event that everyone was waiting for, the conformation show judged by John D. Johnson. With our dog's new nickname "Pinocchio" we were sure we would get creamed in this event. The first part was puppy conformation. There were four young dogs entered, all about eight months old, one of them was Stumpy. The pups walked around the ring and Mr. Johnson scrutinized their movement. He made them sit still and looked in their mouths. After some deliberation he picked Stumpy as the winner then, uncharacteristically for a dog show judge, he explained why this dog was superior to the others. Mainly he was impressed with Stumpy's rock hard muscles and physical conditioning. The losers were grateful to have this explanation and I overheard some of them say that they were going to get into weight pulling.

Never good at politics, Mark Landers has a reputation for losing confirmation dog shows, which is why he got into weight pulling in the first place. Before this event he was heard muttering darkly that showing was all subjective anyway. Afterwards he was beaming and capering like a six-foot-seven, 300-pound kid.

A weight pull dog needs a strong rear end.

The adult males were up next. There were several good dogs but the highest quality dog was also the smallest. Dailey's Tug O' War only weighs 88-pounds. There were other dogs there that weighed 120-pounds and were still good quality if not the very best, specifically - none had as thick and as muscular rear as the first place dog. Tug is a full brother to Lander's Bam Bam, the IWPA champion. In fact these two dogs are littermates. Tug had entered an amateur weight pull contest a couple years ago that he won handily without one day of training. Again Mr. Johnson explained his decision. And again it seemed to be a matter of conditioning, this dog has received a lot more exercise than his competition and it showed with greater muscular development and less fat. Some people were shocked that Mr. Johnson picked the smallest dog. He once said that the ideal size for a Bulldog is one big enough to throw a saddle on. Hearing this a friend of his laughed and said for John D. the ideal Bulldog is big enough to have his own zip code.

The adult bitches were next and the dog we had to beat had a muzzle the same length as Bully's. This dog shared three grandparents with Bully and was genetically almost a sister. She was a famous bitch, Boyd's Morena, a very well built dog. Mr. Johnson was hard pressed to decide but finally gave Bully the nod. He liked her physique and the way she pulled weights earlier plus she was a quarter-inch undershot, while Morena had a scissors bite. So our dog won best bitch. We now had three first place ribbons.

Now the best bitch had to compete with the best dog, which meant we had to go up against the formidable Tug O' War. His conditioning was equal to Bully's and he was pure Johnson, one of the best in the country. So we could hardly feel disappointed when Tug beat Bully. We got to know this dog pretty well when Bully romped with him in the open field outside our hotel. He's the fastest, most agile, pure Johnson dog I've ever seen. Incidentally, Tug's kennel is located in Eureka, Missouri and is called Dailey's American Bulldogs.

Even if you are in bad shape, your Bulldog can be in top condition.

Drag pulling is essential for conditioning.

The show was over and several breeders hung around the park for two hours waiting for flights. We answered questions about our breed from the crowd and tried to be goodwill ambassadors. One breeder had a litter of puppies that he turned loose among the curiosity seekers. Before he left every puppy was sold. Finally we packed our weary Bulldog into her crate for the flight home. My final thoughts about the Bulldog Extravaganza before taking off were that this was how all Bulldog shows should be run.

Doozey - IWPA Weight Pull Champion

Nikko performing the Bark & Hold

Bully Does Schutzhund

When we got back from Tulsa Martha got an assignment from the local paper that she writes for to do a story on Tyson Kennels. She found out that not only does this kennel breed some very fine European bloodline German Shepherds, they also have training contracts with 70 police departments nationwide and run the prestigious Menlo Park Schutzhund Club. Randy Tyson-Witmer convinced Martha that our fear of sport protection training was unfounded if it was done under quality professional supervision, like the kind her club provided. They wouldn't even agitate Bully in the old fashioned sense. Instead they would stoke her prey drive in gradual steps. I told Martha that Al Banuelos had finally put a Schutzhund title on a female AB.

"That clinches it," she said, "let's make Bully into a Schutzhund." From talking to people that had actually done it, I knew it wouldn't be as easy as that, especially if Bully was going to keep competing in weight pulling. But it would be interesting to try.

We entered the intermediate obedience class before doing any protection training and I could immediately tell that the Menlo Park Schutzhund club was vastly superior to our old obedience club. One of the first things the instructor taught us was a technique for getting Bully to run during a recall not just trot or walk. If I had known it before we went to Tulsa I would have been spared the snide remarks. The technique was simple, make the dog come to you from a distance of about 50-feet, as soon as she gets moving praise her for her initial effort then turn 180 degrees and run as fast you can, naturally she lights up like a sprinter at the starting blocks. With just a few repetitions I got her running full speed on every recall. Another technique we learned was a subtle method for manipulating her choke collar while going into a sit or just after sitting that made the dog line up smartly and squarely. These are the sort of things that allow you to win an obedience contest, not just have an obedient dog.

Several of our classmates had German bred German Shepherds; one was a working police dog. Their owners gave all commands in German. This helped lend an air of seriousness and professionalism to the class, which helped all the dogs perform better.

At the end of our first obedience class we were issued a chew toy made out of jute, the same material that a protection sleeve is made out of. Bully retained the puppy habit of chewing into adulthood. She chewed on this toy every day and got use to the taste and texture of a sleeve.

Bosco shows commitment to bite

After our second class there was a protection evaluation, to see which dogs have the right temperament for this kind of training. There was also an advanced protection class for experienced dogs. Most of the obedience dogs cleared out quickly before the protection people arrived. I soon understood why. Protection dogs were locked into crates on the back of pickups. When you got near one of these crates they lunged forward, barked and snarled. This would set off a chain reaction and soon the whole parking lot sounded like the hounds from hell had been let loose. Adding to this impression was the 100-degree weather that day, which is unusually hot for the San Francisco peninsula. Between classes I had taken Bully swimming and gave her a hard work out, this was a mistake.

The candidate dogs were supposed to watch experienced dogs hit a sleeve before they were evaluated, which in itself was a mini evaluation. There were three rookie dogs: a Belgian Malinois, Bully and a big AKC Rottweiler. Bully and the Malinois got very excited when the Schutzhund dogs hit the sleeve and worried the agitator. Bully especially strained on her leash in an attempt to join in the fun. The Rottie seemed disinterested.

The Malinois went up before the evaluator/agitator with his owner holding him on a leash, all dogs were wearing wide leather collars that didn't pinch or constrict. The evaluator waved a burlap sack before the candidate dog. This sack was rolled up and sewn together like a giant cigar. The Malinois immediately grabbed it with fury and shook. The evaluator let go and told the dog's owner to run a lap. Despite the heat, they both streaked across the big open field that Tyson uses for training.

The decoy is training the dog to target the middle of the sleeve.

They came back to the evaluator, who was a muscular yet nimble man named Terry. He wore heavy leather protective clothing despite the heat. His balance and stance made me think he might be a martial arts expert. I would later learn that Terry had been a champion wrestler in high school and college and a runner up for the Olympics. The exercise was repeated again and the Malinois went for the sack with equal gusto. They raced across the field a little slower. The exercise was repeated one more time with excellent results. They ran off the field, the dog was put right into his crate and they left after the owner had been assured that her dog had passed easily. The dog was put away to create an air of expectation, the last thing it was supposed to remember was this exciting exercise, not sitting around watching other dogs.

Now it was Bully's turn, she watched Terry dully as he waved the sack under her nose. He kept doing it. She ignored him. He fastened the sack to a long rope and whipped it past her at high speed. She did nothing. Bully's lazy

streak was coming through. I sputtered in embarrassment and said that she was a holy terror earlier today chasing sticks that I threw into a lake. Terry fastened me with a chastising stare. "Maybe that's the problem, you've worn her out. You should bring your dog to these training sessions fresh." I stared at my feet, abashed. Terry tried a new tactic, flicking the sack at the end of its rope so that it hit Bully lightly in the face. She snarled at it the first time, snapped at it the second then lunged and grabbed it the third. Terry gave her a game of tug of war, let her win, then yelled at me to run with her. We galloped around the field and returned to home base. I cradled Bully as per instructions until she reluctantly spit out the burlap. Terry picked it up and waved the sack. Bully went for it without preamble. Again he gave her a good hearty tug of war, which he hadn't done with the Malinois, and we were off. We repeated the exercise a third time and he told me to run off the field and put her away. I was so excited that I ran smack into a fence and wound up flat on my back. Everyone watching roared with laughter. I didn't care because Bully had passed her test. Martha put Bully in her crate and I climbed shakily to my feet.

The dog is given a miss, so he will be hungry for the sleeve.

I decided to stick around and see how the Rottie did. His performance reinforced all my notions about AKC breeding. He was afraid of the sack and shied away from it whenever it got near him. He looked big and tough but two decades of show breeding in America had destroyed the heart that the German breeders had so painstakingly put into this breed over hundreds of years. Not surprisingly, the owners of this dog are now intent on getting an American Bulldog.

Before Bully's second day of protection training Martha and I kept her quiet all day and even put her in a crate for an hour before she got out in the field. She was like a caged tiger as she began the new exercise. Martha was in charge this time, she was instructed to hold Bully on a long leash and not move while Terry flung a small sleeve toward them. This sleeve was attached to a long leather lead. Terry jerked it back before Bully could bite it about three times. Bully lunged for it each time and snapped at air. Martha was barely able to hold her back.

A deep bite is the result of excellent training and genetics. Bosco is Bully's half brother and is training with Al Banuelos.

On the fourth time the sleeve was close enough for Bully to reach and she snatched it out of the air and shook it viciously. Terry gave her a short tug of war then let go. Martha ran around the field with Bully on lead in a kind of victory dance. Bully had beaten the sleeve in mock combat.

This exercise was repeated three times with Bully catching the sleeve in midair each time, which was the whole idea, getting the dog to go up in the air after a sleeve. I noticed that Terry was training Bully differently than the other green dogs. He wasn't concerned that the European dogs learn to bite high up off the ground. After the last bite Martha ran Bully on lead into her crate on the back of our truck. Bully was aching for more action but wasn't going to get it. This was intentional, to increase her prey drive and desire to go after the sleeve. Afterwards, I asked Randy Tyson if we should practice with Bully at home. She said no, twice a

week here at the Schutzhund club was enough. This was a different kind of training and over doing it would decrease the frustration level that we were deliberately stoking.

Terry gives Bully a solid bite

Randy was pleased with the progress Bully was making. This was the first American Bulldog the club had worked with and everyone liked the apparent hardness of her bite. "There's just one thing" Randy said, "she needs to lose a little weight. I'd like to see at least four ribs showing on either side. You should get her down to 80-pounds."

It struck me that we were going to have to choose between weight pulling and Schutzhund. The experienced pull guys in Tulsa had told me not to lean Bully down. I informed Martha that I wanted to keep Bully at 90-pounds and in a harness. She told me that Bully was half her dog and her half wasn't going to pull weights anymore. She thought Bully's sprained shoulder was due to weight training and eventually the harness would prove crippling. I tried reasoning with her by explaining that Schutzhund was a breed test designed for German Shepherds not Bulldogs and that it entailed going over six-foot A frames, which is hard on shoulders. My arguments fell on deaf ears and she informed me once again that her half of Bully was never going to pull weights again. Since I couldn't pull weights with half a dog that seemed to settle it. She did compromise on one point, I could train our new puppy we were planning on buying from Boyd's Bulldogs any way I wanted if I would help with Bully's Schutzhund career. The next day I got up early and took her for a long run. I would have ribs showing in no time.

Kevin White trains Turbo in the finer points of bite work

Bully didn't mourn the loss of weight pulling because she soon grew to love protection work. On her third session she got to bite the sleeve while the agitator wore it on his arm. Terry skillfully set up these bites by having Martha hold Bully back as she lunged for his arm. This built up the dog's frustration level. When he could see everything was just right, he got close enough for a good bite. He gave Bully a small tug fight, quickly slipped his arm out of the sleeve and told Martha and dog to run with the trophy. Bully shook it with fierce joy, circled back toward Terry, spit it out and then snapped at him. Those civil agitations were still haunting us. Martha kicked the sleeve to refocus Bully's attention on it and not the man. Terry put the sleeve on his arm and Bully bit the proper target.

One of the criticisms of Schutzhund is that dogs can become 'sleeve-happy' and may not bite a real bad guy who isn't wearing a sleeve in a combat situation. We wanted Bully to become as sleeve happy as possible, to view the sleeve as her enemy. A lack of real world combativeness was the least of our worries.

One thing Terry didn't like was the way Bully pulled Martha around like a rag doll when he was trying to set up the bites. In this case, the dog was stronger than the woman. He suggested that I should be the primary handler. Martha wouldn't hear of it though. She was becoming a Schutzhund junkie.

I wandered away from the dogs doing sleeve work and over to some others dogs that had started at the same time as us but weren't as far along in protection. I should hasten to add

that these dogs were blowing us away in obedience, would probably demolish us in tracking and would certainly turn out to be better Schutzhunds. Today they were struggling with the idea of actually biting a man with a sleeve. One dog would bite hesitantly, shake the burlap sack aggressively, run around with it like he was supposed to, then bring it back to the agitator and spit it out. The agitator set the sack down then walked around it sneakily, making furtive gestures every couple of steps. The dog froze and stared at him suspiciously. The man suddenly stole the sack. The dog lunged for it, gripped solidly, shook it and ran around the field triumphantly. This time the dog didn't spit it out in front of the sneaky sack thief. I could see that being a good agitator required acting ability. I gained even more respect for agitators on our next lesson. Several beginning dogs were going after the sleeve in only a half-hearted manner. With these dogs Terry would throw the sleeve down and agitate them directly with just his body. In this way he could stoke their defensive drive and ignore their prey drive. He wanted them to feel a little threatened.

There was another beginning dog, a European German Shepherd that had Bully's problem but to a greater degree, it wanted to attack the man and ignore the sleeve. Terry did finally manage to get this dog to bite the sleeve and hold it, he then ran around the field with the handler/dog team. If he didn't the dog would spit out the sleeve immediately and go after the agitator again. This technique kept the dog focused on the sleeve.

On our next session I was surprised to see Terry put away the sleeve and take out a long tube made out of jute (burlap), filled with foam rubber and tied to a leather lead. Before he started, Terry showed Martha a technique for holding back a strong dog on leash. He had her put the leash behind her rear, hold on with one hand in front and one behind, flex her knees and get a low center of gravity. When Martha was set he flung the tube toward just out of reach, several feet above ground. Bully leaped for it with a determined blast of power but Martha was braced and held her back. The next time he let Bully catch it, then (holding the leather lead) he gave her the most ferocious tug of war yet. She tore at the tube, jumping off the ground and twisting her whole body in violent whip saw maneuvers. Terry was barely able to hold on.

Terry trained Bully differently than the German bred dogs. He taught her to out (stop biting on command) much sooner than our classmates. He also was more concerned about her sleeve sureness and unconcerned about her inability to bark. Terry was very concerned about her targeting. If she didn't bite the exact center of the sleeve she was not rewarded with a tug of war. Martha and I were surprised to learn that Terry's insights came from the fact that he'd owned an American Bulldog as a teenager named Blinky that apparently looked and acted like Bully.

Bite suit training keeps a Schutzhund decoy honest, i.e. he can't hide the sleeve from the dog and not get munched.

We were about two or three months into the Schutzhund regimen when our first unfortunate incident occurred. By this time we had established a routine where Bully would ride to protection class in a crate in the back of our pickup and ride in the cab for obedience. For protection she would stay in the parking lot, in her crate, until Terry was ready for her, then she would go directly from the crate to the field and get some bite work. Typically we would steer her around the aggressive protection dogs en route on a tight leash. Some of these dogs would clearly attack her if they hadn't been restrained. She would snarl back at them but her correction would be mild, partially because her protection collar didn't constrict or choke her no matter how hard you tugged at it.

On the day in question I took Bully to obedience class in her crate instead of the cab. Bully had gotten muddy right before class and I didn't want to muck up the inside of my truck. I was dimly aware that something was wrong when Bully failed to jump down and stroll out onto the field for a leisurely spot of obedience work. Instead she was lunging at the end of her leash, expecting to get a bite, strangling herself on the choker.

I made her sit in the middle of the dog pack and waited for class to begin, holding the leash loosely. Bully didn't see Terry and his sleeve. She wasn't use to sitting around uncrated before the protection work began. I noticed her body was tense and ramrod straight. Her head was shifting left to right, searching for Terry. I still hadn't put two and two together. A tough female Rottweiler walked by and probably noticed Bully's body posture. The Rottie lifted a lip and emitted a soft snarl. Bully leaped into the air and pounced on the Rottie with all four feet. I had the presence of mind to immediately pull her off but was too stunned to give a reprimand. Our instructor screamed at me, "give that dog a correction." I gave one so harsh that the instructor smiled with satisfaction.

A Schutzhund III dog must be able to withstand hard stick hits.

I was mortified. Bully had never started a dogfight before. It seemed that the endless hours I had spent explaining that she was not a giant Pit Bull to everyone who asked went down the drain in one incident of unwarranted dog aggression. After a moment's reflection, I realized that as usual it was my fault not Bully's and there wouldn't have been any problem if we hadn't been inadvertently training her to bite every time she got out of her crate. On further reflection maybe using the crate in this manner was acceptable since we were trying to isolate her protective behavior, we just had to be more aware of what we were doing. Lack of awareness is the biggest mistake novice protection trainers can make.

Boyd's Hammer training for Schutzhund I

After a while we noticed a new routine had set in, we'd split up our training duties since Schutzhund was so time consuming. I was doing obedience while Martha did protection. We decided to continue along these lines. With this decision made Martha went out and bought a pair of soccer shoes with long cleats, she was tired of Bully dragging her around the training field every time she lunged at an agitator. Bully had claws to dig into the turf and now Martha was similarly equipped. The shoes were a good idea, the split in training duties was not.

At our next class, Bully was agitated by someone other than Terry for the first time. The club was breaking in a young agitator named Tim and Randy decided to let Martha and the Bulldog have a shot at him. During this session Randy supervised everything very closely. It went smoothly until Tim tried to get Bully to bark. This was a problem with Bully and almost every other AB in this sport, ABs rarely bark, which makes it impossible to perform the bark and hold exercise, an integral part of Schutzhund.

Tim's solution was to growl at her and use menacing body language after dropping the sleeve on the ground. This fired up Bully's defensive instincts, the very instincts we had tried so hard to keep dormant. Bully didn't bark, instead she growled, lunging for the man not the sleeve. Martha strained at the leash. Randy Tyson inter-

vened and instructed the decoy to use only prey techniques with Bully, not civil agitation. Randy took the leash from Martha and expertly nipped Bully's wayward response in the bud. For the rest of the session Randy handled Bully and instructed Tim and Martha at the same time. She didn't let the sleeve touch the ground or even get close to the ground the whole session. When Tim slipped the sleeve off his arm and Randy ran around the field with Bully, she kept the dog's head up. By the time the exercise was over our Bulldog was completely refocused on the sleeve. Schutzhund is sport training, not personal protection. We have never worried about Bully having insufficient civil drive if a situation warranted it.

At our next protection class everyone was talking excitedly about the upcoming German Shepherd breed survey and conformation show that was being sponsored by the club and would be held on our training field. A judge from Germany was being flown in. He would preside over the whole affair.

Martha and I soon realized why our fees were so low for all this training. We were expected to roll up our sleeves and help put on the show. I arrived at the training field early that Saturday and helped pitch tents, set up tables and mount flags along the chain link fence that surrounds the field. The flags were from the countries and regions that may be participating in the upcoming activities. There were flags representing Mexico, Canada, USA, California, Germany and Bavaria. I unthinkingly put the Bavarian and German flags at the far end of the fence near the outdoor toilets. One of the senior club members noticed my faux pas and hollered at me. "Dammit, don't put German flags by the toilet, put them in front, here by the gate where the judge will see them as soon as he enters the field." He mumbled a dark curse in German. I did as he said and put the Canadian flag by the toilet, which seemed politically correct.

Martha had made her famous Santa Fe style bean salad and was helping man the food booth. All the other food items seemed to have a Teutonic twist, smoked pork chops, Bavarian potatoes and German beer. I looked at the parking lot and noticed all the cars parked near the entrance were German makes. The Toyotas and pickups were all tucked away on the side. This is what America would be like if Germany had won WW II.

The German judge arrived on the scene followed by one of the many club members who spoke fluent German. She carried a microphone and translated everything the judge said over the PA system. He was tall and imposing but the pink unprotected skin around his face, neck and bald head soon started to burn in the hot California sun. No one dared to suggest he was only human and offer him a hat or sunscreen.

The loudspeaker blared. "We will begin with adult dogs and the temperament test." This was to be the first event of the breed survey, a process that would eventually determine which of the ten assembled adults would be suitable for breeding under the rules of the German Shepherd Club of Germany and the United Schutzhund Club of America. Before a German Shepherd can even compete in a breed survey it must first have three things: 1) A working title, in this case every dog was a Schutzhund I or II. 2) An endurance title, which means it must be able to jog twelve-miles at a fast pace. 3) The dog's hips must be certified dysplasia free by German radiologists.

The judge walked slowly past the row of breed survey Shepherds sitting at attention, suddenly he whirled around holding a revolver loaded with blanks and fired in the air. Not only did they not flinch some of them seemed to wear expressions of contempt at such a transparent ploy at intimidation.

Their scores were recorded in some sort of ledger book and the next event was announced. "Now we will have the courage test." Menlo Park's top agitator hid himself in a blind in a far corner of the training field. The first dog was sent running toward the blind with a send away command. When he neared the blind the agitator leaped out and threatened the dog. The Shepherd launched into an impressive attack, clamping onto the sleeve, withstanding blows from a baton and being whirled around with all four feet off the ground. The handler yelled "Aus" from a distance of twenty-yards and the dog went into the bark and hold. This team then went through all the protection exercises required in Schutzhund I.

The same sequence was repeated with all ten dogs. Nine passed with flying colors and one was failed for not pressing his attack boldly enough after the agitator accidentally stepped hard on his foot. This dog probably was naturally courageous enough to pass the breed survey

under normal circumstances but the man who had him before the current owner was abusive. That he had come this far was a miracle. However the German rules do not make exceptions or special cases.

The next test was the conformation show. In this event not only did the dogs pose in striking show stances, they also had to trot and run around a large ring for great distances with their handlers so the judge could examine and evaluate their movement. This was actually a mini-endurance test that wiped out the handlers much worse than the dogs since it was over 90 degrees that day. The handlers were allowed to run their dogs in relays, spelling each other with more than one handler per dog.

The man standing next to me was born and raised in Germany. He scoffed that back home relays were not permitted, the handlers had to be in as good a shape as the dogs. "In Germany both man and dog are tested."

Bully training for her WST

After each dog was finished a lengthy critique was given over the loud speakers highlighting its strong and weak points. Not only were points of confirmation discussed but also each dog's fighting spirit and controllability. If the judge wasn't satisfied he didn't pull any punches either, using words like "disappointing" for the dogs that didn't cut the mustard. Other dogs were described as "excellent" and were given the highest breed survey score possible, Corp one for life. These dogs were real life Rin Tin Tins.

After witnessing a European style working dog show and breed suitability test I was forced to amend the high marks I'd given the Bulldog Extravaganza in Tulsa. I was impressed with this Bulldog show only because I was comparing it to the AKC shows I'd attended for years where there were no working events at all. Now that I had seen how Europeans evaluated dogs I was forced to admit that the Tulsa show was hopelessly inadequate in three ways: 1) Working tests such as Weight Pull and Protection were not mandatory. Only one, two or three Bulldogs had competed in working events while dozens paraded around the show ring. 2) There was no hip evaluation required for Bulldog beauty contestants at that time. 3) There was no authority that could pass or fail a breed candidate in a working event.

Bully went a week without protection training because of the German dog show. I spent that week addressing her most obvious weak point - she wouldn't bark. I called up an experienced Bulldog Schutzhund trainer, Steve Visuddhiadham, and asked his advice. He told me to starve her for one night and one day then tease her with a piece of meat, give her a command to bark and when she complied give her the meat, then try again. Steve is training his Bulldogs in Swahili. I couldn't pronounce the Swahili word for bark so I settled on the word "Ruff" as my command.

A Schutzhund III Bulldog needs to be in great physical condition.

When I dangled the meat in front of our starving Bulldog I thought she was going to take my arm off when she leaped for it. I raised it high above my head and her snapping jaws got only air as a reward. She sat down and cocked her head, trying to figure out what I wanted. I gave the command, "Ruff." She went through her whole obedience repertoire in a vain effort to please me and get the meat. She stood, sat, went down and heeled at my side. Finally she growled in frustration and barked. I gave her a small amount of meat and a large amount of praise. I pulled out another chunk and said, "Ruff." She tentatively gave out a small experimental bark. She received the same proportion of meat and praise.

I tried successfully three more times to get her to bark on command. This technique worked great except each time I was able to elicit only a single bark. Two days later Martha took Bully to class and was paired up with a very good agitator who is also a police officer. She told him that we were focusing on barking and they went to work. He threw the sleeve back and forth in front of Bully to get her riled then put it on and taunted her just outside leash range. Martha was now wearing shoes with cleats and practicing the art of Zen immovability with her legs shoulder width apart and flexed. Bully did not drag her around the field, as she was accustomed. After the frustration had built up Martha gave the command, "Ruff." Bully emitted a heartfelt bark. The agitator immediately moved in closer and Bully was rewarded with a bite. He fought with her for a short while then slipped off the sleeve. Bully paraded around the field with her trophy. Martha told her, "Aus" and Bully spat out the sleeve. They repeated this scenario two more times with the same results. Bully had barked for the first time in protection training. A small cheer arose from our friends. Since then I have learned that most ABs involved in Schutzhund need to learn to bark for food away from the protection field and without a decoy present. Decoys that try to get ABs to bark during early protection work by defensive techniques that threaten the dog can ruin a potentially good Bulldog.

Barking (if properly installed) does help Bulldogs do better in the guard exercises. Barking is mandatory in Schutzhund but optional in the BST. At that time the BST didn't exist so we had to get Bully to bark. The newly vocal Bulldog was exhibiting much more intensity with her sleeve work, barking seemed to focus her on the decoy and forget everything else.

Terry began using a flexible stick, giving her light stinging blows on her flanks and rump.

This revved Bully up even more. He started to teach Martha how to set up full mouth bites, where the dog's entire mouth engulfed the sleeve before she clamped down. When Bully got a deep bite, one that stretched her lips back to her ears, then Terry would give her a good fight, wrestling like mad and a few light swats with his baton. When she got a shallow or a 'cheap bite' then there would be no fight at all. I could see as the practice session went on she got more deep bites. Terry's tactic was working.

With all this intensity flowing around we thought it wise to give Bully some extra tenderness training. We let her frolic regularly with my two-year old nephew. We let her play with other dogs at parks. At first she was a little sharp with the soft gentle dogs that she rough-housed with during these encounters but the word, "Aus" would make her disengage instantly. After a few such commands she got the idea and we foolishly thought we could trust her to roam freely on these excursions.

On one trip to an off leash dog park we encountered a couple who were trying to rescue a fighting Pit Bull. This dog was one of many that the San Francisco Police had confiscated from a high stakes professional dogfight. These people had no business taking a hardened Pit Bull to this park and didn't know what the hell they were doing even though they did keep this rescued dog on leash.

Bully raced ahead of us as Martha and I jogged along the beach. She initially approached (off leash) the battle scarred female Pit with a wagging tail, soon Bully's tail froze as stiff as an iron rod. The Yuppie at the other end of the Pit Bull's leash wasn't paying attention to his charge. The Pit tore into Bully with buzz saw jaws, keeping low to the ground. Bully lowered her body and buzz sawed back. The Yuppie was dragged out of his daydream and forward about ten-feet in the soft sand as the two bitches tangled. I was stunned for several seconds. It was the first time I had seen fur literally fly. The Yuppie screamed, "this is the third time today" and kicked his dog savagely, pulling hard on the leash. Martha and I yelled, "Aus" at the same time and Bully broke off from the fight. She looked at us with a manic glow in her eyes then disobeyed the out command and tore into the Pit Bull again. We yelled, "Aus" a second time and ordered her to come. Finally when she saw me running toward her she obeyed.

I will give the Yuppie credit for what he did next, which was to pull on the choke collar until the dog went limp. Afterwards Bully sported several deep slash marks on her head. I don't think the Pit Bull received any real damage. I should have given Bully a firm correction after this incident but didn't. She showed signs of increased dog aggression for two weeks, hampering our training immensely. On the protection field she would turn away from the agitator and lunge at one of the green dogs tied to a stake. After several stern corrections I finally exorcised the dog aggression demons brought on by the Pit Bull fight, but psychic scars remained. I have never let her run off leash around strange dogs since that incident.

Spinning the dog in helicopter-like turns, instills a tenacious grip.

The protection phase of Schutzhund was proving to be a cakewalk for Bully but advanced obedience work was more challenging. Not only did she have to perform commands that she already knew with precision and speed, at about three months new commands started piling up. Martha had been shrewd to opt for protection training. At this time I found myself having to teach Bully the send out and retrieving. I decided to work smart not hard. The bark on command had been the fastest exercise Bully had ever learned. She had gotten it right in one day and had never missed barking at the word, "Ruff" ever since. I decided to starve her before attempting the send out.

After she was sufficiently ravenous I put her in the stay command in the middle backyard and placed a biscuit on a towel about fifty-feet away, toward the back of the yard, near a fence.

When I placed the biscuit I made grand gestures so Bully knew it was there. I gave her the German command, "Voraus" while pointing at the towel. She sprinted toward it and wolfed down the treat. I said, "Down" and she flopped onto the towel.

We had to do the send out exercise in class; in front of and along side other dogs. Obviously the dogs are off leash during the send out and therefore can not have any dog aggressive tendencies. After that second week had gone by Bully was fine, even if another dog growled at her. Still, I can't emphasize strongly enough the importance of avoiding dogfights with this breed. If they get in enough fights and find out they like it you may not be able to compete in canine sports like weight pulling or Schutzhund.

The Bark and Hold is usually trained in a sit position, but ABs often do better in a down.

Bully had been in her Schutzhund regimen for several months when Martha and I had to take a business trip to Seattle, naturally we brought our four-legged surrogate child with us. That proved to be a good thing.

Between conferences and meetings Martha and I took turns walking Bully in the various parks of the city. I was under the impres-

sion that Seattle was a low crime metropolis. Our experience there dissuaded me of this notion. On one walk Martha had just left a park in a seedier part of town when she met a dog enthusiast. This guy had been studying the American Bulldog ads in Dog World for months. In addition, his father use to breed Old English Whites in Tennessee in the 20's. He was thinking about buying a puppy and was asking when Bully was going into heat when a very large, belligerent and deranged homeless man emerged from the park. He bellowed at the dog enthusiast, "quit talking to my wife!" He walked toward them, then started running and screaming. "Leave her alone. She's my wife!" The crazy man's face was contorted with rage as he continued insisting that Martha was his wife.

Martha whipped the leash around behind her butt, got a good grip and flexed her legs. Bully hit the end of the leash with a thump as she lunged toward the mad man. At first Bully gagged, strangling herself against the choke collar. Her claws scratched against the dry pavement of the sidewalk. She stopped straining against the leash and emitted a steady harsh growl as if she'd swallowed a giant electric razor. Every hair stood straight up on her back like a porcupine. Teeth gleamed under snarling lips. Bully's hair had never stood up like that for a man but it always did against serious animal foes like Pit Bulls or raccoons.

The big homeless man stopped his charge abruptly as he saw the dog for the first time. His eyes snapped open wide and he stammered stupidly, "that s-sure looks like a mean dog." Martha glared at him and hissed through clinched teeth, "it is a mean dog." Bully lunged at him, confirming the statement to be true. The interloper turned on his heel and ran away quickly and anticlimactically.

The dog enthusiast was impressed. After all it looked like he was the focus of the big man's rage, not Martha. "I want to buy one of her puppies," was his parting comment as he took our name and phone number down.

When we got back from Seattle and took Bully to protection class Terry knew something had happened. After practice he said, "every single bite was full mouth, deep, hard, perfect. She has much more confidence." It occurred to me that the encounter with the homeless man had actually been a sort of defensive agitation session as opposed to all the prey drive work we'd been doing. I didn't get a chance to tell him about Martha's adventure and my theory about defense though because he brought up another subject. "You've got to teach her to bark using the German word, 'Geblat,' not 'Ruff'. When you take her to a Schutzhund trial German commands are going to be much more impressive to a German judge than these weird commands you keep making up."

In Schutzhund trials a padded baton is used, however in training a bamboo clatter stick is sometimes useful.

His admonition deflated the pride I felt about Bully's great training session and her real world heroism. I felt I had no choice but to comply because Terry was just ranked the number one catcher (agitator) in the Western Schutzhund region. At the time I thought his expertise and hard work had saved Martha from a mugging since Bully probably couldn't have stopped that attack without his training. I now believe that sport training has little to do with real world personal protection. I didn't know that then so I felt deeply indebted to Terry. I started all over with barking on command in German. It took longer to retrain to a different command than it did to train her initially. The moral of the story is to start your Schutzhund dog in German.

After these great training sessions Bully's third heat was getting close. She became moody and had her worst protection class ever. One of the young agitators asked if he could work her instead of Terry. Martha reluctantly consented even though Terry had given her a short list of agitators to use if he was unavailable. This young man was not on the list. Bully had worked with him once before and didn't like him because he couldn't give her as good a fight as Terry. They went out on the field and Bully

wouldn't even bite the sleeve. She turned away to face Terry and barked as if begging him to come out and put on the sleeve. Martha tried jerking her back, got tangled in the leash and stepped hard on Bully's foot. Now Bully started barking angrily at Martha. She fumbled with the leash, trying to line Bully up on the agitator. The session degenerated even further and became a total fiasco.

The next dog up was the Malinois that we had been informally competing against since our first day. This dog had been making great progress lately and turned in a stellar performance.

After it was all over Terry approached Martha and asked her hotly what she thought she was doing. "I've put a lot of blood, sweat and tears into this dog. Not to mention a bad back because she's so heavy and that can all be wasted with what you were doing out there." He pointed to the Malinois and said, "I can't believe that dog looks better than Bully." Martha mumbled an apology, her face red with embarrassment. "When the last dog is done," Terry continued, "you and I will go out there and Bully will have some fun. That's the way we're training her and it is the only way that will work." Bully then put on an acceptable if not great performance, biting the sleeve eagerly but without the full mouth bites she had been getting. Her lazy streak or Bulldog quirkiness was showing. No well-bred German dog would show this much inconsistency in sport work.

When we got home I gave my take on some of the problems Martha was having with Bully. "Because I'm doing all the obedience training you have less control over her. No one else in the club does it that way, in fact - it's illegal to have more than one handler in a Schutzhund trial." ABs are reluctant to take orders from strangers. They also tend to obey the family member they perceive as dominant better than any other. This is why Bully will drag Martha out onto the protection field without heeling. I realized there really isn't as clear a division between protection training and obedience as I had assumed. Because there is such a division between weight pulling and obedience my judgment had been compromised.

Motivated by Terry's tongue lashing, Martha enthusiastically agreed to take over all facets of Bully's Schutzhund regimen. The next few training sessions were great, not only was

Bully getting good bites, Martha had her under control on and off the field.

The onset of her heat put all training at the Schutzhund club on hold. We took advantage of this hiatus by starting Bully in tracking. For the next seven days we would all get up early and Martha would put a leash on Bully while I put on a protection sleeve. Just the sight of me wearing the sleeve would drive Bully wild with anticipation. I would rev her up even more by hitting the sleeve loudly with a protection baton. Then Martha and Bully would go into a barn and I would close the door. My next move was to walk with a heavy shuffling gait down wind to a hiding spot about 100 or 200-yards away. Martha would give the command, "find him" and Bully's nose would go straight down to the trail I had just laid. She couldn't air scent me with her nose raised because I was careful to keep the wind to my back. Air scenting is illegal in Schutzhund. Even with my precautions, from time to time Bully would raise her head in a vain effort at air scenting. Martha would tap the dirt and refocus her on ground scenting.

An example of a Schutzhund courage test

Within a few minutes Bully would come snuffling to my hiding place, Martha in tow. When I was sighted the leash was dropped, the bite command given and Bully got her grip, a reward that now meant more to her than a food treat. Other than the sleeve, I was wearing only a T-shirt and jeans for the first bite. I soon learned why agitators wear the heavy leather overalls called scratch pants. The dewclaws on Bully's front legs ripped my T-shirt and left scratches on my belly. The next day I wore three layers of

thick sweatshirts. After a few days of this routine it occurred to me that we were using an English command again instead of German. At least it wasn't a weird made up one. I vowed not to be bullied into retraining her with a different command no matter how much pressure was applied once we started back with the club.

On the seventh day of her heat all training necessarily came to an end because we were all driving to Colorado where Bully would be bred to Bam Bam. Our plan to get a female from Boyd's Moleque and Tyson and keep the pick male from Bully/Bam Bam was, I thought, iron-clad. From out of the blue Martha didn't want to breed Bully because senior club members had told her that if she kept training at her current pace Bully would have an outside shot at a Schutzhund I in three months, the tail end of the current season.

If Bully became pregnant it would take another year to get the title. In my heart I knew the senior members were being overly optimistic. They watched Bully's protection work but not her obedience. She was doing terrible on the retrieve for instance. I felt that at our current pace it would take so long (if ever) to get a title that interrupting the regimen for a pregnancy would hardly make any difference.

I told Martha that my half of Bully was getting pregnant. I wanted a male weight pull dog and one of the pups would fill my desire. So in the fall of '95 our bitch became pregnant and her Schutzhund career was temporarily put on the shelf.

After our few months of Schutzhund training we hardly qualify as experts but we did gain enough insight to offer novice Bulldog owners some tips. This is a breed test for German Shepherds so be prepared to face some prejudice on that score. It is probably a good idea to find a club that has at least a few other breeds besides Shepherds. Because Schutzhund is not designed for ABs some things will be very difficult. At one trial we attended the German judge expected each dog to bark 40 times in the bark and hold. Bulldogs have been bred to hunt silently so barking while in defense or prey drive is unnatural. The German sport requires dogs to bite the exact center of the sleeve, also unnatural for Bulldogs. The linear, nose to the ground, style of scent tracking is another difficult task.

Some AB protection sport enthusiasts have opted to compete in Ring Sport, which emphasizes protection work using a body suit (biting anywhere is acceptable), speed, jumping ability and control in obedience without the fussy precision of Schutzhund. ABs are temperamentally better suited to Ring Sport though oversized Bulldogs will have trouble with the jumps.

If your personal security requirements are very high, another advantage of Ring Sport is that it is closer to personal protection or street training than Schutzhund. A dog with a Ring III title is more suited to police K-9 work than a dog with a Schutzhund III. As a breed test the two sports are roughly equivalent.

Boyd's Hi Jumpin'Mikie, Sch I, BST, OFA

Tomahawk's Cindy - a brutal bite dog

Blue Heaven working Sammy Holloway

Bulldog Jamboree

On March ninth and tenth of 1996 the Powerhouse American Bulldog club of Fresno, California under the auspices of the ABA hosted an AB show (The Bulldog Jamboree) that was as close to a German breed survey as anything the fancy had yet done. This show was to be the biggest working AB competition ever held up to that point and would eventually lead to the creation of the Working American Bulldog Association. The Powerhouse club is a group of ten Bulldog enthusiasts who train for obedience, very hardcore personal protection and tracking as it relates to protection, i.e. to find a bad guy in a warehouse, yard or home. Under the leadership of Kevin White their breeding scheme is to use mainly Suregrip blood, out cross heavily, OFA certify and protection test on a high level.

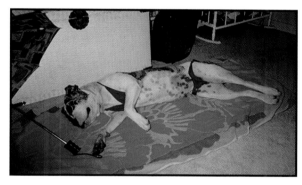

A properly trained bite dog is also a good family dog. Flo loves to play dress up as much as she loves protection work.

For Martha and me the Bulldog Jamboree experience actually began in December of '95 when the Powerhouse club invited us to join in a weekend long training seminar that they were using to tune their dogs up for the big competition in March. Al Banuelos was running the seminar.

Bully was pregnant at that time so we could only participate in the first part of the seminar, obedience. Al's advice for us on obedience was similar to Mark Landers' advice on weight pulling, quit being so reserved, fire the dog up more. He also showed me how to use food to keep her eyes focused on my head.

The Powerhouse dogs and a few other top ABs from the West Coast went through some

very advanced obedience routines. Everyone learned a lot but it was pretty boring. Then the protection part of the seminar began and the fireworks started to fly. Kevin White asked Al's main helper, Mario, if he thought he could back down his prize protection dogs, Blue and Flo. Blue is 115-pounds of rock hard tiger meat. Flo's nickname is 'Flo the psycho.' She tips the scale at 67-pounds but hits like she weighs 300 and is running on nitroglycerin. Flo is a balanced dog, her favorite sport after tearing apart agitators is playing dress up with her real owner, Kevin's daughter - Ashley.

Flo takes everything Mario can dish out.

In the middle of the bite field Mario set up folding wooden chairs that were designed to collapse at a feather touch. This was a diabolical invention of Al Banuelos, who is known to invent weird bite scenarios to test deep man gameness, things and situations a dog has never seen before in its training. The first dog up was Flo. She caught Mario on the arm of his body suit and he dragged her toward these chairs. Mario racked her across the first chair and it snapped around her like a bear trap. She only bit harder. He kicked the first chair away and racked her across another. He then pummeled her with a gallon sized plastic orange juice bottle filled with rocks. I had never seen agitation work this rough before. In our Schutzhund club dogs are hit with a padded baton on the shoulders and flank. Mario was pounding Flo's head with rocks. Flo is a very hard protection dog and this sort of punishment was child's play to her. Kevin finally outed Flo when she started biting through Mario's suit and drawing blood.

95

Helper Mario Erazo testing Butcher

Blue went through the same routine. Mario is a big guy, in good shape, lifts weights and works dogs all the time. He was unable to dish out enough punishment to slow Blue down, let alone back him off. The other Powerhouse dogs were all put through some tough paces. Luckily there were no animal rights activists watching. I'm sure they would have been horrified when blood flowed down Taz's (Flo's son) muzzle. They would really have been horrified to see the swollen eyes and bruises the dogs sported the next day. I'm also sure that they would want one of these thoroughly tested dogs protecting them in a dark ally on the wrong side of town.

The Fresno guys were truly testing the depth of their dogs' man gameness. When the protection work was done the Fresno Bulldogs were brought up to the crowd of strangers that had gathered to watch all the canine fireworks. Little children rushed forward to pet them. Dogs that minutes earlier were biting through body suits wagged their tails good-naturedly and gave the children tender licks in the face.

When Al was done with the seminar he had this to say, "I've never seen so many good Bulldogs together in one place." At that time there were a handful of working AB clubs across the country but the Powerhouse club of Fresno was the one that everyone else was measured against. Any protection club is only as good as its agitators or decoys. The three main decoys for Powerhouse at that time were: Kevin White - who can bench press 365-pounds and run the 100-yard dash in under ten seconds, a man mountain named Dave Hannah who simply lifts the entire gym when he works out and Peter Valentino, who is as sinewy as an eel.

The Bulldog Jamboree would be a significant notch up from the Bulldog Extravaganza and would feature weight pulling as well as other performance events. Bully's pups were weaned in early February. After the pups were out of the way, Martha and I renegotiated our understanding of what we intended to do with our separate halves of Bully. Martha caved in and conceded that I could have control of the entire dog for one year.

Testing a dog this hard should never be done by amateurs.

I began training in earnest for weight pulling. This time I was determined not to repeat the mistakes I'd made in Tulsa. I worked Bully less strenuously, giving her muscles more time to recover between weight pull sessions. I still let her run every other day but she had to walk a mile first before she could run. Bully was warmed up prior to any exercise. Before she pulled the weight cart I held her still and worked her up until she was whining to surge forward against the harness. When I finally let her go she pulled with explosive power. I was training her the way people train for protection, winding her up with frustration and anticipation. I was concentrating on her attitude, not her physical condition, because in one month, right after a pregnancy, there was no way I could really get her in top shape anyway.

By the first week of March Bully was able to pull over 2000-pounds on my cart over carpeted asphalt. This would be the equivalent of 6000-pounds on the rail system we used in Tulsa. On paper she was nearly three times stronger than she had been for that first weight pull. Of course she was really only a little bit stronger. I had just trained her better this time.

When Bully and I pulled into the Fresno SPCA grounds on the first day of the show I couldn't believe my eyes. There must have been 100 Bulldogs and 300 people there. I asked the Powerhouse folks how many dogs were in each event. There were about 30 dogs in the seven different shows, 12 in the weight pull (with four separate weight classes), 20 in the two obedience competitions and 40 in the five different protection events. Besides the weight pull Bully was entered in senior female conformation, on leash obedience and on leash protection using a sleeve.

Blue ready for muzzle work

Her first event was confirmation as judged by Kyle Symmes. We did the usual conformation things: ran our dogs, trotted them, stacked them into a show stand. What was unusual was Mr. Symmes temperament tested each dog by poking its head in between the eyes as well as making startling noises and movements. A few dogs flinched, which he mentally eliminated.

The three finalists in our category were Bully, Bully's sister 'Flo the Psycho' and Maco (a daughter of Bam Bam and Tulsa). Mr. Symmes told us that these three bitches were very similar in conformation and temperament. All three were protection trained. Mr. Symmes almost got them to bite with his temperament test. He picked Bully for first place almost with the flip of a coin. The only confirmation edge that she had was a tighter bite than the other two, who were extremely undershot. If Mr. Johnson had been

judging he would have picked Maco or Flo because they were more undershot.

For best overall female Bully lost out to a very good bitch named Missy. Mr. Symmes explained in great detail why he made this choice, which I appreciated. What he said boiled down to Bully's back legs needed more angulation, her stifle was too short. A short stifle is a serious structural defect since dogs built this way are more prone to knee ligament tears.

By denying the dog a bite, muzzle work increases his drive.

The best overall male was Blue. Since males at this level of competition are usually better than females that meant that Blue was the overall confirmation champion. The second best adult male was Boyd's Mickie. Boyd's dog had very good confirmation but I think Mr. Symmes liked Blue's physical conditioning better. Blue's body fat content is about 3%.

Bully did terrible in the obedience competition. I wanted to crawl into a hole when she came to me on the recall at a snail's pace just like she did in Tulsa. The other Bulldogs were all fantastic. The number one obedience dog was Brody, owned by Tom Riche. This dog had a Schutzhund I title at the time and represents three generations of Schutzhund breeding. Brody would go on to get his Schutzhund III and compete nationally. Al Banuelos bred him. Brody's obedience work was beyond belief. When he was told to finish an exercise, the dog would jump through the air and land in a perfect sit in a precise spot at Tom's side. The crowd clapped madly at this dog's military precision.

Brody took first in both protection and obedience.

Kevin White's Blue Heaven took second place in obedience. Blue was almost as good as Brody, glued to Kevin's side on the heel, staring into his face attentively, man and dog moving together as though choreographed by Hollywood.

After obedience the main event for Bully and me was next, the weight pull. There are two ways a dog will pull a weight cart, on voice command or by lunging after some sort of bait that is held in front of him. All but three dogs in the whole competition were pulling after bait, which meant this pull was not using official ABA rules. Flo was the best lightweight dog. She pulled a few hundred pounds without being baited but quickly lost interest when the weight got heavy. Bear in mind that she has received no weight pull training, Flo is a protection dog. When she stopped pulling, Kevin had his 12-year old daughter, Ashley, walk in front of the finish line. He then got a loutish looking man to grab her. Ashley screamed, "Flo, Help! Help!"

Flo coiled up like a cobra and flew through the air at the loutish man. Of course her harness and the heavy weight cart checked her flight in mid air. The cart did move forward several inches. The man's eyes grew wide with fear. He wasn't wearing a bite suit. Kevin told him not to worry; he and Dave Hannah would grab onto Flo if she got close enough to bite. The worst that would happen was a little ripped clothing, nothing for a true Bulldogger. Reluctantly the loutish man grabbed Ashley again. The little girl pre-

tended to scream in fright. Flo continued propelling the cart forward with each leap until she crossed the finish line, earning her first place in the lightweight category.

Butcher put through the paces

The middleweight class was Bully's event. There were several dogs who pulled weights through baiting in this category and one other, Valentino's Ammo who pulled on command, though he had only received a couple weeks worth of training, like Flo he is primarily a superb protection dog. The bait dogs were quickly eliminated. Ammo did a great job for the amount of training he had. He peaked at 900-pounds, which would have been well over 2000-pounds on steel rails. Bully simply tore up the weight track. I stopped her at 1200-pounds, which she pulled in twelve seconds. I already knew that she could pull all the weight that Powerhouse had brought to the competition, just under a ton. In other words, Bully could pull twice what even the biggest dog there could pull. But I thought we would be competing in protection the next day so there was no sense in risking an injury.

Bully and I couldn't watch the light heavy and heavyweight pulls because all the baiting was beginning to fire her up, which would be bad for her training. Boyd's Mikie, who was voice trained, (but only to the extent that Ammo was) won the heavyweight class. Mikie did about as well as Ammo, which is to say fantastic for that level of training. Flo's son,

Taz, won the light heavy pull. Blue took third place in the heavyweight division which earned him valuable points for the ultimate competition, overall champion, an achievement Powerhouse had dubbed Baddest Bulldog on the planet, a precursor to Irondog triathlons.

Rattler shows good weight pull form.

The next day was to be devoted almost entirely to protection. The four different competitions were the main event for most of the people and dogs in attendance at the Jamboree. At eight in the morning Al Banuelos assembled 30 handlers together to explain the routine we would be going through. This routine would be the same for the easiest class, on leash sleeve, as for the most advanced, off leash body suit. By the time Al was finished I knew that Bully was no way near ready for this competition. She would need another year of training to get through it. We would have to bow out. The routine Al put those advanced Bulldogs through that day would a few years later be slightly modified and called a BST II, the most advanced title issued by the WABA.

The dogs were expected to be sent away from their handlers and search two blinds for a decoy. Once they found him they would have to do a bark and hold, out of sight of their handler, pinning the bad guy inside the blind but not attacking. The decoy would try to escape and the dog would attack, withstand punishment from the baton and hold the decoy again while the handler disarmed him.

The dog would then have to attack him during a running escape, hold him again and then withstand a full courage test with gunfire. After this the dogs would have to face Mario (who I was now calling super Mario) for an even harder courage test. As in December, Mario would try to back the dogs down with some hard testing involving a bamboo cane. To really make the contests interesting some very good Pit Bulls, Rotties, one tough Bandog and a killer Malinois were also entered to match the ABs up against other breeds as well as each other. These other breeds were not tested as hard as the Bulldogs though.

Mikie shows bad form, but wins on sheer strength.

Al Banuelos was supervising the complicated procedures to make sure that the testing didn't get so brutal that a given dog would be backed down so hard his training was ruined. Al is known for his ability to read a dog. Throughout the day Al would cry halt and a dog that was failing would be disqualified before any permanent damage was done. Al would then instruct his decoys to work the dog in prey and build him back up again. Once they had restored his courage the dog would walk cockily off the field, a better dog than he was before. The agitation work was so rough that one Bulldog decided to cheat and bit a suited decoy in an unprotected spot, his foot, which was only covered with a light running shoe. As soon as this dog got this dangerous bite Al's team sprung into action and pried him off immediately with no one any worse for the wear. Like I said, true Bulldoggers think nothing of a little pain.

Kyle Symmes was the protection judge. He rated each dog on a 100 point scale that naturally included fighting spirit and courage but also points for control such as how well the dog outed and how well he heeled at his handlers side while a decoy/prisoner was being escorted from point A to point B.

Blue pulls for a tug toy, pulling for bait is illegal in a sanctioned competition.

The overall protection champion was Brody with Blue a close second. Al's Malinois scored higher than these dogs but this was a Bulldog show so that didn't count. While it is true that the Malinois had better control, it seemed that the Bulldogs were able to absorb more punishment. But that could have been due to the fact that they are heavier and the stick hits sounded louder against their big carcasses. Flo could absorb more punishment than any dog out there and received the highest rating for courage. Unfortunately she earned her nickname by refusing to out. Kevin had to tear her off the decoy physically before she hurt someone. He later confided to me that Flo was in heat and her judgment was clouded with hormones. This was too bad because Flo was outing perfectly in December when we last saw her. If she hadn't been in heat she might have taken first place. I asked some of the experienced protection guys which dog would be the one to have in a dark alley filled with muggers and they all agreed it would be Flo.

Flo getting ready to out

After the four protection contests were over Kevin White had scheduled a protection event for novice Bulldogs or intermediates at Bully's level. He tied five totally green dogs to a fence and ran Bully through her paces on a sleeve in front of these dogs. Kevin was disappointed at what a poor protection handler I was. I would give Bully the command, "Faus" and stand back to watch her bite the sleeve. "Encourage her," he shouted at me. "Praise her for that bite." Al Banuelos started calling out advice as well. I regretted my decision to let Martha do all the protection work. Kevin stared into Bully's eyes as she clamped down on the sleeve. She returned his stare unblinkingly and growled. He waved a fist over her head and she fired up more convincingly. Kevin peeked at the five dogs on the fence out of the corners of his eyes and liked what he saw. Most were lunging at him, straining against leads.

Bully was the only dog to be fully trained to pull on command without bait. She pulled more weight than any other dog at the Jamboree.

Once all the green dogs were fired up from watching Bully, Kevin told me to leave the field and began to train. He teased them up with a special sleeve that could be unrolled into a bite rag or rolled up and fastened with velcro then put around the arm like a regular sleeve.

He managed to get every dog to first bite the unrolled sleeve and then eventually to bite it on his arm. I'd never seen green dogs brought along so rapidly. Kevin then gradually introduced stress to the green dogs as they bit his arm sleeve by rubbing their heads. He talked soothingly to blunt the stress, creating a balance that brought out the best in each dog. When the beginners were done they marched off the field. Both dogs and handlers swelled with pride.

100

The last part of the show was a second round of conformation classes to be judged by Casey Couturier. The insiders all knew that Casey would pick smaller performance type dogs as winners and that Kyle would pick bigger dogs with a non-exaggerated Johnson look. Even though Kyle would never pick an extreme Johnson type dog, it was ironic that even within the ABA the perennial Scott verse Johnson schism was still alive. At this time there was only one standard so Johnson and Scott types had to compete directly.

Superior jaw strength means ABs can bite through a bite suit.

Sure enough, the winners of the second day were much smaller and more Scott-like than the winners of the first Day. Casey picked a 70-pound daughter of Flo named Lady as best female and the 85-pound, long legged, big headed, Ammo, as best male.

The dog with the most cumulative points, the grand champion and Baddest Bulldog on the planet was White's Blue Heaven.

The Bulldog Jamboree finally brought American Bulldog competition within spitting distance of the best working shows of Europe. The protection testing was actually more arduous than what I'd seen at local Schutzhund trials. The problem was that there was still no formal structure or organization to repeat these tests in the future and on a nation wide basis. Plus there was no hip requirement. Shortly after the Jamboree the Working American Bulldog Association was founded by Kevin White to correct these deficiencies. Tom Riche was installed as the president and quickly became the driving force behind WABA, which now has a national scope, is internationally recognized and is equiv-

alent to such organizations as the United Schutzhund Club of America. WABA is run by experienced Bulldoggers that have designed various working tests uniquely suited to the American Bulldog.

Tomahawk's Lucille has produced hard bite dogs.

Caleb - UCD III, OFA Good

Hunting with Don Matthews

During one of my numerous phone calls with Don Matthews (Konfederate Kennels in Florida) the subject of a chapter on hog hunting came up. Don gave me this advice, "no book on the American Bulldog can claim to be comprehensive without detailed information on hog hunting, Dave, this is the heart and soul of the breed." I already had come to this conclusion but knew of only one serious hunter on the West Coast, Kyle Symmes, and he was always very busy and hard to get a hold of. "Well heck, son, come on out to Florida. We'll show you what hog hunting is all about."

Don Matthews plays tug of war with Scarlet

A few weeks after that conversation I found myself on a jet, headed deep into the heart of Dixie and one of the most exhilarating experiences of my life. I couldn't help thinking that hog hunting with Don Matthews was like tossing a football with Steve Young. On further reflection I decided that I better not say that to Don, he would be offended unless I made the comparison to Dan Marino of the Miami Dolphins. In any case, he was probably the best man in the country at this sport.

I scrambled out of the plane, into a rental car and settled down for a long drive to Fort Pierce. I was so excited I hardly noticed the heat, which in late July was only a degree or two less than a blast furnace. Old Florida is swiftly being paved over and turned into shopping malls but in the rural community where the Matthews live there is still a fair amount of country left. Alligators swim in ponds near their house, bald eagles soar overhead and most importantly, hundreds of wild boar root through the dense jungle like thickets called palmettos that dot the countryside.

I finally got there, knocked on the door and met Don for the first time. Usually when you meet someone in person that you've talked to extensively on the phone a mental picture is formed of that person that usually doesn't match reality. I knew a lot about Don, he'd won the bronze star and purple heart in Vietnam, he'd started an arm wrestling club that produced national champions, his family had lived continually in Florida since the Civil War and his great great grandfathers had fought for the Confederacy. Don looked exactly like my mental picture, about six-foot-two, lean and muscular with a craggy visage burned brown from the hot Florida sun.

We shook hands. I walked inside and met his wife, Sandra. She greeted me warmly then looked at her husband. "Don, don't get him hooked on hog hunting." She looked at me. "Dave, are you married?" I answered, "yes, my wife's name is Martha, we've been married three years." Sandra looked back at Don. "It wouldn't be fair to Martha if Dave became an addict." Don's face screwed up into an expression of mock puzzlement as if to say, "addicted to hog hunting? Who had ever heard of such a ludicrous notion?" I was soon to find out that it is not a ludicrous notion, this sport provides one of the greatest adrenaline rushes known to man. Don said, "throw your bag in that room, Dave, and we'll go meet some of my hunting buddies at Jim Huck's country store."

Matthews' Speck - A great hog dog killed by a wild boar in 1976

Built for the Florida heat, Jackson has a four-inch muzzle and weighs 100-pounds.

Jim Huck's place was a combination deli, barbecue pit and general store. Inside, hanging on the walls, were several trophy mounts of wild boars and paintings of hunting scenes. While Huck was busy barbecuing several racks of huge meaty ribs I got the opportunity to pick the brains of two experienced hog men, Don's son Travis and Eddie Richardson, a.k.a. Rabbit. Huck and Rabbit also come from families that have lived in Florida since the Civil War and their ancestors have been hunting hogs with dogs for just as long.

One of the first things I learned is the most important part of a wild boar is his teeth. The lower teeth are called cutters or tusks. The upper set are called whetters, their purpose is similar to a whetstone that sharpens a knife. The boar grinds his tusks against the whetters to keep inner edges razor sharp and tips needle sharp. Commercial hunting lodges buy boars from people like Don and knock out the whetters, this allows the tusks to grow up to seven-inches long because the boar can no longer grind them down. While impressive looking these long dull teeth are not as dangerous to a dog as the sharp two or four-inch tusks of a true wild boar.

As I talked to these men I realized that the hog hunters in Florida had informally developed a long established and complicated system of game management. They release 80% of the boars they catch. Before they release one they decide if he had put up a good fight and was a worthy specimen. If he wasn't game and strong they will castrate him, disinfect the scrotum, bob his tail and possibly put a notch in an ear. A neutered boar is called a bar. After a month or two in the wild the bar will become plumper and

less gristly than a boar. The next time he is caught he will be fit to eat.

If the boar had put up a tremendous fight and was physically impressive he will be left intact and released. He might be released in a different location though because towns and highways isolate the pockets of wilderness that hogs live in. Local herds have a tendency to become inbred which over time reduces their size and overall quality.

Jackson's puppies, future hog catchers

So it seems these men actually breed the animals they hunt. What about the animals they hunt with? There are four breeds of dogs that are used to catch hogs in Florida: White Bulldog, Brindle Bulldog, Leopard dog and Florida Cur. White Bulldogs are unregistered ABs or what I call hill Bulldogs. Brindle Bulldogs are big Pit Bulls specially bred for catch work, really the same dog as a White Bulldog, just a different color. Leopards and Curs are not only able to catch they are also excellent at tracking hogs, because of this many hunters use just them without Bulldogs. Some hunters let the Curs and Leopards do 90% of the work, they find and catch the hogs, but a Bulldog is kept in reserve in case the boar is really bad and the Curs or Leopards need help. The only time Bulldogs will do all the catch work is if you were using hounds to find the pigs (pure hounds can't catch) or if you were hunting with Bulldogs alone. Bulldogs are not good trailers so they can only hunt alone if the hogs are so plentiful that you are likely to stumble on top of them no matter where you turn.

After I'd asked a million questions, Rabbit asked me a few, "so Dave, you're writing a book about White Bulldogs. Are they popular in California?"

I nodded, "they're starting to get real popular." This seemed to puzzle him, "I didn't think you had that many wild hogs." Don smiled in mild amusement, he was the only Florida native present who knew that White Bulldogs are also called American Bulldogs and are becoming common place in suburban America. I said, "there's only a handful of people who use them on hogs in California. Most people keep them as guard dogs."

Bubba is a Florida Cur with coloration like a Coonhound.

Rabbit's brow furrowed into a deep frown, now he was confused. "White Bulldogs? They're too docile to bite a man. They'll inhale a hog but I've never seen one even growl at a man." I wasn't surprised by this comment. I'd heard many times that pure hog hunting strains were not human aggressive. I launched into a dissertation on the different strains of American Bulldog and how the Johnson dogs were being crossed into the hog hunters to produce watch-dogs. This is exactly what Don Matthews is doing with his strain of pure hog hunters.

It was my turn to ask questions again. "What is a Florida Cur?" Rabbit answered, "a cross between a Bulldog and a hound, but this happened a long time ago. Curs have been a pure breed for over a hundred years. Maybe longer."

The coloration of all the Florida Curs I would see that weekend bore testimony to this lineage. They ranged in color from mostly Bulldog white to that of a Black and Tan Coonhound. Many of them were long and narrow like a Coonhound but the ones Don bred were thicker with heavy crushing jaws like a Bulldog. The Curs would give voice much less frequently than a hound but they weren't dead silent on the hunt like a Bulldog.

Then I asked Rabbit what other names he knew for White Bulldogs. He knew of one other, Alabama Bulldog. My next question involved the nuts and bolts of tonight's hog hunt. On our first hunt we would use only Leopard dogs and Curs. We would need to keep the wind in our face so the dogs could scent the hogs but the hogs couldn't smell us, they had poor eyesight but good noses. We would have to be careful to let only two dogs get on a hog at any one time. If there were two dogs hanging on to each of the hog's ears a third dog would go to the hog's nose or face and get cut up. Another thing to watch for, sometimes the ranchers in this area would catch hogs in traps and release them after cutting off both ears. This was a sick joke played on the hunters, the dogs had nothing to grab onto and could get cut bad. They also warned me to be careful not to get hog bit because wild boar eat carrion and their mouths contain deadly bacteria.

These Florida Curs are colored like Bulldogs.

The hunt tonight would be at a place called Southern Fruit Properties, a cattle ranch interspersed with citrus groves. Rabbit said he couldn't participate in this hunt but he would lead the next one tomorrow morning. Don had back to back hunting lined up for me the next three days. I wouldn't get much sleep but would pack a month's worth of hunting into a short time period.

It was past ten when three Curs and one Leopard were outfitted with huge leather cut collars and loaded into two pickup trucks. We were all equipped with small pocketknives, lengths of rope and high powered flash lights. Nobody carried a side arm.

When we had driven past the citrus groves and into the rough terrain of the cattle ranch the two trucks stopped. The men got out and searched for hog signs. Don motioned me to where he was standing and shined a light on the ground. There were several hoof prints, like a deer's but three times as big, more rounded and wider. The other hunters gathered near the tracks. Jim Huck almost whispered, "I think this is Big Boy." The more notorious boars that they had tracked and seen but never caught all had names like Range Line Red or Two Socks. In this area Big Boy was the most notorious one of all. We followed the tracks down a dirt road until we found the spot where the boar had entered the forest.

Two dogs were let loose at this point. They tore silently into the woods. Everyone strained to follow their progress with our ears. After what seemed a long time but was probably only a few minutes, Don's big Cur, Bubba, barked three times. "That's unusual," Don muttered.

"Isn't that what he does when he's found a hog?" I asked. "No," Don replied, "he usually will just go into it. We'd hear the ruckus as they fought but not any barking. It must be a real small pig."

Hog sign, a big boar's hoof print

After 15-minutes the dogs came back to the trucks. They must have run several miles and had lost their quarry. Trailing through the inky blackness and thick brush was harder work for the dogs than for the pig because all the porker had to do was run, plus he knew where he was going. It was still close to 90 degrees and the dogs were winded. We loaded them up and drove on, past palmettos and open pastures, shining the high powered lights as we went.

Travis and I were in one truck, Don and Jim Huck were in the other. Don's dogs were also in his truck, these two were more experienced than the dogs Travis and I had. Also our truck had a longer wheel-base and couldn't go as fast through this rough country as Don's. When Travis' flashlight picked out a small pig Don's truck was 300-yards away. Normally this wouldn't be a problem but this clever hog was hiding in the middle of a herd of cattle. Travis' inexperienced dogs couldn't be trusted to get the hog and leave the cattle alone. He cursed softly and tried to signal the lead truck with his light to no avail. "Oh well," he said gloomily, "no sense fooling with a small pig anyway."

As we circled around the cattle herd the wind brought hog scent to our dogs. They each let out a small woof. We knew where that scent came from and ignored it. We continued bouncing and bumping along until we came to an electrified fence that ran next to a large pond. Near this pond there were plenty of hog signs, earth torn up by their rooting as though plowed by a tractor. Don unloaded the two experienced dogs and put them on leads. "I think I know exactly where that big hog is," he assured me. The two Matthews men almost tip toed around the pond, quickly disappearing into the darkness. Suddenly we heard the massive commotion of dogs on a big hog. Jim Huck and I ran toward the disturbance with the next best dog on lead.

As we got closer we could see the action at the end of our flash light beams. Don's dogs had the hog caught by the ears but the big monster flung them off, one hit the electric fence and yelped. Huck let loose a dog that sailed into the hog and got a hold, another dog joined in. Travis grabbed the hog's back legs and tried to flip it over, belly up. You can't easily flip a hog and dogs, so Don pulled the dogs off and tied them to a small tree. He was ten-feet in front of the brute when it kicked out and flung Travis to the ground. The hog rushed toward Don with its mouth open, tusks gleaming cruelly in Huck's flashlight beam. Don twirled his rope overhead like a lariat, flung it toward the boar's head and caught him around the neck. He side stepped the charge like a matador and tied the other end of the rope to the electric fence, shocking himself in the bargain. The hog hit the end of the rope and its charge was aborted.

A dog reattached himself to the quarry. Don got around behind this mass of animals, took a deep breath, grabbed the hind legs and threw the boar, dog and all, onto its back. Travis and Huck rushed forward, removed the dog and grabbed for legs. Don put his knee into the prone boar's jowl, neutralizing its teeth and holding it down. Together all three men tied the boar's legs together and the four of us dragged it to a pick-up.

"Well, its not Big Boy, but this is sure a good hog." Don announced. "So you won't castrate this one then?" I asked. The three experienced hog men laughed at my naivete. "No, this one's a breeder. We'll turn it loose somewhere else. See this perfectly straight tail? The black color with just a little reddish yellow in the face? This boar is probably pure Russian. There was an old farmer who released a bunch of Russians in this area a few years ago." That would explain its extraordinary fighting ability. This boar weighed about 200-pounds but fought like a 300-pounder.

We untied the dogs from their tree and saw the results of the Russian's fighting ability, the cut collars were all gouged deeply and Bubba's chest bore a four-inch gash. Luckily it was mostly skin deep and only bleeding slightly. We then loaded the dogs and reexamined the trophy. The boar was grinding his teeth together with a loud angry clicking noise, this was not only the way it kept the tusks sharp it was also a warning to stay away. The dogs didn't heed this warning, they kept trying to bite the boar through the steel bars that separated them. Travis yelled at them to stop, "the hunts over!" Huck uncorked a bottle of Crown Royal and everyone took a swig.

By the time we 'd gotten back to Don's house it was four in the morning, our next hunt would start at five, so there was no sense in trying to sleep, as usual I asked questions. "How did you know there was a hog on the other side of the pond?"

"There is a mess of pink root growing over there and the hogs have little else to eat this time of year, there aren't any oranges on the ground anymore and the berries in the palmettos aren't ripe yet." I pondered this awhile before asking my next question, "do you think a trained Bulldog would have been thrown off the boar the way Bubba had?" Don grew reflective, "you may be right, a Bulldog may have held on better, but with all the cattle out there, for this hunt, Curs and Leopards were a safer choice. Its hard

enough finding places to hunt nowadays. You have to be careful not to antagonize the landowners. Don't worry, you'll see Bulldogs in action soon enough."

Different situations call for different dogs. Our next hunt was off an airboat, which meant only one dog could accompany us. Obviously this dog would have to trail and catch. Don brought his champion Cur, Bubba, who was eager to go despite his hog cut from the last hunt.

We stopped in front of Rabbit's house and hooked the airboat and trailer onto Don's pickup. Rabbit had built this boat himself and it was a work of art. The 220 horsepower continental airplane engine could propel it up to 70 miles an hour over water or marsh. Its underside was coated with a special polymer that was so slippery the boat could actually traverse dry land or grass. The prop was about four-feet wide and was mounted five-feet off the ground.

Hog sign, a broken branch

Our hunt took place in Fish Eatin' Creek which fed into lake Okeechobee. This creek snaked labyrinth-like through a beautiful and vast wetland called Cow Bone Marsh. The airboat ride was exhilarating. We saw more alligators than I ever dreamed existed, but no hogs. Rabbit idled his boat slowly past some matted vegetation and said, "look Don, airboat signs. Those Okeechobee boys have found our secret hunting spot." He powered ahead then slowed at a turn in the creek, there were more signs that another airboat had been in Fish Eatin' creek during the night. It looked as if some other hunters had either gotten what hogs were in this area or had scared them away to higher ground.

Not willing to throw in the towel, Rabbit pointed his airboat toward a line of trees and skimmed across the marsh. Occasionally we would bounce onto and over dry land. We checked out every island of trees that popped out of Cow Bone marsh to no avail. Don and Rabbit were disappointed. Just the ride had been a blast for me.

A Matthews Bulldog from the 1920's

Now we had several hours to kill before our next hunt, which would be at night again. I spent part of the time talking to Don's father, Don Matthews senior, who is a spry 80-year old. He regaled me with stories of what it was like in old Florida, when you could drop a hook into any body of water and instantly catch fish or just wade into the ocean and scoop up lobsters. I was especially interested in stories about White Bulldogs he had owned as boy in the 20's. Unlike the dogs Rabbit described, these ones weren't afraid to bite a man. As far as Don Matthews senior knew for sure his father was the first Matthews to breed White Bulldogs. Since his great grandson Mason had just received a White Bull pup that made at least five generations of Matthews men that kept these dogs. Senior showed me photos of Bulldogs from the 20's, then he pulled out a photo from 1915, the oldest known photo of an American Bulldog.

A couple hours after sunset it had begun to cool off a little and I was delighted to see Don load one of his green but eager Bulldog bitches, Mammy, along with an experienced Cur. We headed off toward a cattle operation called Penawae ranch, where we would hook up with the rancher Billy Padrick and his friend Dave Trudell, a.k.a. Rat.

We were following Billy's truck along a dirt road that led into the heart of the ranch when Don suddenly slammed on his brakes. He pointed a flashlight into a ditch that ran parallel to the road. There was a medium sized boar rooting into a mound of earth only about 20-feet away. "Oh damn," he cursed forlornly and tried to signal Billy's truck by blinking his headlights. The lead truck paid no attention and receded into the darkness. "We're not supposed to hunt off this road because its owned jointly by the two ranches it borders. But if I could get Billy's attention..."

He tried his lights again, no luck. We both stared at the hog, so close we could smell it, literally. Don yelled at it and shined his light. The boar glanced at us briefly but wouldn't be spooked and kept on rooting. "This is a perfect opportunity for a Bulldog catch, and that looks like a good tough boar." He seemed to be engaged in an internal wrestling match. "The thing is, like I said, its tough to get these ranchers to let you hunt..." His voice trailed off. I chimed in, "let's not break any rules. There's plenty of hogs up ahead." He nodded and gunned his truck, shining the light one last time on the fearless boar. Even though the beam caught the boar squarely in the eye there was no telltale reflection. Wild pigs are the ultimate stealth animal. I have no idea how Don spotted this black hog down in a ditch in almost pitch darkness.

In the early 1900's, a boar catching Bulldog actually put meat on the table.

In the center of Penawae ranch there is a hunting lodge, next to which sits a huge swamp buggy that is about seven-feet off the ground at its highest point. Like the airboat, this buggy was custom made for hog hunting with steel dog boxes built into the body and a quartz searchlight mounted near the driver's seat.

This is the oldest known photograph of an American Bulldog. Circa 1915

Three of Billy's dogs and Don's two were loaded into these boxes. One dog, an old experienced Cur jumped up next to Billy and rode shotgun. In addition to cut collars these dogs were outfitted with radio tracking collars. As we traversed through meadows, woods and swamps Billy would probe the darkness with his light. The old Cur would follow the beam keenly with his eyes. Every now and then he would lift his head and sniff the wind, find no hog scent and return his attention to the beam.

After a while we went past a herd of deer and the old dog woofed gently. Rat said, "ah, he's just smelling deer." Billy looked at his old friend, shook his head and said, "no, there's a hog out there." The Buggy came to a halt and two young Curs were released. At first the dogs headed toward the deer and Rat made a small "I told you so" noise. Right as he made this noise the dogs veered off and disappeared into some thick brush. After about two minutes we heard the sound of a dog fighting a hog. It broke off suddenly and the chase seemed to recede into the distance. Don and Rat went after the dogs on foot. Billy fired up his buggy, turned on his radio direction finder and roared off parallel to a creek. I hung on to the back of the buggy for dear life as it bounced and swayed madly.

The excitement ended before it began. The dogs quickly returned to the buggy as did the hunters. Apparently it was a small quick pig that had lost the dogs in some impenetrable palmetto.

We traversed the ranch for the rest of the night without seeing anymore hogs. The experienced hunters were frustrated. I stopped following the searchlight and looked up at the star-studded blackness of the heavens. I had never ridden on a swamp buggy and the hot tropical night was so beautiful it was a great experience even without the excitement of the hunt.

As he turned around and headed for the lodge Billy announced gruffly that they would find hogs here next time. He pointed to several 100-pound bags of corn on the floor next to our feet. "Slit those things open and start pouring corn onto the ground." As the corn spilled earthward I could almost feel the stealthy hogs hiding in the nearby ranches begin their migration to Penawae, but it was too late for this hunt.

We got back to Don's house at about the same time in the morning as before, around four, and like before we had another hunt scheduled in an hour. This time we slept during that one measly hour. We left the two dogs in the truck. I imagined they slept for an hour also.

Hog sign, a half-eaten cow carcass

We arrived at Pilgrim's Dairy just after sunrise. The dairy belonged to Travis' wife's grandmother and was mostly abandoned. Travis did raise a few cattle here as a side business but they would be fenced off from where we were hunting. This was the coolest time of day and everyone was energized by the relatively low temperature. The hunters today were: Don, his 15-year old nephew Richard, myself, Travis and his three-year old son, Mason. The little boy was already a fierce hog hunter. He demanded a knife before we set off. When he got one, he pocketed it and said, "let's go catch a hog!" As if on cue we all took off on foot into the lush landscape.

Mammy catches her first big hog

We saw hog signs everywhere, skeletons of dead cows that hogs had eaten, massive earth works from their rooting, hoof prints, small trees with the bark rubbed off and other trees that they had tusked.

Within a few minutes a boar lit off in front of us. Mammy the Bulldog and the Cur took off in hot pursuit. The hunters scrambled to follow. The dogs caught the boar in a creek that was about three or four-feet deep. Don got there first and jumped down the steeply banked sides, he yelled at Richard and me to follow. We crashed into the water and sunk up to our waists. Following directions Richard and I each grabbed a hind leg. Don tore the dogs loose and looked for a place to tie them up. We floated the hog to dry land and dragged it up the steep bank, belly up. Once we had him on level ground we didn't know what to do. Richard was only slightly less green that I was. We were afraid to let go of the hog's legs for fear of getting bit. Fortunately Travis showed up right then. He had been carrying Mason and was consequently a little slower than usual. We handed the hog over and he grabbed the back legs. A quick twist and the 125-pound porker was on its back. He put a knee to its jowl and tied its legs together. I was amazed at how much easier this boar was to handle than the Russian we caught the day before. "What kind of hog is this, Travis?" I asked. It looked pretty much like a smaller version of the Russian but was solid black with a slight curl to the tail and the snout was longer. "This is a wood pig. They are descendants from the pigs the Spaniards let loose in Florida hundreds of years ago."

Now we had to drag this wood pig over half a mile to the pickup. It was starting to get

hot again and I mumbled wearily, "now would be the time to have a weight pull trained Bulldog." Don looked at me in a funny way, "you know that's not a bad idea, these dogs could easily drag this thing back home." He pointed to the two dogs that seemed to be laughing at us sweating humans as they lolly-gagged along.

Bulldogs eager to hunt

It turned out to be a good thing that they weren't hooked up to harnesses because just then they took off after another boar. I couldn't really see how the dogs had caught the first hog down in the creek but now they were on flat land and I could see everything. The Cur went first, his nose down and legs pumping. Mammy was right on his tail, trusting his superior nose to get the job done. They ran the boar up against a fence and latched onto his ears like magnets to steel. As far as I could tell the two were about equally skilled as catch dogs. Since the Cur was much more experienced than Mammy this was an indication of how good she really was. This was the first big hog she'd ever caught. Don was delighted with her performance.

Three Bulldogs on a hog

When the second boar was tied up Travis pointed out something interesting, "normally we'd turn a boar like this into a bar, but look - another boar has beaten us to it." Sure enough, this hog's scrotum had been sliced open in a fight with a presumably tougher boar. It also had hog cuts along its flanks. I put my hand along its side. The skin there felt like armor plating, almost as stiff as bone. These animals had truly evolved to fight.

A hog willing to fight

"Everybody stand back," Don said, "I'm going to turn this one loose. He's already been turned into a bar and he'll mend better in the woods than in a pen." The hog staggered to its feet, turned tail and ran. "All right," Don continued, "since the dogs won't do it for us, lets go get that other hog."

By the time we had it tucked away inside the little pen built into Don's pickup he had another idea. "This area here is so thick with hogs we can hunt with Bulldogs alone. What say we drop off this boar and test out some of these new dogs I've been raising?"

As I mentioned, Don is in the process of introducing Johnson blood to his hog catching Scott dogs in order to increase size. Unlike some other breeders who have crossed the two lines, Don is making sure that anything he uses in his program has the stamina, agility and courage to do real hog work.

I was especially eager to see how his eight-month old stud, Jackson would do. This dog is about 75% Johnson and will probably weigh over 100-pounds when he's full-grown. He's an unusual Johnson Bulldog since his muzzle is over four-inches long. It's as if he was custom made for the Florida heat. However, his head is so wide he still looks Bulldoggy. Don was more interested in another male (named Hammer) who is about 40% Johnson and hasn't

shown much interest in catch work so far. If he failed again he would be removed from the Konfederate program and sold as a pet. We would also bring along two Scott females who Don knew could catch but needed a workout. Hogs were so plentiful at Pilgrim's Dairy we would need another experienced hand. Don's youngest son, Shane, would accompany us. Shane is 15-years old, quick, wiry, a star baseball player and an accomplished hog catcher.

By the time we got started on our 'Bulldogs only' hunt it was close to noon and seemed hot enough to roast meat without an oven. The dogs were panting like steam engines before they jumped out of the truck. Fortunately Pilgrim's Dairy really was hog heaven and the two bitches caught a 100-pound boar right away. It was like shooting fish in a barrel. This boar was turned loose and every dog was held back except Jackson. He was fleet of foot despite the heat and barreled into an ear like an old pro. This was only the second or third hog he'd ever seen. This boar was a mean one too; he broke the hold and bit Jackson in the shoulder. Jackson broke this hold and got an ear, this time not letting go. Shane and I had to break him off the hog and had a hard time doing it. When we finally got him off, the boar was so mad it wouldn't run away but stood its ground, clicking its teeth and emitting a pungent odor.

The boar has Jackson in a shoulder hold

Hammer was turned loose. He went up to the boar casually and sniffed at it. The boar charged him. Hammer danced out of the way nimbly but wouldn't bite. He didn't run away either. He wasn't afraid of the boar but could see no reason to try and catch it. Everybody coaxed him on, to no avail.

Jackson, OFA Good, is tired after a hunt.

Finally Don said, "let's get the dogs out of here and this hog can go back into the woods." When we were all loaded up into the pickup, the boar glared at us defiantly and walked slowly into the woods, he stopped one last time to challenge us before disappearing completely. I could see that he deserved to breed.

On the way back Travis started complaining about the heat. He told me about plans he and his wife were making to move to Montana. "There's just one thing that makes me want to stay," he added wistfully. I thought I knew, "the winters are too cold?" He shook his head, "no, we love the cold, winter sports, skiing, all that. It's that there are no wild hogs there."

Jackson charges a bad boar

"I wonder why they don't have any. Is it because they freeze out in the winter?" I asked. Travis got a sinister gleam in his eye and said, "yeah, any kind of hog would freeze out except a pure Russian boar, the kind that can even survive in Siberia."

"Do you think a hog hunter could introduce some hogs like that into Montana?" I asked innocently. He gave me a speculative nod. It was within the realm of possibility.

After going on just a few hunts I could understand why Travis and the other Floridians I had met were so dedicated to this sport. Not only was there the joy of man and dog working together, which can also be found in Schutzhund, there was also an element of danger and unpredictability missing from other canine sports. I also understood why Bulldogs that have been bred for so many years to catch wild hogs could adapt so quickly to protection work with humans.

Jackson gets his grip. The boar tries to cut him. Jackson dodges while holding on.

Outing a dog after he has just gotten a good grip on a boar's ear is exactly like outing one from a sleeve. Coincidentally, the two sports have evolved similar terminology, a Schutzhund dog that engulfs the entire sleeve in his mouth is said to 'swallow the sleeve,' when a hog dog does the same thing to a boar's ear he is 'swallowing the ear.'

As far as a breed test, it is obviously very good. When Don flunked Hammer as a potential stud and passed Jackson he was measuring many different things. Both dogs are physically sound and have great structure. Jackson has more heart and gameness. Not only was he willing to wade into an animal much bigger, stronger and more formidable than himself, he kept going after the boar had tried to take a piece out of him. Jackson was nimble and quick enough to avoid getting hurt.

This is Don's major concern regarding the introduction of Johnson blood to the smaller strain that he has bred for 25-years, he wants to retain the quickness and other qualities needed to catch wild boar. The way he is going about it is performance breeding at its best. There is nothing theoretical or abstract about a dog's abilities after being tested in this manner.

Hunters immobilize the boar then out the catch dog

Scott's Dixieman - Don Matthews started with Bulldogs like this.

Voodoo - extreme weight pull dog

Life with Bully

Our second trip to Mountain Gator Kennels was even more informative than our first. Martha, Bully and I climbed into our van for a cross-country jaunt when our Bulldog bitch was in her eighth day of heat. We drove nearly nonstop, so we hit Colorado early in the heat cycle. We put Bully's hot pants on and pitched camp in a dog friendly hotel. Not only was Bully going to be bred, the three of us would spend the next few days watching Mark Landers condition his young weight pull Bulldogs, his IWPA rising stars, for a competition that we were invited to attend in a few days.

The next morning we drove the five-miles to Mountain Gators Kennels, arriving at the crack of dawn. Mark Landers met us in the driveway and told us to keep Bully in the van for the next hour. This time would be spent watching weight pull conditioning. Stumpy, Brahma and Proud Mary were harnessed and yoked to 30-foot chains festooned with lead weights. The MGK Bulldogs licked their noses and whined in eager anticipation of a vigorous work out.

Brahma usually drag pulls his own weight for a mile.

There was a well-worn path that wound through the rolling Rocky Mountain foothills behind the kennel. The pull dogs were lined up like one long living freight train with three locomotives. Big Mark ordered the dogs to work. Toenails dug into packed earth, lead weights rattled against steel and the canine railroad was in action. The dogs moved smoothly out of the station and drag pulled as a unit, away from where we stood.

Stumpy drag pulls past a Greyhound/Pit cross.

Huffing and Puffing, lowering their heads and heaving forward under the monster loads, the pull dogs were forced to keep roughly the same pace. All we needed was a whistle and the illusion of a railroad would be complete.

Bully stuck her head out an open window and wore a puzzled expression. Mark, Martha and I stood in silence as the dogs exercised themselves. I would need to walk next to Bully and encourage her if I expected that much weight to be dragged. Plus I darn well better have savory treats in my hand and be quite liberal with tidbit dispersal while singing constant words of praise. These MGK dogs were scratching, panting and laboring on a single command. Mark was standing impassive and reserved. There was no food in sight, though I'm sure they would get breakfast after the work out.

Minutes rolled by and all I could do was marvel at the pull dogs struggling against the lead-weighted chains. It was an endurance workout that could go on for over an hour. This workout wouldn't be that long because these dogs would be pulling in a tournament in four days. It was still more work than I would care to do. The MGK dogs grew small with distance. The winding course made a turn and the canine train slowly got bigger. Finally, Mark began calling out encouragement and the three living locomotives poured on the steam. Lead weights were carving grooves in rocky soil. The dogs were almost plowing a field. Bully whined for permission to join the fun.

She wouldn't be doing any pulling for a long while. It was time for Bully to get pregnant. When the drag pulling was over we turned her loose in the central enclosure surrounded by dog kennels. A dozen Bulldogs barked and carried on. Mark ordered them to shut up and go back into doghouses. Amazingly, after a few more commands the entire kennel was silent and disappeared from view. No other AB breeder that we'd visited could order his dogs to be quiet and expect to be obeyed. Bam Bam refrained from barking but he was leaping against his steel fence, whining, licking his chops, smelling heat pheromones and raring to go.

Bully finally stood naturally for Bam Bam and Martha declared that they were in love.

Bully and Bam Bam ran together for a few minutes. The stud dog made several attempts to mount her but Bully whirled each time and nipped. It was plain that she wasn't going to stand for him, at least not today. I wanted to get three ties over five days. To do this I had to get a tie today, so we were forced to muzzle and hold her still.

When it became obvious what Mark Landers and I were doing Martha cried in alarm, "oh no you're not. Bully is not going to be raped." Bully was a maiden bitch and this was the only way to initiate the pregnancy short of artificial insemination. I'm no biologist but I distrust artificial insemination to send the best sperm to ovum. Sperm are not all alike, just as brothers and sisters are different genetically. We got our first tie over Martha's protestations.

Forty-eight hours later, on the second attempt at mating, I held Bully but didn't muzzle her. On the third try she flagged her tail and was willing to stand for the male naturally. Martha smiled and declared that this final mating was morally acceptable because she could tell Bully was in love.

The day before we left we watched MGK dogs dominate a high level IWPA weight pull in Bighton, Colorado. They took first in every division entered. Brahma was so young that he couldn't even officially enter and could only do

an exhibition pull. This exhibition pull would have won his weight division.

A half-dozen American Bulldogs competed besides the three MGK dogs. These were mostly dogs bred by Landers and owned by Colorado weight pull enthusiasts. ABs dominated the pull and swept Huskies, Rottweilers, Malamutes and Pit mixes aside in toenail digging, muscle popping, glory.

Bully and Bam Bam stay tied for a half-hour.

This is where I learned that a Johnson phenotype was not necessary to win weight pulls. Mark has bred and helped train a few Scott type or performance ABs. Locals have taken these performance ABs to the top in weight pull tournaments. Mark's own breeding program at that point was for a Johnson appearance and superior weight pull ability, others have bred for a performance build and weight pull ability. Bam Bam was the current world record holder in the 100-pound weight class. The next world record holder could have a Scott phenotype; outward physical appearance does not determine which dog is the strongest. The DNA that we were buying would hopefully contain the inner strength of Bam Bam as well as Bully. Since one was a Scott type and the other Johnson, the puppies could look like either parent. Mark told us that the males would look exactly like Bam Bam and the females exactly like Bully. This turned out to be an accurate prediction. We had one female pup that looked and acted exactly like Bully and one male was a recreation of Bam Bam - physically and temperamentally.

When the two puppies were weaned and out of the way, I focused our training on the Brickyard club's Baddest Bulldog on the planet competition held in conjunction with the big ABA confirmation dog show they sponsor once a year. As you recall, the Bulldog that scores highest in four competitions (obedience, protection, weight pull and conformation) is declared Baddest Bulldog on the planet and White's Blue Heaven was the first AB so crowned in 1996.

Bam Bam set the world's record right before our breeding.

I learned a great deal about drag pulling on our trip to Colorado and soon had Bully pulling logging chains through horse and cattle pastures at the crack of dawn. We kept Bully's male puppy and he routinely walked behind his mother during these morning excursions. The puppy, Bear, almost seemed to pretend he was weight pulling as he trudged the worn path winding over hill and dale.

Two things happened that would eventually lead to mortal danger for Bear. Unbeknownst to me, he began walking the drag pull track by himself when released from his small yard for an unsupervised romp. And a horse that hated dogs and cats was put in the pasture nearest our house. This horse was the kind that will chase down a cat and stomp it if possible, a horse that could survive in the wild. Bully's drag track bisected this dangerous horse pasture.

One day at noon I took a break from my metal work, let Bear loose to play and gave Bully an obedience lesson in the front yard. She was in a down stay when suddenly her ears perked. She stood and started trotting toward the horse pasture. It wasn't like her to break a command. I took a few steps to get around a tree and looked in the direction Bully was traveling.

Bear was cowering in the shadow of the dog hating horse. I had seen this horse cripple a feral cat a week earlier, in a different pasture. This monster was pawing the ground and preparing to crush Bear.

A vicious horse endangered Bear's life

Bully emitted a nervous whine as she kicked in the afterburners and broke into a sprint. The killer horse saw Bully and turned to face the larger carnivore. I thought about yelling a stay command or an out. This mare was the mother of champion cutting horses. She was worth at least fifty thousands dollars. The puppy was worth one thousand dollars. To my credit, I bit my tongue. Bully would have disobeyed anyway since she'd already broken the down stay.

Sadie Mae has a performance build and excels at weight pull. Photo - Bob Toye

Bully accelerated. The nasty mare raised her head high and shifted weight to hind hooves, preparing to strike with front hooves. The evil horse knew what Bully was capable of. The mare momentarily forgot Bear. A fight with Bully would be nothing like stomping a cat or a puppy. Bully slowed to crawl under a fence, popped up on the other side and broke back into a gallop. As the mother dog got closer the mare lowered her head and pinned ears back tight against her head. Bully clenched her teeth and zoomed to within several feet of the quivering mare. The Bulldog leaped like a guided missile and smashed the mare in the head with the tip of her snout, jaws clamped tight to create a flying battering ram. Horseflesh was punched, not bitten. The mare reared into a two-legged stance and clipped the air with front hooves in a spot where Bully had been, head weaving in a nickering and confused fury.

Stumpy has a Johnson build and pulls like a locomotive. Photo - Bob Toye

Bully spun in midair and landed facing the mare. Bear was behind his mother, shaking. With cold murder in her eyes Bully locked stares with the horse and communicated silently. Hair was standing on end but she wasn't barking or growling. Other than bristly hair, there was no threat display or posturing, just a promise to fight to the death. Yet the Bulldog didn't launch into an attack. Bully was aware that this was a favored horse. She was acting like an intelligent farm dog. She could only be pushed so far though or she would attack.

The horse lacked gameness. The mare's eyes rolled until the whites flashed like surrender flags. Her whole body shuttered as though an earthquake were rocking the land. The Quarter Horse spun on heels and galloped up the hill. Bully and Bear calmly walked to the front yard as though nothing had happened. I consider that moment the high point of Bully's career.

Her next milestone occurred a year later when Bully finally had enough training to compete in all four phases of the second Fresno Baddest Bulldog on the planet competition (in

1997). She did a super job in weight pull and obedience (finally sprinting on the recall) and racked up another first in confirmation. She never does well when a performance event is coupled with a competitive weight pull and turned in an average performance in protection that day. Still, it was enough to carry the torch from White's Blue Heaven and earn a WABA working title. For one year Bully reigned as the Baddest Bulldog on the planet. Our goal was achieved. My tenure over her career was over. Now it was Martha's turn to pursue a Schutzhund I with Bully. Within weeks of taking over Martha had put a Sch Bh title on Bully under a strict German judge. This was another high point.

The low point of Bully's career occurred on Christmas Eve of that year. Martha and I were out of town for the holiday. Our good friends and fellow Bulldoggers, Rob and Kim Boyd, were dog sitting for us, along with their dogs. The Boyd's two dogs, Hammer (100-pound AB) and Summer (65-pound Colby Pit Bull), have stayed in our guest kennel many times without any problems. The guest kennel shares what I thought was a sturdy, dogfight proof, fence with Bully's kennel.

Lucero's Handsome wins in Bighton, Colorado

Bully decided that her alpha status was being threatened. Belle was in heat and Bully thought that Hammer was going to be bred to Belle. When the dog sitters were preparing to leave Christmas Eve morning Bully managed to thrust her head and shoulders through the fence and into the guest kennel. As Rob and Kim were motoring away to work Bully must have started goading the guest dogs into a fight.

Hammer and Summer fence fought with Bully for hours. Idiotically, Bully kept her body thrust into the opening she had created in the fence and absorbed all the punishment of the fight. The male AB and the female Colby Pit were too smart to thrust themselves into Bully's kennel. When Rob and Kim came back to our house Christmas Eve night they found Bully laying in a heap, ripped to shreds, suffering from dehydration and blood loss. Hammer and Summer were unscratched and seemingly sorry for what Bully had forced them to do.

Gator kicks into four-wheel drive

Bully was rushed to the hospital and doused with antibiotics. She couldn't be sown together because her wounds were swollen, ragged, blood clotted messes that would have to heal on their own.

When we got back Christmas night I inspected the fence after Martha and I gave the battered Bully a thorough once over. Bent wire cables were coated in gore, dried blood and fur, all of it Bully's.

My years spent with Bully had convinced me that she might possess the highest level of gameness and would fight to the death against formidable foes. If this were true then Hammer and Summer should have killed her. On the other hand, it was possible that she had continued pressing her body into the fence to the bitter end but Hammer and Summer grew tired of chewing on her and relented.

I was deeply ashamed of the fences I had built. I am a professional metal worker and should have fences built to the standard of a zoo enclosure. In a perverse way I was disappointed with Bully. If she was dead game she should be dead. Of course, I love her and was infinitely glad that she was alive but the analytical part of me had to know if she'd given up or if the other

two dogs simply stopped fighting because she couldn't hurt them and she'd then collapsed from blood loss. I built a zoo enclosure fence (which I called the super fence) inside the guest kennel and left Bully's fence intact, including the hole that she had wormed her body through to get at Summer and Hammer.

Rob and Kim were scheduled for a fishing vacation. They dropped their American Bulldog and Pit Bull off at my house a month after Christmas so I could dog sit. Hammer and Summer were put in the guest kennel. Bully was turned loose in her yard. A heavy steel-mesh super fence, sunk deep into the Earth and strong enough to hold back the first armored division separated my Bulldog from her two enemies.

Bully didn't know this though, to her one fence looked like another. She walked stiff legged up to her old fence with a hole in it and growled at the female Pit Bull and male AB on the other side. Bully was only partially healed. She was still oozing crud from imperfectly sealed wounds and limping from torn muscles. Her body and spirit were not doing that well. If there wasn't a super fence in place and she tried to fight again, the guest dogs would kill her.

OEA's Coory pulling in competition

Gameness does not mean intelligence, actually it is closer to the opposite - stupidity. Bully paced back and forth, seemingly muttering to herself, "dead game dogs are usually dead but can I tolerate this insult to my honor?" She stopped pacing and stared at Hammer and Summer. She made up her mind and savagely thrust into the hole in the old fence, trying to squeeze her body into harm's way, breaking scabs, aware that the odds were against her but not caring. The peace loving guest dogs picked up noses from the wild flowers growing in my guest kennel and stared in exasperation at Bully. They'd already kicked her ass three ways to Monday, were they going to have to do it all over again?

Bully continued to thrust her head and shoulders madly into the hole and screamed a challenge from behind her flimsy fence. She didn't notice or understand that beyond was a layer of steel reinforced wire mesh that a beetle might crawl through but not a dog. Hammer and Summer wandered casually to this wall of impenetrable mesh and halted. Hammer jumped up on the super fence, let loose a single bark and turned away. Summer followed his lead.

Suregrip's Freddie Kruegger, Gator's brother, Bully's grandfather, was also a good weight pull dog.

Bully barked in delight, taunting them. Ha, you're cowards! After a few minutes of apparent unwillingness to meet the challenge Bully concluded that Hammer and Summer had learned their lesson from last time and were now sufficiently cowed. The limp that had been plaguing her was miraculously gone. Her head was raised high in triumph. Wounds that had been healing slowly now sealed up and disappeared in a few weeks. Apparently, Bully considered a tracery of white scars on neck, shoulders and chest a small price to pay to affirm one's gameness. Bully correctly assumed her alpha status was restored. She was queen of all she surveyed, game on man or beast.

I have included accounts of Bully's accidental dogfights not to boast of her toughness but as examples of what to avoid. Understanding dog aggression in ABs is a must for Bulldog owner/handlers. I can now and always could trust Bully not to attack a submissive dog. The world is full of non-submissive dogs, so responsible AB owners must take precautions. When I walk Bully in any public place where other dogs may be present she is always on leash. Because of my training she will not lunge for any dog while on leash even if it is lunging for her. I can walk her right up to 90% of all dogs. I can turn her off leash with 90% of all dogs and she will play as peacefully as a Collie. But with the ten percent (or so) of truly dominant dogs she must be on leash and under voice control or behind a well made fence. I never feel the need to be an ambassador for the breed when in public with Bully. If someone with a dog asks, "is your dog okay with other dogs?" I answer firmly, "no, she is not."

Putnam's Bear, OFA Good, Freddie Kruegger's great-grandson.

Bully, Belle and the author

Lucy - BST, OFA Good

The Redwood AB Show

The following paperwork must be on file with the WABA before your dog may take the BST: 1) A copy of the dog's registration papers with a minimum three-generation pedigree. 2) A photograph of the entered dog taken from a ¾ side view. Photo will not be returned. 3) The appropriate entry fees in cash, cashier check, money order or personal check made payable to the WABA. 4) Copy of an OFA or Penn-hip certificate with current WABA acceptable scores. 5) Vet certified weight dated within two months of the test date. 6) Copies of official documents or certificates of any titles previously acquired by the dog (i.e. show champion, Sch titles, TTs, etc...) that you wish acknowledged. Paperwork requirement is the same for the WST, except OFA or Penn-hip documents are not needed.

Falsified or fraudulent documents discovered at any time will cause all titles awarded by the WABA to any and all dogs owned by the guilty party to be permanently revoked with no refund of any fees previously paid.

To earn a BST or WST your American Bulldog must do the following exercises: Obedience/Temperament portion of BST/WST. The dog shall wear either a fur saver or choke chain with leash attached to the dead ring. All leashes and collars must be inspected and deemed suitable by a WABA official prior to the beginning of each test.

The test is pass/fail, however, a minimum of 30 points must be achieved in order to pass this test. Additionally, each dog will be evaluated with regard to its temperament as outlined on the test sheet. This test may be repeated two times (total of three tries) by dogs who fail, with no less than two months between test.

Each individual exercise ends with the basic position (dog at a sit at handler's side). The judge will signal handler to begin, and, if requested beforehand, handler may call out instructions during the test.

Exercise 1 - Heeling on leash with gunshots (20 points). From basic position handler gives heel command, handler and dog walk straight ahead 40-50 paces (without stopping) execute an about turn, continue 10-15 paces at normal speed, then fast pace for a minimum of 10 paces immediately followed by a minimum of 10 slow paces, with no normal paces in between. Dog and handler then proceed at a normal pace and execute a minimum of one right turn, one left turn and one left about turn, after which the handler halts. Dog shall automatically sit at all halts, while remaining at handler's left, its shoulder even with handler's knee. Handler influence and dogs that forge ahead or lag behind will incur a point deduction. The heel command may be given when changing pace and out of each starting position. The leash is held in the left hand and must be slack at all times. Two gunshots will be fired at five-second intervals, at a distance of approximately 15 paces, during the heeling pattern. Dogs exhibiting gunshyness will be disqualified. Indifference is the ideal reaction, however mild reaction or excitability will not disqualify the dog.

To pass the obedience portion of the BST your dog must heel closer than this to the handler. Photo - Bob Toye

Exercise 2 - Sit in motion (10 points). From the basic position the handler walks straight ahead, dog heeling, about 10 paces and gives the sit command, drops leash, and without changing pace or looking back, continues forward another 30 paces, halts and turns to face the dog. At judges order handler returns to dog and resumes basic position to the right of the dog. Five points will be deducted if dog stands or lies down.

Exercise 3 - Down in motion with recall (10 points). From the basic position dog and handler walk straight ahead a distance of approximately 10 paces, handler gives the down command upon which dog should quickly lie down, and continues to walk straight ahead without looking back, another 30 paces, stops and turns facing dog. At judge's signal handler calls dog. Dog should run to handler, sit directly in front, and at the heel command return to the basic position. Five points deducted if dog sits or stands.

WABA decoys such as Mario Erazo tend to test dogs intensely.

Exercise 4 - Heeling through a group (10 points). At judge's order, handler heels the dog through a group of four people, halting in the middle of the group. Members of the group calmly move amongst each other while dog and handler maintain the basic position. Judge will dismiss the group. Obedience/Temperament test is completed.

WABA Protection test:

Only dogs that have passed the obedience and temperament test may take part in the protection test. Dogs who fail the protection test due to training/control problems (i.e. refusing to out) may repeat the entire test a maximum of two more times (a total of three) no less than two months apart. Dogs taking the BST that fail the courage test, however, will be prohibited from repeating the test. WST dogs that fail the courage test may repeat the entire test. Not guarding cleanly, re-biting after the out command, and loss of focus during the guarding do not constitute failure, but will be reflected in the dog's evaluation.

The dog shall wear either a fur saver or choke chain with leash attached to dead ring. The helper may be outfitted with a sleeve or full body suit, depending on the dog's training.

Exercise 1 - Surprise attack on handler (out of blind). Dog and handler approach blind on leash. When dog and handler reach a point approximately 12-feet from the blind (this point marked on ground). The judge will instruct the helper to come out of the blind and attack the handler, upon which the handler drops the leash. The dog should immediately engage the helper and continue gripping while being driven by the helper. Dog shall receive two moderate stick hits (padded stick) with an interval of two or three steps between hits. If the dog fails to grip the helper or comes off at any time, the helper must continue to drive the dog. If the dog returns to the helper and re-grips, the test will continue. If the dog fails to re-grip, the judge shall stop the test and the dog can not pass.

Boyd's Mikie hones his guarding skills

Upon signal from the judge, the handler outs the dog and picks up leash or holds dog by collar. A total of three out commands are allowed. If the dog refuses to out after the first and second commands, handler may upon judge's instruction, approach the dog to give the final out command. This will reflect in the dog's final evaluation. Handler may not touch the dog. Following the out, the dog shall guard the helper for a period of five seconds without re-biting. During that time the dog must stay intensely focused on the helper. Barking is not required.

Exercise 2 - Courage test. Upon signal from helper, handler takes hold of dog's leash or collar, while helper runs away to a distance of approximately 30-yards then turns and runs at dog in a threatening manner. Upon judge's signal, handler gives one command and sends dog on helper. Dog should run toward helper immediately, without hesitation, and show full commitment to the bite. Dogs who fail to engage the helper, come off the grip and do not immediately re-engage or leave during the guarding, will not pass the test.

Helper then drives the dog, freezes, followed by a signal from the judge - instructing handler to out his dog. Once again the handler is given three tries to out his dog and the dog is required to guard the decoy for five seconds after the last out command is given. When the guard is completed, handler picks up dog and leaves the field, dog heeling. The protection test is completed. Congratulations, you have put a BST on your American Bulldog!

By May 30, 1998, Working American Bulldog Association Breed Suitability Tests were routinely taken before the three or four big ABA shows that occurred every year in Florida, Ohio, Virginia or California. The WABA was awarding more working titles than any other organization, although a steady trickle of Schutzhund and Ring Sport titles were being added to our breed roster every year.

Bulldog politics didn't make any difference to me at eight o'clock on that May morning. My Chevy S truck was careening down the highway at 90 MPH. Bungee cords creaked as we swerved in front of minivans. Bear and Belle were leaning into the turns while sitting in strapped down plastic dog crates in the pickup bed, sniffing the wind and enjoying the buffeting breeze. Belle didn't know she was going to take her BST and Bear didn't know he was going to be shown for the first time. They did know I was freaking out.

I was late for no good reason. The Redwood ABA club that I was a member of was hosting this major regional show and working trial. My responsibilities for helping set up the event were myriad. I should have been at the park two hours ago, but had simply overslept. I didn't have the strength of character to admit that in front of the hundred people that would be waiting expectantly at the trial grounds in 60-minutes.

Bully would have to take the rap. I would tell everyone that she escaped, got into

the street and was mauling a neighbor dog. My friends would nod grimly and grumble, "that damn Bully did it to you again, Dave." WABA officials would note this reaction, believe my story and hopefully excuse me for being late. Since most people in the crowd (WABA officials included) have ABs, everyone would murmur in sympathy.

Belle begins to learn to guard, note the long line

The Royal Oaks field trial was 80-miles from my house. We had an hour before the trial was scheduled to start. We would barely make it or be only a few minutes late if I drove like a maniac and didn't get busted. A crucial step in setting up the BST field would not get done because of my lateness. Spectator parking was supposed to be diverted by signs on sawhorses in the back of my truck. When I finally arrived, pickup trucks, open vans and crates full of Bulldogs would be lining the field. The people/dog teams taking the trial would be furious at me despite my lie about Bully being the cause of this screw-up. If they knew the real reason why I screwed up I'd probably get lynched. The BST teams (Belle and me included) would have to take the test in combat conditions because Royal Oak's largest parking lot was adjacent to the trial field.

My truck pulled into the main parking lot in a dust cloud. We'd evaded the highway patrol and gained a few minutes. Instead of being absurdly late we were just plain late. My truck's tires were smoking and my Bulldogs' ears took a second to flap down against their cheeks.

My heart pounded in fear and my jaw dropped when I saw the field. It was a zoo. Flimsy yellow police tape was holding a huge crowd from surging onto the square grassy surface devoted to the trial. People were packed shoulder to shoulder, truck to truck. Crates of snarling Bulldogs were literally touching the sidelines of the trial field. Because of the unruly crowd the registration table was mobbed and the trial was delayed by an hour. My own ineptness was aiding my cause.

Belle breaks the guard and receives a correction.

I had enough time to take each dog for a short walk and didn't have to lie to WABA officials. Only my friends were angry about my lateness. Four or five Redwood club members accosted me as soon as the two Bulldogs and I had returned from a short walk. I told the phony story implicating Bully. My story was believed. Irritation was transformed into sympathy. Minutes passed. Belle and I found ourselves doing the obedience routine in the combat conditions I had created.

Brian Rice, the judge, warned me to avoid a spot on the turf where an in-heat bitch had peed. My overloaded brain didn't quite register the exact spot where he was pointing.

Belle's heeling was strong. Her change of pace was nice. I sprinted as hard as I could and her head remained within inches of my left knee. I came screeching to a super slow pace from full speed with her nose glued to my knee. We continued with the heeling pattern at a normal walking pace and awaited the gunfire. Our obedience partnership was functioning smoothly. Belle was ignoring the human and canine crowd and hanging at my side as we walked.

Snap had nearly perfect obedience when she passed the OB I. Photo - Michelle LeNoir

The obedience portion of the test is nearly identical to the Schutzhund Bh, except it is done on leash. Every dog on the field was required to be on leash or locked in a secure container because the potential for a dogfight with these many American Bulldogs packed cheek to jowl was very high. However, during the BST the leash must be so slack and the turns so crisp that the judge will conclude this dog could do the heeling off leash.

Belle gets airborne on a practice long bite

Belle carries the sleeve

We heeled up and down the field, made the turns and there was no gunshot. We made more turns and continued the pattern. The starter pistol didn't work. Someone yelled at me to keep heeling. We marched up and down the field like an airliner without permission to land until a back up pistol was found. Her work was nearly flawless so far. The shots were fired and Belle didn't flinch.

A group of six or seven prearranged strangers walked onto the trial field and milled in a disorganized bunch. We heeled into the crowd smoothly. Belle wove among the strangers with a bounce to her step and a gentle wag of the tail. We came to a sit stop. The crowd surrounded her and pressed in from all sides. She sat at calm attention and let them push against her. She was steadily ignoring the aggressive dogs and boisterous people beyond the pressing mob of strangers. The prearranged crowd left the field and we prepared to do the final exercises.

The combat conditions were worse than I thought. I tried to recall where the judge had said a female dog or a raccoon in-heat or something had urinated on the grassy carpet. Royal Oaks park is near a wilderness area. Maybe a bear had urinated on our trial field. Every dog taking the test had reacted to this spot. I was told the two dogs that had taken the test before us had blown it because of this spot. Judge Rice warned me to do my in motion exercises well away from this part of the field. Now that we were out here I was confused as to where the invisible spot was.

Our sit in motion was good. I was three quarters through the routine. Later, I would realize our down in motion was right next to the raccoon urine spot. From the crowd's reaction I deduced that Belle went down nicely as I marched up the field without turning to see if my command was obeyed. Trial rules dictate that the handler march forty paces, turn and wait for the judge's signal. I turned around. Belle was in a slightly different location, still in a down but smelling the turf near her front paws. She'd broken the command. When my back was turned she'd crawled on her belly to this seductive odor. We would loose major points but could still pass if the rest of the routine was flawless.

The judge signaled for recall. I shouted, "come." She sprinted hard on the recall command and zipped to a good sit directly in front of me. She did a crisp finish. We heeled to the judge and obedience was over. We passed with the equivalent of a B minus or C plus. Our score was 37 out of 50. The dog after me (the last in the trial) was Dave Hannah's Mack. After the officials scanned the sidelines for uncrated Bulldogs, Dave was given permission to do the routine off leash because the judges had seen Mack's work and knew he was at the level of a Schutzhund III in obedience. Mack and Dave got a score of 50 out of 50.

A deep, steady, bite well help your AB pass the BST. Photo - Michelle LeNoir

Agility work will build a dog's confidence and help obtain working titles.

The bites were next. I didn't want Belle to watch the two dogs in front of us do bite work. So we hid behind a concrete building, cooling our heels. My heart was pounding like a jackhammer, palms sweating like Niagara Falls. It seemed as though only seconds had gone by when the third place in the rotation rolled around and we were running toward the field. Rob Boyd ran alongside us and presented a trial sleeve. Belle didn't break stride as she leaped up to meet his high presentation and clamp down for a solid bite. Running toward the field, Rob slipped the protection arm and peeled into the crowd. The warm up bite had gone well. Still running, I told her to spit out the sleeve and praised her for a good out when she obediently complied. We entered the field. On the judge's signal we moved slowly toward the blind. She could smell the decoy behind the canvass and was straining on her dead ring, which meant point loss. We should be heeling as though this were an obedience routine. Belle was over excited, as was I. Twelve-feet from the blind Dave Deleissegues popped from behind the tent-like structure. Mr. Deleissegues has done decoy work on an international level in Schutzhund and took first with his Rottie, Hark, in the North American finals, the first non-German Shepherd to ever do so.

This formidable decoy raised his stick and attacked the handler, running directly at me. I gave Belle the bite command and turned her loose. In high drive, tufts of grass flew from her feet as she went into action. The decoy was charging at her as fast as he could. A roar rose from the sidelines. Now the crowd worked in my favor by revving Belle up. She sprinted too fast; hitting the sleeve so hard she jammed slightly, bounced back and was forced to bite mid way to the molars. The decoy didn't stop running. He drove her and she crossed her back feet to move smoothly and stay in front of the man. She timed her re-bite and finally got a deep grip. She took the stick hits with eyes open and feet moving. The decoy froze and stopped fighting. I gave the out command. She outed smoothly but was dirty in her bark and hold, snapping and bumping at the sleeve but not re-biting. I was forced to wait several seconds. Belle went into a cleaner bark and hold, sitting squarely and barking alertly, one eye on the decoy's head the other on the sleeve. On the judge's signal I approached Belle to pick her up for the long bite. As I drew near she got dirty and started circling the decoy. I gave her a down command and finally got her under control.

If this were a Schutzhund trial, I would be losing so many points failure would be looming. Fortunately it was a breed suitability test where the dog was being judged, not her training or handling. Belle had done okay because of the good stick hits, deep re-bite and immediate release on the first out. The BST allowed the out command to be given up to three times before a dog failed for refusing to disengage. There is no shame in passing the test after the third out was obeyed. Belle was headed toward a low score on control, for dirty guarding.

The Judge nodded when the decoy was twenty or thirty-yards away. The decoy charged us. I gave the bite command. Belle flew down the field and got a better initial bite but had to re-bite to adjust for rapid lateral driving motion. The last few steps of the driving were absorbed smoothly because of a good re-bite. The fight stopped. I outed her. She popped off and went into a clean bark and hold. I was able to collect her more easily than the attack on handler bite. My control score should go up a tad.

With all her bite energy expended Belle finally came under complete control. I heeled her to the judge and put her into down stay. Brian Rice gave a lengthy evaluation to the crowd. Belle was high in courage and fight drive but only medium in hardness. Her control was deemed only adequate. We passed with an average score. That meant that Belle's one litter (ten and a half months old that day) was retroactively the first BST to BST breeding. The people who had bought puppies from me would be ecstatic. Two were in the crowd. My puppy customers hooted and the half-grown puppies woofed as though understanding the reason their masters were so happy.

Bully class winner, Souza's Dixie, PD2, OFA Good, 1st place in hardest hitting dog

Belle's mate, Hammer, was also in the crowd with his owner Rob Boyd. Hammer had been rated very hard after his BST with a near perfect obedience routine. Rob and Hammer both howled. The last dog in the protection phase of the trial was Hannah's Mack. This dog did his protection routine at Hammer's level. The team before me in the rotation was Mark Griffin and Lucy, fellow members of the Redwood club and our training partners. Lucy had passed her BST with scores roughly the same as Belle's. I was glad that we had ended our trial on such a strong note.

The rest of the dog show meant two confirmation classes for Belle and three for Bear, her kennel buddy. Martha would be showing the 78-pound Bear in the bully class, which was fitting because he is ¾ Johnson and looks it, with a head like a basketball, solid bone, fantastic movement, tightly built and springy. He moves like a Kentucky trotting horse and is one of the few short-muzzled Bulldoggy Johnson ABs that can run 12-miles and beg for more. Martha and Bear were considered a real threat in the show ring. While many East Coast ABA bully or ABNA classic judges would automatically discount him for being too small and not extreme enough, in

California even the Johnson crowd does some bite work and understands the athletic advantage to a smaller, tighter, Johnson Bulldog.

I didn't have high hopes for Belle. She is as heavily built as Bear and almost as Bulldoggy but has to be shown in the standard class because she has a scissors bite. The ABA bully class (Johnson) disqualifies any dog that isn't undershot. The standard (Scott/Painter) class is more liberal, allowing undershot, even and scissors bites. Because Belle has a tight scissors bite I had to show her in the wrong class. That didn't bother me because of her crooked tail. I could never win show points with her under any circumstances because her tail is shaped like the sickle in the old Soviet flag. While this flaw does not affect functionality it is enough to prevent first or second in any ring. Because of her straight legs and good working structure Belle usually takes a third in a standard class show with a big turnout.

The standard class winner was Ellie Rock's Diesel, Sch I and OFA.

The disqualification clause that forbids even or scissors bite ABs from competing in the bully class was and is misunderstood by most novice ABA show handlers. A novice will read that a bully class dog must be undershot and that a standard Bulldog can have any kind of bite (the preference going to a tight reverse scissors) and interprets this information wrongly, believing that any undershot dog should be shown in the bully ring. They are correct in assuming that all even bites or scissors bites must be shown in the standard class. They are hopelessly wrong to take an only slightly undershot, non-wrinkled, long muzzled, medium boned performance AB and compete against Johnson dogs in the bully class. These performance dogs that are voluntarily shown in the wrong class may have taken a first place in the standard ring but end up scoring zero in the bully ring. Nine out of ten ABs should be shown in the standard class. The rule of thumb is - if you're debating what class to show your AB in, sign-up for the standard class.

Standard judges are asking themselves if a Bulldog has the correct structure to hunt wild hogs in the broiling sun of a Dixie summer. ABA judges in the bully class are looking for a larger version of the Philo-Kuon Bulldog of early 19th century England: blocky, big headed, estate guard dogs. The ABA confirmation blueprint does not say that the bully (Johnson) type AB should be bigger than the standard type. In other words, bully class judges want a reasonably sized, fairly athletic Bulldoggy specimen with a large but not exaggerated head, medium/short length muzzle, manageable face wrinkles, quarter-inch undershot and great movement. The bully confirmation standard does not say: "Everything being equal the larger dog is preferred." In fact, it says that if a bully dog and a standard dog weigh the same, the bully dog should be shorter because he is supposed to have heavier bone.

Bear shows great movement

This description matches Bear to a tee. Martha was blowing through her confirmation classes like Sherman's march to the sea. She and Bear racked up two firsts. The second blue ribbon was awarded in the prestigious hip class; a show ring where every dog has certified hips, another ABA innovation. Judge Kyle Symmes was impressed with Bear's movement and said so twice. I was proud to have bred him.

The highlight of the confirmation show was when Judge Sheila Couturier picked Souza's Dixie (a female) as best in show bully class. I'd never seen an ABA judge pick a female for best in show. The call was a good one. Dixie has exceptional confirmation. This is the West Coast Johnson type, blocky yet athletic. On the East Coast, Dixie would be shown as a standard. The best in show standard AB was Ellie Rock's Diesel. Both of these show champions have passed OFA and have working titles.

Belle took third place and was spared from fourth only because she truly has good structural confirmation to go with muscle too heavy for the standard class and her oversized head. Our poor showing didn't make any difference because the next event for Belle and her human partner was the race. I believed that the race would show more correctly what kind of structure a dog has than a visual inspection. This event was a timed recall at fifty-yards. The dogs would be running against the clock, one at a time. The fastest time (obviously) wins. The event was open to any dog with a BST, WST or OB title. Even though Belle's BST was only a couple hours old she could participate in the world's fastest Bulldog competition.

The race was scheduled Sunday afternoon after the last confirmation winner was given the final bouquet of roses and the last raffle item handed out. The racers were: Rob Boyd's Hammer, my dog Belle, Tom Riche's Brody and Dan Guerra's red nose Pit Bull - Sonny. The smart money was all on Brody. Working people insist that he is the fastest Bulldog on the West Coast. There were a few BST/WST Bulldog handlers in the crowd that refused to race their dogs because Brody was considered a ringer. I was outclassed. It was déjà vu. I was in the same position in the Belle versus Brody race as I was with the Bully versus Stumpy weight pull years earlier in Oklahoma. Belle was a ten-to-one underdog among the betting crowd.

The gamblers betting against us didn't realize that I had a card up my sleeve. I was in charge of setting up the fifty-yard racetrack and testing the stop watch system with any dog I wanted. I would chose Belle as the test dog. I thought this gave me a huge advantage.

Ostensibly my dog would do a trial run to just make sure the timing equipment worked properly. She would perform this function but she would also be warming up. The other dogs would walk cold muscled straight from their crates to the starting line. My dog would be limber as a cheetah.

Brody - fastest AB in the world, that day

The race rules state that the competing dog is put into a stay at the start line, then the handler walks fifty-yards downfield and as many paces past the finish line as he wants, turns and gives one recall command. The stopwatch starts on his voice command and ends as the dog's nose crosses the finish line. Belle blazed on her trial run at 4.88 seconds. It should be noted that dogs don't achieve top speed without a prey object, losing almost one second without a moving object to chase.

Now my dog was loose and warm and the others were stiff and cold. A few minutes later and Belle was the first entrant in the race. I walked down the field away from the crowd. Belle was in a rock solid down stay, oblivious to all these people. In her Zen-like state the barking Bulldogs in trucks and crates didn't exist. If she had been this focused during the trial I would have gotten a much better score. I suddenly realized our control problems were my fault not Belle's. She had been feeding off my uncertainty and frustration at being late. Now, during the race, I was cool and confident because I had utter faith in the card up my sleeve and this was all just for fun. My 84-pound bitch could beat Tom Riche's 75-pound Schutzhund III male pocket rocket because I'd stacked the deck.

I yelled the recall command and Belle sprinted the fifty-yards in 4.99. The crowd went oooh! Sounded like a tough time to beat. I was surprised that her practice time was better than her race time. My scheme had backfired on me. Perhaps her foot had gotten caught in a gopher hole on the second run.

Hammer was next. He plopped his beefy frame at the start line and watched Rob walk down field. The 100-pound Hammer looks a yard wide and doesn't appear to be very fast. Don't be fooled, he is much faster than he looks and had the possibility to be a dark horse, a spoiler. Some kids in the crowd knew the big dog's name and started teasing him and giving him voice commands by name. A few adults tried to hush the brats, only making them worse. Hammer whined and looked away from Rob.

Belle - second place in race

Parents grabbed their kids and the teasing stopped. A man that was Rob's height and build and was dressed in a similar gray shirt and faded blue jeans was standing in the sun five-yards away from the finish line. The real Rob was standing ten paces beyond the finish line, under an oak tree and was swallowed by shadow. He didn't notice that his dog was looking at the wrong person. The wind was in Rob's face so Hammer couldn't smell him.

The kids started giving commands to Hammer again. The big dog glanced at the kids and away from the man who looked like Rob. The real Rob shouted, "here" and Hammer streaked to the look-alike man. He came to a crisp sit in front of the wrong person. The stopwatch was still ticking. Hammer sat for several seconds with a puzzled expression on his face. What the hell? Swinging his head, he sighted his true master. Weight pull winning muscles bunched into action as he sprinted again. The big wide Bulldog bounced to a sit in front of the right guy. Final time, over ten seconds. Not bad considering the mishap. Hammer moved pretty fast for a light heavyweight but was out of the money.

Hammer BST II, 1st in hardest hitting dog

Brody was next. Tom Riche put his dog on the start line and trotted downfield fifty-yards. He didn't go the full ten paces past the finish line and was standing dangerously near the stopwatch trigger point when he turned and took position. No one seemed to notice Tom's mistake except me. I should've said something but showed weakness of character by keeping my mouth closed. Tom yelled a recall command and Brody was a streak of white lightening, obviously faster than Belle. The smart money laughed. I was chagrined. Even with my dog warmed-up Brody was still faster. In the last four strides Brody slowed and slammed into a sit. Half of his slow down was done on the racetrack and half was done past the finish line. My slow down was mostly past the finish line. Ha ha ha. The timekeeper called, "five point two." Belle had beaten Brody by fractions of a second. On paper I had California's fastest American Bulldog. Belle and I both howled triumphantly. This made up for third place in the beauty contest and the C plus in obedience.

Dan Guerra told me to stop crowing as he led his red nose Schutzhund III, OFA good, super Pit to the start line. Pit Bulls can take the BST and a few have done so. The 63-pound red nose lined up on the racecourse was WABA titled and eligible under race rules. Sonny was revving his motor like a jet waiting at the runway. The Pit's mouth was open and panting despite the cool weather. No fair, the Pit jet fighter was hyperventilating, in effect engaging a turbo charger. Dan left Sonny on the start line and walked downfield past even where I had stood and gave the recall. Sonny was an AA fuelie dragster: a red flash that was sitting down field in the blink of an eye. Time: 4.44 scorching seconds. He was the winner, but as a Pit Bull didn't factor among the highly partisan Bulldog crowd. Dan had the fastest Pit Bull in California. I had the fastest American Bulldog.

Fans cheered Belle as she pranced off the field. Tom Riche said loud enough for the peanut gallery to hear, "how about a rematch. Unofficially. Doesn't count. Just to see who really has the fastest Bulldog?" Dan Guerra's ears perked up at these words. He demanded a rematch as well, even though he'd beaten every dog entered. He knew Belle was the only dog to take a warm up lap and thought he would get an even better time. I don't know why everyone was getting so upset. I hadn't done anything to prevent them from taking their own hot laps. In any case, the mob wasn't interested in seeing the Pit Bull get a second shot. They wanted to see a rematch between the two top American Bulldogs.

Ivan - Hammer BST II x Belle BST, 118 lbs

The crowd started clamoring for a side by side race. The Bulldoggers would have gotten ugly if I didn't put Belle in a down stay at the start line next to Brody. Both Tom and I walked fifty-five-yards downfield and lined up parallel to each other. Dave Hannah followed closely to act as judge. The rules for the official fastest Bulldog competition explicitly state no baiting with food or movement. There were no rules for the unofficial just-to-see-who-really-is-fastest American Bulldog race, only a stopwatch and a voice command. Tom decided he would clap his hands during the run. I decided to be a statute since that's what Belle is used to from her trial training. Looking back, I realize standing still was bad strategy.

To earn a BST your dog must bite tenaciously. Photo - Michelle LeNoir

The two dogs lay in perfect down stays lined up two-feet apart on the exact same line. Both were intently following their master's retreating backs. They looked like dragsters ready to rumble. We turned at the same time and stood parallel, three-yards apart. Dave Hannah hollered, "One two three!" We yelled recall commands. Both dogs got off to fast starts. For the first few yards Belle was almost neck and neck with the small white speedster. She managed to achieve fair speed. Paws gathering under and stretching to full extension. Halfway and Brody started to accelerate. He gathered steam and left her in the dust. Her face looked earnest as she tracked her rival's departure. She looked ahead at me and gave a speed burst, too little, too late. Brody's best time was 4.66. So, truthfully, he was the fastest Bulldog in California as tested by the Redwood American Bulldog club in '98. Brody and Belle would race again at the '99 Redwood Irondog triathlon and achieve much better times. Brody and Riche's Brindle would still beat Belle by .2 seconds. Rats!

The show was over. Belle and I trudged back to the vehicles. Bear was sitting in Martha's van next to his blue ribbons, a gloating expression on his big wrinkly head. He acted as though his show wins were more noble than Belle's BST. Martha and I drove home at a sedate speed.

As the sun set in the redwood trees of our backyard that evening. I wandered into the kennel of Brindle (the Hammer/Belle puppy I had kept) and thought how great the show was and considered the infrastructure behind the confirmation and working trials. It was made possible to some degree by the ABA, the organization nine out of ten Bulldoggers register their ABs with and the parent club of the WABA. If I we were to have gone to an ABNA show back East the experience would have been much the same since WABA is welcome there.

The ABA bully and ABNA classic confirmation classes have been producing champions that are less exaggerated and more athletic than the extremist splinter breeders that produce dogs that deserve nicknames like porch Bulldog. ABA bully and ABNA classic show winners are leggy and tight but still Bulldoggy. The Johnson breeders that don't show in the ABA or ABNA have created various small registries that are seeking to produce 150-pound Bulldogs with inch long muzzles. Giant English Bulldogs. Non-exaggerated Johnson dogs will live longer and healthier lives than caricature oversized extreme Bulldogs.

It must be admitted that ABA and ABNA standard classes are producing champions that are blockier than some old time performance Bulldogs. Hundred pound dogs like Turbo, dogs with jowls and a big head, are winning the standard class. ABs such as Boyd's Mikie have won both bully and standard ABA shows.

The gradual melding of two types to evolve the Hybrid type is working well. This is the standard class AB. It has become the dominant force in the ABA and ABNA. At the same time the minority of breeders that are producing pure performance (non-typey) dogs are relatively happy even though the standard ring actually favors dogs with some type. Standard and Johnson breeders are lucky to have separate show rings. If anything, there is a need for a third class and a third show ring, an extreme performance class where smaller heads and less blockiness is tolerated. No one wants a third ring except radicals like me, so it will never happen. Two ring ABA and ABNA shows that produce standard and bully (classic) class champions are routine. The war has been largely settled. We should continue to breed dogs that range from a coarse, leggy, square headed Pit Bull type to a tight, lean, muscular, white Bullmastiff, always trying to keep the muzzle length close to three-inches or longer. Breeders should use a wide head to make a medium muzzle look short, never an actual short non-functional muzzle. Also, we should never allow small hindquarters or pushed out elbows or any truly exaggerated features.

Throughout history Beardogs and Bulldogs have genetically mingled yet remained separate, refreshing each other's gene pools periodically. That is the secret to a traditional working Bull breed. That is why a 60 to 120-pound weight range is acceptable as are two or even three types within one breed.

Suregrip's Jack the Gripper catches a large and nasty wild Russian boar. This would have earned him a Catch Dog III title.

Whether one agrees with my reasoning or not, that is the state of affairs with the American Bulldog community. As always, working ability takes precedence over breed type. The major AB working organizations and the titles they issue are:

1) Al Joye's American Bulldog Weight Pull Association (ABWPA) issues the WPD I, II and III. To get a WPD I your dog must pull twelve times his body weight under IWPA rules. ABWPA titles mirror the weight pull titles issued by the IWPA.

2) The Working American Bulldog Association issues the Breed Suitability Test I and II, Working Suitability Test I and II, Weight Pull I, Obedience I and the endurance title or AD. The OB I is similar to a Sch Bh, except the heeling is on a slack leash. The WABA WP I is similar to Al Joye's WPD I (see above). The BST is the test described in the preceding section of this chapter. A dog must have hips certified non-dysplastic by OFA or Penn-hip to take the BST. The WST is the same test as the BST but requires no hip check. I believe it is implied that WST dogs will not be bred despite high working aptitude. The WST II and BST II are off-leash advanced protection and obedience tests involving Ring Sport style stick hits and gunfire in various bite scenarios. Either suit or sleeve may be used for the four suitability tests. The AD endurance title is a 12-mile run. The dog must maintain a speed of 7.7 to 9.5-miles per hour. The AD also includes a heeling/obedience test after the 12-mile run.

3) Lemuel Miller's Utility Catch Dog Association (UCDA) conducts hog catching trials to issue Catch Dog titles. Your dog must have the ability to do real catch work on a tough medium sized wild boar to earn a CD I. Approximately half the ABs that try for the CD I fail. To earn a CD II and CD III the wild boars are more formidable, hunts are longer and go into deeper brush, which makes conditions more taxing. The UCD titles are even tougher, reserved for professional catch dogs and can involve catching cattle. The UCDA and WABA are sister organizations, so UCDA titles are transferable and equal to WABA titles.

The first AB to earn a BST and a CD I was Marco Zapparilli's Bronx. Al Joye's Stonewall was the first to earn a BST and a WPD II. No AB, as of 1999, has received all three: a BST, WPD I and CD I. Any working Bulldogger would consider the first AB to rack up all three titles ultimately breed worthy. A special name should be created to describe an AB that earns all three, such as the BWC I (Breed Weight Catch One). Soon there will be a BST III to compliment the WPD III and CD III that already exist. Sometime early in the next century an American Bulldog will be titled with a BWC III. Perhaps midway or toward the end of the 21st century there will be pink-papered AB puppies that have several generations of BWC III ancestors. Can you imagine how much working ability those Bulldogs will have?

I am training Belle for the BST II, WP I and Irondog triathlon. Looking any further than these immediate goals is counterproductive. The BST II is tough - entirely off leash, involves running blinds, blind searches, advanced guarding and other advanced Schutzhund/Ring Sport tests with multiple decoys. If and when we get the two titles and win an Irondog, we'll start thinking about a Catch Dog one.

To earn a UCD III, a Bulldog can catch wild cattle.

Turbo - BST, CD I, ABA Champion, OFA Good

AB Breeders

This chapter covers a few breeders prominent in 1995 or earlier that have produced foundation dogs for other programs. Since then I have come to feel that too much emphasis is placed on breeders and not enough on individual dogs. A good breeding depends on the animals being mated. One breeder may have a litter on the ground that comes from superior parents and next to it there may be another litter that is inferior. The secret to picking a good puppy is having the knowledge to judge the quality of the parents (and grandparents) yourself. When knowledgeable breeders buy dogs from lazy or ignorant competitors they will often do the testing themselves. Consider Matt Boyd, a pioneer in board certifying AB hips. He has probably paid for more hip examinations of other breeders' Bulldogs than anybody; if the hips come up good he may breed one of his bitches to the stud in question, if the hips are bad he moves on. Al Banuelos has bought dogs from the rural South where protection sport is a rarity. He acts as a decoy and courage tests Bulldogs directly. He may then have to take a promising Bulldog to a local vet for an X-ray because the hillbilly owner has never even heard of OFA. Such obstacles are trivial to a dedicated Bulldogger facing a prize specimen.

WAB Katie

The following breeders appear in random order. Breeder information is delivered in their own words as much as possible without me acting as a filter, except the section on Larry Koura, where I base my observation directly on dogs that he has bred.

Working American Bulldogs

A.J. Baldwin owns Working American Bulldogs (WAB) in Richmond, Ohio. His bloodlines are approximately 75% Johnson and 25% Painter. Mr. Baldwin is an expert on hip dysplasia. He estimates that 10% of Johnson dogs have significant dysplasia problems and is concerned that poor breeding could increase it to 50%, as has already happened with large AKC breeds such as the St. Bernard.

WAB Slammer, OFA Good, trained in weight pull, protection, obedience and agility, Gator x Doozey

Eliminating dysplasia is more like a war to Mr. Baldwin than a technical breeding challenge. He attacks with a three pronged assault: 1) All his dogs over two-years old are OFA or Penn-hip certified. 2) He uses drag weight pulling as a breed test. 3) His original stock consisted of sound Johnson/Suregrip dogs with a genetic history of soundness.

Mr. Baldwin is currently expanding his program and acquiring different bloodlines, looking for dogs that have solid structures. His breeding goals go beyond just structural integrity though to include working ability. Slammer (his 107-pound stud) is protection trained, weight trained, and works out on agility and search courses. WAB has only nine dogs and they are treated like pets, interacting with the Baldwin children on a daily basis.

WAB Grizzella nuzzles Brutus

Every litter goes through elaborate temperament tests at about seven weeks. These tests include such activities such as rolling a pup on his back and restraining him for 30-seconds then measuring the degree of dominance or submissiveness exhibited. Nine different characteristics are tested. Studies by animal researchers have proven that carefully crafted testing at this age can accurately predict the temperament of adult dogs. Puppies without steady nerves are culled.

WAB Thor at 10-weeks old

While protectiveness is important to his breeding program, Mr. Baldwin feels that if there ever is a personality defect it should be toward a dog being overly friendly. This is important to bear in mind because breeding is an imprecise

art and a breeder can not simply dial in the exact qualities he's looking for. Mr. Baldwin's general goals are to breed a Johnson type dog that looks Bulldoggy, yet is still athletic.

Vanguard's Stonewall, BST, WPD II, OFA Good

Vanguard Kennels

Vanguard Kennels of Manassas, Virginia is owned and operated by Al Joye and his wife, Lorraine. Al has been associated with American Bulldogs for over 40-years. Having served 26-years of active duty in the Marine Corps, he was often temporarily out of the fancy while serving in Vietnam or elsewhere overseas. Never the less, he remained involved and in love with the breed. Vanguard kennels is an active effort to produce athletic, performance oriented and sound tempered American Bulldogs for the discrete owner. Specific bloodlines are not as important as the qualities and characteristics that blend to produce great companions. Should there be a more prominent type of dog produced it would be a Scott/Painter cross. Al is quoted as saying, "in contrast to what many may think, Joe Painter should be given a medal for his contributions to the American Bulldog and the breeders of the grossly oversized Mastiff type dogs should be embarrassed."

Vanguard kennels produces approximately two litters each year. He is very discriminating who he will sell to and thus questions a potential owner specifically about how the puppy is to be treated. One recent customer claimed that it felt like he was getting a top security clearance to buy a puppy. But Al is determined to avoid the stigma associated with the Pit Bull and feels that responsible owners are the key ingredient to the breed's survival.

Vanguard's Stonewall

Stonewall receives the first BST

Al prefers to produce dogs with thick wedge type heads and without heavy, thick loose lips. He feels that the American Bulldog should have an expression of determined confidence, an expression that looks nothing like the English Bulldog or Mastiff. Another difference between smaller performance bred ABs and the larger Mastiff type is longevity. The performance type will live 12 to 14-years if kept in shape and fed properly.

Although his own dogs are not actively involved in hog hunting or Schutzhund this kennel has produced dogs that are active in both of these arenas. Al feels that these sports test the very fiber of a Bulldog and help keep it a true working breed.

Vanguard's Block Buster

Al has serious misgivings concerning the grossly oversized Mastiff type dogs. It is his understanding from extensive reading and numerous candid conversations with other breeders and veterinarians that 75% of the American Bulldogs weighing over 120-pounds will likely have some degree of genetic weakness in their hips or shoulders with 10% of those being strong candidates for euthanasia. He acknowledges that there are many who will disagree with him on this but challenges those who do to a four hour hog hunt in a South Carolina swamp or easier yet try their dogs on a 12-mile brisk jog (a routine requirement in Germany for working breeds). Al feels that in addition to hard physical testing of adult dogs, responsible breeders must be willing to cull weak specimens as puppies and be actively involved in temperament testing in a manner similar to that described in A.J. Baldwin's program. Al states that as of 1995 he has never had a reported case of hip dysplasia. He attributes this to a very selective breeding program with the quality of the total dog, not size, foremost in mind. He admits that he has been very fortunate for sometimes the very best breeding programs will produce negative results.

Without fail, Al will pay tribute to Al Banuelos as the premier trainer and breeder of some of the best American Bulldogs available.

He appreciates Banuelos' honesty and integrity as much as he does his great dogs. He is also quick to compliment Matt Boyd and A.J. Baldwin. Al often says, "there are so many good breeders out there, it is a shame for someone to buy garbage from a puppy mill." The Vanguard slogan is - "The Cutting Edge of American Bulldogs."

Suregrip's Freddie Kruegger

Several Vanguard American Bulldogs have passed the WABA Breed Suitability Test and earned Weight Pull titles. Every year Al continues to put additional working titles on Bulldogs in his program.

Suregrip's Rattler as a pup, star of the movie Homeward bound, posing with Klayton Symmes

Suregrip

Kyle Symmes of Suregrip kennels in Temecula, California is one of the most influential Bulldog breeders of the 1990's. Most of the other breeders in this section have used his dogs for foundation stock. He uses all major bloodlines but is moving away from Johnson and toward the performance lines.

Dutton's Maxine of Suregrip, 102-pounds, OFA Good

Mr. Symmes got his first Bulldog in 1982 from a truck driver who had moved to California from Alabama. The truck driver (and Bulldog) moved in with a girlfriend and her six cats, within a week she only had two left. This dog was offered to Mr. Symmes who gladly accepted. At the time he was training Shepherds and Rottweilers in protection and obedience. In three weeks the Bulldog could do everything that it took two years for an average Rottie to accomplish. This dog only weighed 85-pounds, which was too small for Mr. Symmes at that time, so he sold it to a soldier who was shipping out overseas.

About one year later he got two dogs from John D. Johnson. One of them was Bulldog Drummond, who became one of the all time great performance dogs. Mr. Symmes was to find out later that Drummond was half Johnson, half Painter. This dog stimulated his interest in breeding ABs. Drummond was 93-pounds of courage, brains and total devotion, capable of many tasks: stock dog, catch dog, protection, baby sitter and 22 other training behaviors. He bought a total of eight dogs from Mr. Johnson and used three as breeders.

Freddie Kruegger smoking a cigar

He tested these early dogs hard in catch work and protection. One of them passed away in 1995 just shy of 12-years old - Rip'n Woody, another all time great and the most prolific stud in American Bulldog history.

Rattler as an adult, on a boar

His next acquisitions were three Painter dogs - Mad Max, the Jet Bitch and Sheena. The cross between Woody (pure Johnson) and Sheena (pure Painter) has been an important one. The offspring of this union have been the foundation for many excellent kennels. I will mention just five. These five dogs have excelled in personal protection, sport protection and weight pulling. Despite their big size (105 to 120-pounds) they have done well in hog catching under less than rigorous conditions. When crossed with smaller females their progeny have excelled in hog catching. These five dogs are Banuelos' Sonja, Watchdog's Whitefang, Mt. Gator's Gator Red, Big Bull's Grimlock and

Suregrip's Freddie Kruegger. Many breeders have coveted Woody blood because if he was crossed to the right bitch you were almost guaranteed a strong, hard hitting, man dog with courage and fire.

Rip'n Woody - most prolific AB stud ever

Choi's Terra Shark of Suregrip

In its early phase Suregrip acquired dogs from the original Scott, Williamson and Tate. Out of 33 dogs he kept only seven, culling through hard testing. A big part of this testing process involves catching wild hogs. Mr. Symmes is one of only two Bulldog breeders in the nation who also breeds purebred Eurasian wild boars. He likes to test his dogs on the toughest possible hogs and ones with domestic blood aren't as tough as pure Eurasian or Russian boars. The other breeder is Casey Couturier who not only got foundation dogs from Suregrip but foundation hogs as well.

Suregrip dogs have appeared in over a dozen movies and TV commercials. The most famous is the Disney film Homeward Bound. Rattler (Chance) was only six months old when he performed all those feats on the silver screen.

One of the things that excites people about Suregrip kennels is that large (but not gigantic) Bulldogs have been produced that are athletic and sound. Bulldog Drummond, Jack the Ripper, Hog Dog and Misdemeanor were all world class hog catchers while weighing between 80 to 100-pounds. Hannibal was a decent hog dog and weighed 122-pounds at 27-inches tall and had no Johnson blood. He was ½ Tate and ½ Scott.

Suregrip's Bulldog Drummond

Suregrip Ammo of Valentino, OFA Good

Mitch Allison's Polar Bear, White Fang son, Woody grandson, after a tough hog hunt

Rattler is now full grown at 116-pounds, he is becoming the world's first Bulldog to certify as an arson alert dog (Mr. Symmes is a fire chief). Rattler will alert firemen to the presence of 18 different flammable liquids at a given fire scene. His testimony will be considered valid in court. Some offspring of Rattler have proven to be equally trainable.

Suregrip dogs are used in hospital therapy for the elderly and disabled. Suregrip breeding has produced top Schutzhund dogs in Germany, Austria and Hungary as well as the first Schutzhund titles in America. Even though Mr. Symmes does not breed for show purposes, his breedings and his own personal dogs have produced plenty of show titles. I have already mentioned that another of his breedings, Gator Red, was one of the greatest weight pull dogs of all times.

Many of these awards have been won by people who bought dogs from Suregrip, then trained for years, shedding blood, sweat and tears. They complain that Mr. Symmes unfairly benefits from their efforts. This is why I have differentiated in the above paragraph between dogs that he owns and has trained and dogs of his breeding - which other people own and train.

This knife cuts both ways and perhaps Suregrip should get credit for providing the right raw material that others can work with. A breeder's worth can only be measured in how well his dogs perform irrespective of who trained them. Suregrip sells 30 or 45 puppies a year.

Junk Yard Dog

Louis De Naples is a physician in Michigan. He calls his kennel Junk Yard Dog and it consists of two Bulldogs (a breeding pair) kept in his house and a couple more that he keeps with close relatives. His purpose in breeding is not to sell dogs but to insure a supply for himself and his family. You and I will never get a chance to buy a Junk Yard Bulldog unless one of us lives next door to Dr. De Naples. He is an example of the very small but excellent breeder that an astute Bulldog enthusiast may be lucky enough to come across if he turns over the right rocks. His bloodlines are almost entirely Painter, the male, Matto, is a son of Sergeant Rock. Pure Painter Bulldogs often represent excellent genetic material for protection. Dr. De Naples is an authority on the colorful and bombastic Joe Painter. He relayed the following information to me:

Painter and his partner Margentina were selling dogs to the four-corners of the Earth out of Chicago. At one point they claimed to be selling 80 Bulldogs a month. They had their own registry and treated these dogs like a separate breed called the Game American Bulldog. Painter's breeding goal was to create the gamest animal possible. When dog men use the word game they don't mean aggressiveness, they mean a combination of courage, tenacity and the ability to absorb punishment. A game dog will refuse to give up a task no matter how injured or exhausted he gets. The technical definition is - 'to unflinchingly absorb and withstand punishment and keep fighting.' There are different forms of gameness. A man game dog will protect his master from a 300-pound maniac wielding a sledgehammer. A completely animal game dog will theoretically fight to the death with any animal no matter how injured he gets. The highest form of gameness is called 'dead game.'

This trait is not as unnatural as many people claim. A Great White Shark will fight to the death if netted or hooked by a fisherman. There has never been a Great White captured alive, so this pelagic species has the highest form of gameness. Many Pit Bull men have grudgingly admitted that some of Painter's dogs were dead game. Unscrupulous people took advantage of this strain's gameness and used them as dog fighters. This association with dog fighting has unfairly hurt the image of the Painter dogs.

Often good Painter Bulldogs are advertised as Scott or Williamson, a more honest but still unfortunate code name for the Painter line is Sgt. Rock. This dog should be eagerly sought in pedigrees, not avoided.

Junk Yard Dog's Hanna, Painter bloodline

Contrary to popular belief, these Bulldogs were not extensively crossed with Pit Bulls. If you examine the photos of early and late Painter ABs they are unmistakably Bulldogs. Toward the end of its existence the Game American Bulldog Club employed incredibly tight inbreeding, several generations of father to daughter crosses were performed. Much of this tight breeding was not actually done by Painter but by other people who got hold of his dogs and had their own agenda. Due to the inbreeding the dogs declined in size by up to 20%, which made them the size of a Pit Bull, yet they remained predominantly white in color and Bulldoggy in appearance. Many health problems arose from overly tight bloodlines. In defense of the inbreeding scheme it should be pointed out that even a Pit Bull breeder can achieve the ultimate level of gameness only through this method. The larger Pit Bull gene pool makes tight line breeding feasible.

In 1990 there was a police raid in Chicago and several dog fighters were busted. Joe Painter was not directly involved. The Game American Bulldog Club survived for another couple of years under the direction of John Tappe. In the early 90's there was even bigger trouble and Mr. Tappe was forced to disassociate himself from the AB community. The Game American Bulldog Club still exists, but it is a shadow of its former self.

Junk Yard Dog's Matto, son of Sgt. Rock, pure Painter

Dr. De Naples made it clear to me that he has the utmost respect for Joe Painter and that if Painter were breeding dogs today Junk Yard Dog would buy every Bulldog available in a heartbeat.

What is it like living with a pure Painter Bulldog? First of all don't be afraid of the few years of dog fighting that this line went through. It is nothing like the 300-years of intense fight breeding that the Pit Bull represents. The 95-pound male, Matto, is no more dog aggressive than a German bred Rottweiler or any other good guardian breed. Matto will run off leash through a city park full of dogs without hurting a single one. If he starts after a cat, one word of command will stop him. The 95-pound female would be better left on leash in an environment like that, but she is trustworthy none the less.

These two dogs are completely obedience and protection trained. According to their owner they hit a sleeve harder than a Rottweiler (he has extensive experience with both breeds) but little kids can use his Bulldogs as pillows. Around the house they are as friendly as poodles to welcome guests. If an intruder were to break in, he would have to shoot the dogs to stop them. They are not especially aggressive dogs, just completely fearless. When they do protection work their attitudes are more like professional boxers than street fighters. As an example of this, Dr. De Naples mentions a game he plays that starts with the two dogs play fighting, he waits until it reaches a fevered pitch than quickly inserts a hand between crashing jaws, teeth and skin never connect.

Von Sanctuary

Bill Hines of Harlingen, Texas is one of the few breeders today (1995) who still combs dogs out of the woods the way Alan Scott did two and a half decades ago. He considers his Bulldogs pure Scott not only because he uses the bloodlines developed by Alan Scott in the 60's and 70's but also because he searches out rural enclaves in the mountainous regions of the deep South and finds Scott type dogs. These are areas where people still use them as farm utility dogs. Mr. Hines was born in the 1920's and has been around this breed all his life. He is certainly the most influential breeder of the Scott line in the country. Perhaps the greatest tribute possible was made by Alan Scott himself who is getting back into breeding for the general public after 14-years of breeding only for his own needs. The tribute is simple: Scott is getting foundation dogs from Bill Hines.

Sanders' Kombat, an important addition to the Hines bloodline

I can understand why both men have focused on this strain after hearing a description of a typical day in the life of an old time Bulldog from the hill country: When you pull your car next to the farmhouse, if the dog's master is out he won't let you set foot on the property. If the master is home the dog will look to him to find out what to do. If the man of the house is friendly the Bulldog will tolerate the stranger.

144

If this farmer needs to milk a cow that is a half-mile away he tells his Bulldog to go fetch her. The dog herds the cow gently to the milking shed because he knows that's what his boss wants. The farmer's next task is to ear notch semi-wild hogs that have been left loose to forage. The Bulldog has to hold a big tough sow immobile while its ear is being notched with a sharp knife. That night a raccoon breaks into the barn, the Bulldog chases him away. The same thing happens to a fox trying to get into the chicken coop. The next morning the farmer and his wife go to town, the Bulldog has to keep an eye on the farm while they're away.

Pure Bulldogs from the hills are a vanishing species. Mr. Hines has seen several strains disappear. Years ago he used to see white Bulldogs with pink noses and yellow eyes. Another extinct strain had a red nose and amber eyes. These colors are extremely recessive and this is a powerful piece of evidence supporting the 17th century origin theory.

There are only a handful of Bulldogs still kept by mountain folks today; these people tend to be distrustful of outsiders who are often referred to as foreigners. You can imagine how city slickers or Yankees would have no chance of finding these dogs. Mr. Hines not only speaks their language he has a friend whose business takes him to the backwoods where he hunts down likely dogs. Sometimes he even brings a video camera along to film some of the better Bulldogs. Mr. Hines reviews these tapes and checks out the most promising prospects himself. The process is not unlike a talent scout for a baseball team reporting back to a head coach. This is how he found Snowbird, a beautiful pure white female that has caught over 500 wild hogs before she became a brood bitch for Hines. She is considered to be one of the greatest catch dogs of all times.

Using dogs like this who have survived the rigors of not just one or two hog hunts but years of combat with these monsters is hardcore performance testing. In the words of Mr. Hines, "a wild boar has a switchblade on either side of his mouth." Athletic ability alone is not enough to survive this ordeal, brains and good judgment are essential. A game Pit Bull, for instance, might tackle one of these juggernauts head-on and try to fight it rather than catch it. He might survive a time or two, eventually though he will get torn up.

Mr. Hines' Bulldogs have a reputation for dealing with wild hogs. Ranchers as far away as Australia have contacted him about finding a canine solution to their feral pig problem and have now (1995) began an elaborate breeding program involving frozen semen shipped to the land down under from Hine's Von Sanctuary Kennels. If you have a similar infestation, Mr. Hines recommends a cross between Ladybird and Hobo. "These dogs have heads like shoe boxes and bite like alligators." Hobo is a full uncle to both of my adult bitches and I know that they get prey drive and animal gameness from his bloodlines.

Kombat x Bossman litter, bred by Dave and Tanja Sanders.

Mr. Hines hunted wild hogs for a living in the 50's. His many years of experience have made him disdainful of Johnson blood. He dislikes Johnson traits such as back legs that are longer than the front because this makes the dogs less agile. A short muzzle and smaller teeth (most Johnson strains do have small teeth) means the dog's grip is more easily broken. He has seen dogs like these chewed up by wild hogs and has had to sew them up himself miles from the nearest veterinarian.

When asked why he breeds hog hunting strains when so few people use Bulldogs for this purpose he laughs and replies, "I'm like a guy who makes good swords when there are no sword fighters left. However, if a dog can shake and rattle with a 400-pound wild boar he is certainly going to be able to deal with a burglar."

Screaming Eagle Bulldogs adapt well to the Alaskan winter. In cold weather Bulldog coats grow thicker.

Some of his males are too big for hunting wild hogs in the woods. Country Boy is 110-pounds (one of the larger Scott dogs) but moves like a cat. Mr. Hines looked for years to find this big, tightly built, stud to increase the size in his hog dogs because most of his customers want guard dogs that weigh over 90-pounds. Country Boy is always bred to a hog hunting sized bitch, so even his sons usually won't be as big as he is. Mr. Hines wants males under 100-pounds. In this weight range a Bulldog is still agile enough to do catch work and is a better man fighter as well. A 90-pound dog can bite just as hard as a 120-pounder but is much quicker, can jump higher and has more endurance.

His dogs have short backs because this provides less side to side motion when running, which increases endurance. Mr. Hines believes a Bulldog should be able run three or four-miles without getting winded.

Screaming Eagle Kennels

Mark Oathout and Ralph Gaston own Screaming Eagle Kennels in Wasilla, Alaska. Screaming Eagle dogs are known as the epitome of high performance. Oathout and Gaston started in the early 80's and have gone through many generations. Foundation dogs were bought directly from Joe Painter as well as dogs with Williamson blood and a small drop of Johnson. By now Screaming Eagle has developed its own line which is more or less a perfected version of the Painter line. Though Mr. Oathout is quick to point out there is no such thing as ultimate perfection. He and Mr. Gaston are always striving to improve their stock. To them perfection is a moving target.

Oathout's Pep Pepper, Dick the Bulldog x Hoffman Lady

This kennel has 40 dogs (some of them placed nearby with friends) and no longer out crosses to other lines. Mr. Oathout believes that out crossing is a crutch used to bury bad traits. He prefers to line breed and allow undesirable traits to rise to the surface like cream on milk. He then aggressively culls unsuitable specimens. This technique has eliminated several flaws.

Screaming Eagle Bulldog lunging on the end of his chain

Oathout's Bad Bonnie, Leclerc's Raging Bull x Leclerc's Roxanne

The ideal Oathout male weighs 90-pounds, has long legs and stands about 25- inches tall. His head is large and his jaws meet in an even bite. His palate is clean, which means the dog doesn't snort when he breathes, a characteristic sometimes found in Bulldogs. His rear end is big and strong like a Quarter Horse's. He is not overly aggressive with other animals. More importantly, he is stable with friends, family and children. He is cautious around strangers though not hostile without good cause. A bad guy should have to kill him to stop him. Blows to the head with a baseball bat or broken bones should barely slow him down.

This may seem like hyperbole, but I know of a man who owns an Oathout Bulldog who was charged by a bull moose during the rutting season. His 70-pound Bulldog got a hold of the moose's nose and threw him not once but three times until the moose finally retreated. This dog probably saved his master's life. Another dog has caught over 100 wild hogs in Florida, so they do well in the lower 48 as well. Mr. Oathout courage tests his dogs on a sleeve in the Schutzhund style. Puppies also go through a battery of temperament tests to eliminate shyness or over aggression. When he says he culls aggressively he means it. One dog growled at an Oathout child and was immediately shot. This is why all the dogs in his breeding program are kept with families, to insure good temperaments with children. Some breeders are crossing

Screaming Eagle bitches to Johnson studs to recreate the Suregrip combination.

Boyd's Moleque and daughter Morena. Moleque (in foreground) is OFA Excellent, TT and Register of Merit. She has produced more BST Bulldogs than any other female.

Boyd's Bulldogs

Matt Boyd owns Boyd's Bulldogs in Sacramento, California. His bloodlines include Scott, Williamson, a big dose of Johnson and a small amount of Painter. He has foundation stock from Hines, Symmes, Oathout and breeds out to stud dogs from around the country to vary his gene pool. Mr. Boyd praises Bill Hines for locating old type Bulldogs from the remote southern hill country and making them available to breeders like himself.

Boyd's Fire Engine Red

Bleu's Tatanka of Boyd, Sch I, OFA

This kennel takes a highly technical approach to breeding. For example, he questions breeding dogs for short faces because this trait has been linked to a deformed thyroid and other problems in the bull breeds. Breed testing includes OFA certification or Penn-hip and CERF eye testing. Boyd's Moleque was the first AB to score OFA excellent. Courage testing is done with a professional sports Schutzhund trainer. All puppies are temperament tested.

Boyd's Rippin'Woodchip, one of the few female ABs to earn a Schutzhund I

His breeding goals are to produce a 90 to 110-pound male that is 24 to 26-inches tall with a Scott type body and an intermediate head like Johnson's old King Kong. Size is completely secondary to good structure. Mr. Boyd wants to see heavy bones and straight legs, a free movement with long strides that comes from proper angu-

lation, with a heavy under jaw and a tight undershot bite. A broad muzzle is important in providing a powerful bite and finally a pronounced stop on the forehead to maintain that Bulldoggy look.

Mr. Boyd would like more pigmentation on the lips, nose and eyelids than is commonly found on the AB in order to avoid sunburn and cancer. Endurance is another quality he is focusing on. He is considering titling his dogs in the Schutzhund AD (endurance) program. For novice prospective Bulldog owners, Mr. Boyd is providing some puppies with medium drive. For more experienced clients, high drive breedings are offered.

Tatanka is Belle's littermate brother.

His goals on more general matters include trying to expand the small AB gene pool in order to keep the breed sound. This could be done if specialized breeders would out cross every few years to other breeders with a different specialty. For instance: a strain of weight pulling Bulldogs could out cross to some smaller hog catchers. Mr. Boyd has also actively searched for the last remnants of complete out cross hill Bulldogs and made limited use of these animals to expand the variety in his gene pool.

Another broad goal of Boyd's Bulldogs is to educate the public away from the quest for huge ABs. He breeds for structure not size, on the other hand, he doesn't reject a big dog if it is 100% sound. He has used a 139-pound stud dog from Mountain Gator Kennels that not only passed OFA, the radiologist said the big bruiser had the best hips he'd ever seen on an American Bulldog. At the same time he was investigating a pure Williamson male that weighed only 65-pounds.

Putnam's Belle Star of Boyd as a puppy

I bought a puppy (Belle Star of Boyd) out of the 73-pound OFA excellent Moleque and the 139-pound OFA good MGK Tyson. Today Belle weighs 84-pounds. I was extremely pleased when her hips X-rayed dysplasia free and she earned her BST in 1998. I line bred her to Boyd's Hammer, an agile 100-pounder that has a BST II and good hips. Their puppies are one-year old. Four of them have been X-rayed and have superior hips, super structure and even temperaments. I kept one pup to train for the BST, which we expect to pass in 2000. So my own breeding program is an off shoot of Mr. Boyd's and his work allows me to boast that my puppy represents three generations of certified hips. As of 1999 Boyd's Bulldogs has more Schutzhund titled ABs in their program than any other breeder. The American Bulldog club of Germany gets most of their dogs from Boyd's Bulldogs.

Grimm's Bulldogs

Peter Grimm of Grimm's Bulldogs in New Jersey has a long history with the Bull breeds. He has raised Pit Bulls for over 15-years and his family pioneered the early breeding of the Swinford Bandog, which initially proved to be a failure in its goal of producing a new breed of giant guardian type Pit Bull that would breed true. One of the reasons for this was that Dr. Swinford (who was a close friend of the Grimm family) died early and never completed his work. Another reason is the overwhelming dominance of the Pit Bull's genes over anything they are crossed with.

This failure has repercussions and implications for the AB. Regarding the Bandogs: Mr. Grimm told me that the first generation crosses (if done right) were a fantastic combination of Neo, English Mastiff and Pit. They had the best of three worlds, size and strength from the two Mastiff breeds, structure and toughness from the Pit. These dogs weighed 125 to 180-pounds and could survive the fighting punishment of hardened Pit Bulls, which even ABs are hard pressed to do. Each generation after the third or fourth would shrink in size and would start looking exactly like a Pit. Apparently this tendency could be countered by adding more Mastiff in the later generations. Some of the best Bandogs produced by the Grimm family used this formula.

Grimm's Tomahawk Lucille of Suregrip

Mr. Grimm says that this will also happen to ABs with no Johnson blood. He sees Scott/Painter blood acting in ABs the way Pit Bull blood acts in Bandogs. Similarly, Johnson blood acts like Mastiff blood. So it comes as no surprise that his bloodlines are 75% Johnson and 25% Painter. He definitely feels the strains should be mixed to counter the inbreeding that has occurred to produce them. Mr. Grimm's breeding goal is to have a Bulldoggy look in an athletic family guardian. His males weigh 95 to 125-pounds and are 25 to 26-inches tall with a brachycephalic head.

This breeding program can be characterized by one word, patience. Bitches are not bred on every heat cycle, so they get a rest. They are shipped thousands of miles to breed strategically with select studs from other kennels. All foundation dogs are carefully handpicked; many of them came to Mr. Grimm as pick of the litter puppies.

Peter Grimm gives Buster a bite

Mr. Grimm also offers breedings with medium drive as well as high drive. He realizes that the primary function of his dogs is companionship as family pets, their secondary function is to be family guardians. He breeds with these priorities serving as a guide.

Mr. Grimm is also a Bulldog historian. He believes that the bulk of our dogs came to this country after 1835 when bull baiting was made illegal in England and before 1875 when the sour mug started to dominate in the old country. With this historical perspective in mind, Grimm's Bulldogs strives to maintain what he considers old time Bulldog looks and abilities.

I believe that AB breeders should closely monitor the ongoing work of Bandog breeders. We have many lessons to learn from them. For example, when crossing a Pit Bull to a Neo it is best to use a female Pit and a male Neo.

Similarly, a typey 140-pound Johnson male crosses nicely to a 75-pound Scott bitch, not the other way around.

Grimm AB and Bullmastiff friend

Jaws of Stone Kennels

Al Banuelos owns Jaws of Stone Kennels. He was the first breeder to put Schutzhund titles on ABs. So integral is Schutzhund to Mr. Banuelos' breeding program that a short history of this German sport must precede the section on his kennel.

Banuelos' Sophie was the first female AB to receive a Sch I, rated "A" in hardness.

Schutzhund means protection dog in German. This canine sport was started at the turn of the 19th century in that country as a means of combating show breeding and puppy milling. Schutzhund competition is intended to provide a breed test where three parts or phases measure different things that are essential to police or military dogs. The three phases are tracking, obedience and protection. Tracking is intended to measure scenting ability, trainability and mental endurance. Obedience measures willingness to work, temperament, trainability and physical soundness (because it includes scaling walls and hurtling jumps). Protection measures courage, strength, biting ability and prey drive.

The general public is often confused between the three phases of Schutzhund and the three titles a dog can win - Sch I, Sch II and Sch III. To win any title a dog must demonstrate competence in all three phases. The higher titles represent greater competence. For example, in the tracking phase of Sch II a dog must follow a scent trail that is older and longer than the scent trail in Sch I. In Sch III the trail is even older, longer, has a more complicated pattern and is crisscrossed with other scent trails.

Banuelos' Ike, Sch III, IPO III, FH, OFA Good, Sch III score: 94 - 91 - 98

In the obedience phase of Sch I, a dog must do everything one would expect of AKC advanced obedience trials with some additions like hearing a gunshot at close range and clearing a one-meter jump while retrieving a dumbbell. In Sch II, a dog must do all this and clear a six-foot scaling wall while retrieving a heavier dumbbell. In Sch III, the drills are even more demanding.

For the protection phase of Sch I, the dog must find a hidden agitator and hold him prisoner without the help of his handler. He must stop an attack on his handler without being ordered to do so. During the ensuing fight the agitator (who is wearing a protection sleeve) will hit the dog in a non-vulnerable spot with a long flexible stick. In a separate test the dog must defend himself directly from a threatening agitator, again he is hit with a stick. It is very important that the dog stops attacking when commanded to out. In Sch II, the dog does all this and must also capture a fleeing prisoner. The dog must be able to transport the prisoner from spot to spot. In Sch III, the dog must be able to do all this and attack an agitator in a variety of complicated situations that call for good judgement.

Banuelos' Predator, Sch III, IPO III, FH, WH, OFA, first AB to achieve a Schutzhund title

In all these protection tests a dog may fail if it can not cease attacking on command. A dog that doesn't out crisply will have a hard time receiving a Schutzhund title. Some experienced protection trainers claim that it is difficult for the Mastiff and Bull breeds to out as quickly as German Shepherds because once in attack mode Mastiffs become single minded and obsessed. At least two weeks before a Schutzhund trial a dog must first pass a companion dog test that includes basic obedience plus steadiness when confronting loud noises, new situations and a non-threatening staked out dog. Immediately before the trial a temperament evaluation is given that is designed to weed out overly aggressive animals.

A Sch III dog is usually ill equipped to jump in the back of a K-9 squad car and do police work because sport training is deliberately removed from real world scenarios. The stress involved though is similar to what a working K-9 would encounter. As a breed test this is a very good thing because stress weeds out the weaker specimens. The reason for all this stress lies in the requirement that one dog perform all three phases almost flawlessly. Many working dogs would have no problem excelling in just obedience or just tracking, but to excel in all three can cause even a tough dog to break down, exactly what the founders of Schutzhund intended.

Mr. Banuelos first began training ABs for Schutzhund in 1990. The German hierarchy that runs the sport in this country ridiculed him. It had always been thought that only German breeds could excel in this arena. Their skepticism turned to outrage when Jaws of Stone Ike went from Sch I to Sch III in 4 ½ months. This startling performance prompted the German judges to ban all bull breeds except Boxers from future competition. The American Staffordshire club of Germany was furious, the German Boxer club was nervous since they could be next. Partly through their efforts the ban was lifted and Mr. Banuelos could compete again. He did so with a vengeance and soon his star performer, Predator (Sch III, IPO III, FH, WH and OFA) won a Western Regional Schutzhund championship.

Because the performance strains that he uses were bred to hunt pigs Mr. Banuelos protection trains his dogs by enhancing their natural prey drive rather than stoking their defensive instincts. This latter technique works better on the German breeds and it consists of agitators threatening the dogs to encourage a self-defense mode. The prey drive technique is more the other way around, though both techniques overlap to some degree and Mr. Banuelos will use defense to keep the dogs from getting bored. He has taken his ABs wild boar hunting only once but they performed flawlessly and caught a big boar without any problems.

Mr. Banuelos has found that introducing some Johnson blood into his performance strain makes them bite more boldly when going into an agitator. As far as which lines he likes the best, Scott dogs descended from Mac the Masher are preferred along with Williamson, Johnson and Painter.

Mr. Banuelos trains many different breeds of dogs and offers insights into ABs vs. other working breeds. Two qualities that make ABs better guard dogs than Pit Bulls are less dog aggression and a more developed sense of territoriality. Mr. Banuelos told me about a protection trained Pit Bull he once had who would murder anyone that threatened him in his presence, but if the dog was left alone in its backyard a stranger could put a rope around its neck and lead it away. This would be highly unlikely to happen with a protection trained AB unless the stranger got to know the dog and offered it food over an extended time period.

Al Banuelos, Tom Riche and Brody, training for Schutzhund III

Mr. Banuelos also works with Belgian Malinois, a breed that will consistently outperform ABs in protection work but their temperaments are rarely suited to a home environment. The long and the short of it, a good AB may be the best choice for a family guardian.

If you want to buy a puppy from Jaws of Stone Kennels you better be extremely patient, he only raises one litter a year. You should also have a good deal of experience as a trainer because he may not sell you a dog if you won't work it in some capacity. Mr. Banuelos is not very interested in selling dogs, though he is passionate about perfecting his strain through the sport of Schutzhund. His breeding goals are to increase the AB's drive, strength, speed, nerve, hardness of bite and trainability. As far as hips go, Mr. Banuelos may be the ultimate fanatic, he was the first person ever to OFA certify an AB and has produced many of the original OFA certified Bulldogs. His pioneering efforts in hip testing have blazed a path that a handful of other breeders have followed, which helps guarantee a supply of sound functional Bulldogs for working enthusiasts around the globe. This early attention to hips is now paying off as Banuelos breedings enter their third and fourth generation. For example, the second lowest Penn-hip score ever recorded for an American Bulldog is Sloan's Turbo at .25. This dog is a descendant of Predator. A Penn-hip score that low means the dog has hips as good as a racing Greyhound or an Arctic wolf.

Steve Visuddhidham was a student of Al Banuelos and the second AB breeder to earn Schutzhund titles with Bulldogs.

Mr. Banuelos is influenced by German breeding techniques that involve matings where the dogs are unrelated for three generations. He is leery of out crossing too far however, because even though this can produce tremendous hybrid vigor for one generation, it has been shown that such hybrids will not breed true. In Germany some Shepherds from a Schutzhund strain have been crossed with sturdy show Shepherds and the results have been unbelievable Schutzhund dogs, but the next generation fizzles out. In the Jaws of Stone breeding program each generation gets a little bit better than the next because these short cuts are not taken.

Many of the other breeders in this section are also getting involved in Schutzhund, which will do tremendous good for the breed. When I last talked to Mr. Banuelos he was preparing for a trip to Germany where he studied under the world's foremost Schutzhund expert. Later that summer he flew to Japan

where he was the instructor. Mr. Banuelos is a professional dog trainer and has spent a lot of time working with other AB owner/handlers, helping hone their skills as well as their dog's. His training expertise is rooted in his uncanny ability to 'read' a dog. He can tell with a glance when a dog is ready to give up or disobey an order even before the dog actually exhibits the unwanted behavior, this allows for very rapid progress with any given animal. Mr. Banuelos' skill as a trainer and breeder has created a following in California. This is why all the early Schutzhund titles put on ABs have been on the West Coast.

Protection trained Underground Bulldog

Underground Kennels

Underground Kennels in Sun Valley, California is a spin-off of Al Banuelos' program. It is owned and operated by Steve Visuddhiadham and Jeff LaMonica. Steve did his early training with Al and they keep in close touch. This was the second kennel in America to produce American Bulldogs with Schutzhund titles. Their main stud, Hammer is a Sch III. Another stud, Pubba (Hammer's son), has a Sch I. Hammer is ¼ Johnson, ¼ Scott and ½ Williamson - with Mac the Masher as the biggest component in his pedigree. This kennel uses Scott, Johnson and Painter, mixing all the major blood lines and utilizing line breeding in the manner of German breeding schemes, i.e. with an out cross after a couple of tight generations.

Underground Bulldog pup ready to rumble

For Steve and Jeff the primary breed test is the German sport. If they bred a dog that doesn't have a formal title he or she is still extensively tested in obedience and protection and to a lesser degree tracking. They realize that these dogs were originally bred to catch wild hogs and cattle and that breeding them for Schutzhund will transform them slightly. Schutzhund is, after all, designed to be a breed test for German Shepherds destined for police work or the military. Bulldogs bred to this end will still have the drive, power and agility of a good catch dog but will become more trainable and easier to control. Today, when hunting wild hogs, Bulldogs seldom do any tracking. They let the hounds do that for them. After a few more generations of Schutzhund breeding Bulldogs may develop keener noses and better tracking ability. They may be able to hunt hogs without hounds. This could be a return to the past because years ago some Bulldogs were able to do their own scent work. Even if you don't plan on hunting wild boar this is a useful talent if your child gets lost during a camping trip. Schutzhund bred Bulldogs will better fulfill their new mission as urban guard dogs and companions.

Schutzhund is a good test for structure. The dogs must easily scale six-foot A-frames and jump over a meter high hurdle without touching the bar. Underground kennels trains their dogs on a 42-inch hurdle, which most of them can clear with room to spare.

This kennel strives to provide stable, friendly temperaments in every puppy they produce. Their breeding program is built around Hammer, who has the ability to maul an agitator, then be introduced to a child he has never

seen before and play ball with his new friend for the rest of the day. Hammer has proven he can pass this great temperament on to his descendants.

Clark's Great White, OFA Excellent

Clark's American Bulldogs

Steven Clark owns Clark's American Bulldogs in Moreno Valley, California. His breeding program places an emphasis on foot speed. The Clark family works as a team to test their adult females for fleetness. A BMX bicycle racetrack has been set up in their huge backyard. At the beginning of the test, one of the teenage sons (a competitive BMX racer) takes off with a small head start. He flies over jumps and hills. Then the Bulldogs are let loose, they fly after him, scrambling claws kicking up rooster tails of dirt, legs a blur of motion. The fastest dog reaches the BMX racer first and wins the race. Chase games like this provide good exercise and pack socialization.

Mr. Clark's breeding strategy involves crossing these performance bred, longer muzzled, females to a shorter muzzled, tightly built, Johnson or part Johnson male to produce a fast, heavily muscled Bulldog that will weigh 90 to 110-pounds (for a male).

As with all conscientious breeders, Mr. Clark takes great care to avoid hip dysplasia. Besides X-raying and performance testing, he researches the family history of any possible breeding stock. He looks at parents, grandparents and great grandparents as they run, jump and just stand up from a lying position. Any experienced breeder can tell if a 12- year old dog is dysplastic without an X-ray machine. Even a veterinarian can't do this with a two-year old. He studies lineages of the major breeders and keeps track of incidence of dysplasia, thereby avoiding certain lines that might cause problems.

Clark's Molly Brown, Great White's mom

Mr. Clark attributes the increase in genetic defects that the breed is currently experiencing to an expanding population out of a relatively small gene pool. Because of this he doesn't like inbreeding or tight line breeding. His own program of loose line breeding calls for an individual dog's pedigree to have no more than 3/8 of the ancestry coming from a single dog at the 4th and 5th generation.

Eva Kadane's Diesel of Clark, OFA Good

The Clark family includes five kids from age 4 to 17. They are all involved in socializing each litter of puppies. The first ten weeks of a Clark Bulldog's life is spent interacting with people and dogs, this helps create not only a more stable dog later in life but also a smarter, more easily trained one. Another benefit is that the Clark kids give their Dad an informal personality profile on each pup. This is combined with a

more formal temperament test at five weeks and again at eight weeks, which paints a better picture of what each pup will be when grown up. This allows Mr. Clark to match the right pup to the right buyer. A pig hunter or Schutzhund enthusiast can be confident they will get a dog with extreme prey drive. Someone like myself might want only a high or medium prey drive pup. A low prey drive pup would be neutered and sold cheaply without papers. These tests work, a famous pig hunter in Florida (Don Matthews) has had very good luck with his Clark Bulldog. Not only does this Clark Bulldog inhale hogs - he passed OFA with a rating of good.

One of the other qualities found in Clark Bulldogs is a lack of dog aggression. Like all good Bulldogs, they will get aggressive if another dog tries to dominate them. However Mr. Clark won't tolerate a dog that will attack for no reason and suspects such a Bulldog of having a high percentage of Pit in its bloodlines. Another quality you should find is good trainability because all five of his adult dogs are 100% obedience trained and their puppies have received a great early socialization, so environment and heredity are working together to reinforce this trait. If you want to win obedience trials this may be a good kennel to check out.

This breeding program produced the third AB to receive an OFA excellent, Clark's Great White.

Konfederate Kennels

Don Matthews owns Konfederate Kennels in Fort Pierce, Florida. He has been hunting wild hogs for 45-years. The last time I talked to him, he was preparing to go out the next morning with his Leopard dogs and Bulldogs to bring back some live hogs for a hunting club. Mr. Matthews has probably caught as many hogs as anybody and most of them have been caught with the help of Bulldogs. Twenty-five years ago he would hunt with Bulldogs alone. He wouldn't use bay hounds to find his quarry. The Bulldogs would have to scent the hogs, run them down and catch them all by themselves.

At about this time he started breeding Bulldogs for his own hunting needs. He got dogs from Alan Scott and Scott type dogs from the local community. Back then these dogs were called Old Family Whites or Old Georgia Bulldogs, 95% of them were pure white. A good dog would cost $50. He was the first person to bring pure Scott American Bulldogs into Florida. Mr. Matthews has kept his strain going all these years, always testing breeding stock on wild hogs, which keeps the dogs sound, maintains extreme prey drive and insures against dog aggression because they have to hunt with other dogs.

At least five generations of Matthews have owned ABs.

Mr. Matthews is in the process of expanding his small kennel to sell dogs to the general public. He has introduced larger dogs into his strain to increase their size from 75 or 80-pounds to about 100-pounds because the suburban dog buyer wants a big guard dog. These new dogs have to be able to hunt wild pigs just as efficiently as his old dogs so Mr. Matthews is testing them in the same manner that he always has.

His breeding test is as follows: First the dog must have "attitude," Mr. Matthews must get a gut feeling that the dog won't take any guff from anyone or thing. At the same time it must have restraint, for instance - a small child should be able to gouge its eyes without being attacked. At four or six months, if the dog has the right attitude, it is started on small wild pigs while wearing a protective cut vest. If it shows heart and stands up physically to these small pigs, the dog graduates to bigger and nastier ones. As the dog approaches adulthood it is tried on a full-grown aggressive sow. If that works out, the dog is finally tested on a truly bad pig, a boar with a full set of long teeth. Whether the people who buy his dogs ever hunt hogs or not is immaterial to Mr. Matthews, if they pay $1000 or $800 for a

Bulldog they should get one capable of performing the ancient task for which they have been bred.

He has been looking for some time now for the right big Bulldog. After looking at dozens of likely candidates, he has finally found the right one: a 75% Johnson male with perfect structure, an OFA good rating, a long muzzle, superior catch ability and the name Jackson after Stonewall Jackson. Several bitches are pregnant with this huge, agile, hog hunter. While checking out other kennels, he has been amused with the way some breeders test their dogs on sleeves. To him, a real test is a bad hog putting a six-inch gash in a dog, not a rap in the rump with a little stick.

Joshua's Cowboy, OFA Excellent, 1st OFA AB to father an OFA Excellent offspring

Watching sleeve work did pique Mr. Matthews' curiosity. He had his friend Don Little put on a sleeve, then tied Jackson to a fence. Mr. Little agitated Jackson with a popping whip. Jackson savagely tore into the sleeve because that was the only part of Mr. Little he could get a tooth into. Mr. Matthews asked his friend if they should try it again without the fence tie. Don Little said, "not without a body suit."

Joshua Kennels

Lemuel Miller of Oxford, Florida operates Joshua Kennels and Joshua Kennels Prey-Drive Training Center. Mr. Miller got his first Bulldogs when he was a young man working on his family's farm in the 60's. At that time the breed was called White English. They were slightly smaller than today's dog and were nearly pure white. The Millers would not only catch wild hogs with their White Englishes while on horseback, they would also hunt deer and catch loose cattle. These dogs had better noses than they do now and could be hunted without bay dogs.

Joshua's Caleb and Cracker Cur Doc on a mean boar, Caleb has a UCD III, the highest title a catch dog can achieve.

Back then, rural Florida was infested with wild dogs that often took the form of a large nasty German Shepherd. One day at dinner the Millers heard a pack of wild dogs chasing their cattle and eating the calves. Two White Englishes were let loose on the pack, within minutes they had shaken the lead dogs to death and chased the rest away, without harming a hair on any cow's head.

Today Joshua Kennels uses performance bloodlines from the Sand Valley region with a dash of Woody blood. The focus of this breeding program is hog catching. These dogs are tested in a manner similar to Don Matthews' kennel. Mr. Miller catches up to eight big boars a week, trailing with Florida Curs and catching with Bulldogs. In a year, his dogs will have caught literally tons of wild hogs. Like Don Matthews, Mr. Miller also breeds Florida Curs. He runs a registry for this breed, which in his part of Florida are called Cracker Curs because the cattlemen who originally kept them carried long bullwhips.

There are unique aspects to the way Mr. Miller trains and therefore the way he breeds. He wants to minimize the risk of injury his dogs face while catching a bad boar so they are trained to out on command like a Schutzhund dog. Most hog dogs have to be torn off a boar by force. This is because most hunters primarily value their own safety and want their dogs to hang onto the 300-pound juggernauts like maniacs. For most hunters outing is not a high priority, even if an occasional dog is lost to a boar from time to time. Joshua Kennel's Bulldogs are too valuable for an attitude that cavalier.

At least half the catches are made in water. Caleb and Doc, a great team

There is no problem with Joshua Kennel dogs protecting their owner from a bad hog, however. Mr. Miller once suffered a heat stroke while hunting in the inferno of a Florida summer. A bad boar chose that moment to charge him. His main stud dog, Caleb, tackled the boar and kept him immobile until help arrived.

A bad boar sticks Cowboy, UCD III

How would Caleb do if a human assailant threatened a loved one? A professional protection trainer asked the same question while visiting Joshua Kennels. He agitated Caleb twice. The first time Caleb attacked the sleeve and shook so hard the man tried some advanced bite

157

work. Caleb was launched at him from a distance. The six-foot-three-inch man was knocked down and the sleeve was ripped off his arm.

There are two parts to Joshua Kennels, a small breeding program, which only produces one litter a year and the Prey-Drive Training Center. The latter is a service to urban Bulldog breeders that don't have an opportunity to test their dogs on wild boar. For a very low fee, Mr. Miller will train your young dog to catch. He takes a six-month old pup and spends three or four days just getting to know him and gaining his trust. For the next two or three days your dog will watch experienced dogs hunt without getting a bite. When he is finally ready, a hog that has already been caught is handled in such a manner that it can't get at your dog, the ear is put right in front of his nose. If the dog graduates to catching a loose hog he wears a cut collar and a cut vest. The hogs your dog will catch in the woods will not be fire breathers and they will have small teeth. Not one dog has been seriously hurt yet.

Joshua's Caleb, OFA Good, is being asked to turn loose after hog is thrown.

Mr. Miller is a minister and he has $150,000 worth of TV equipment that he uses in his ministry. The urban Bulldog breeder that uses the Prey-Drive Training Center will receive a professional quality video of his dog catching wild boar. As of 1995, prices for this service start at $200. I'm sure it is not a break-even proposition for Joshua Kennels. The Prey-Drive breeding test is an alternative to show breeding.

As a Bulldog historian Mr. Miller has pursued the question of the origin of our breed. He got a definitive answer from a 93-year old rancher whose family has been raising cattle in Florida from time immemorial. The White Bulldog and the Cracker Cur have been in

Florida for centuries, introduced when the Spanish first brought cattle to the New World. This kennel has three OFA excellent ABs, all with Utility Catch Dog III titles (see page 135).

Owl Hollow Kennels

Alan Scott owns Owl Hollow Kennels in northeastern Alabama. He is (along with John D. Johnson) a principal architect of our modern AB. Contrary to popular belief, Mr. Scott never stopped breeding Bulldogs. He currently (1995) has three dogs and is in the process of expanding his kennel and getting back into it like he did in the 70's.

Mack the Masher of Alan Scott was a foundation stud for the American Bulldog. Picture taken in 1973

In the late 60's Mr. Scott was still in high school and earned money catching wild cattle in the brush and woods of northern Alabama. These cattle had escaped from farms or wrecked cattle trucks and ensconced themselves in the deep woods. The brush was so thick that he couldn't swing a lariat rope, so he bought some local Bulldogs to get the job done. He also got dogs from Ashley and Johnson. Mr. Ashley was a small farmer in the northern part of the state and was known for Bulldogs that could catch cattle exceedingly well. Many foundation dogs of the Scott, Williamson, Bailey and Johnson line came from Ashley. All these early dogs were proven on cattle and hogs for many generations. At the time they usually weighed 75 or 80-pounds, though they could get over 100-pounds. His heaviest dog weighed 105-pounds. They were slightly undershot and had more color than the dogs from north Florida. They had no fighting terrier in them and were pure Bulldog. Some of his foundation dogs included Scott's Bo Bo Bruiser (NKC # R000-123) and Mac the Masher (NKC# R000-118). I have included National Kennel Club numbers because there are so many dogs with similar sounding names such as Bruiser Bo that it is easy to get confused. This distinction is important because Johnson's Bruiser Bo weighed almost twice what Bo Bo Bruiser weighed and was an entirely different kind of dog.

Ch. Gr. Ch. Dixieman of Alan Scott, picture taken in late 70's

While many people used these dogs at this time for catch work, few were interested in breeding and the number of Bulldogs was dwindling. Mr. Scott loved Bulldogs for their spirit and personality, not just their usefulness. He decided this noble breed needed to be saved and started his own strain by combing the hills for the best possible dogs. In '71 he found Mac the Masher, for two years Mr. Scott, Louie Hegwood and John D. Johnson would breed every bitch they had to Mac, he should appear on almost every AB pedigree in existence. Mac was 10 or 12-years old when Mr. Scott found him. He had been an all time great catch dog and because of this his fangs were broken. Even with broken teeth Mac could take a huge beef knucklebone in his mouth, roll it around until he found a certain spot and then clamp down. His jaws would quiver for a few seconds and then the knucklebone would explode into a dozen pieces. For sheer jaw strength Mac was in a league of his own, with mandibles nearly as crushing as a hyena's or a bear's.

Sophia Mae of Alan Scott

When Mr. Scott was hunting for hill dogs he looked for good conformation and gameness. His life could depend on a Bulldog's gameness, considering the unpredictable nature of a wild bull and the rough terrain. This meant the dogs had to be dead game. Most were willing to give their life trying to catch a bull, a boar or anything else. Of these early dogs, 90% were so determined they couldn't be called off a steer once they had a grip and had to be pried off with breaker bars.

Alan Scott's Bruiser Rhoe Ho, picture taken in 1970

In the 70's his breeding program expanded to five or six stud dogs and about 15 bitches, he sold puppies throughout the country. He used his dogs more on cattle than hogs. His training and testing for catch work was similar to the method described by Don Matthews except that instead of starting a young dog on a small pig he would start with a goat and then move up to a 400-pound steer. The catch dogs would be tried on bigger and tougher cattle until they graduated to bulls. Cattle catch work is different than catching boar. A bull can't cut a dog or bite him; even horns aren't much of a threat. The real danger comes from the big beast falling on a dog or stomping him. Many people have told me that it is impossible for a Bulldog to actually throw a bull using his body weight and leverage. Mr. Scott may have more experience with Bulldogs catching bulls than anyone alive and he has seen it many times. Bo Bo Bruiser, for instance, weighed 70-pounds and could throw an 1800-pound Brahman bull. He was an exceptional dog. Most Bulldogs, even good ones, had to wear the bull down through endurance and jaw strength. Mr. Scott also tested chained dogs with a human agitator. Back then you didn't say you were agitating a dog but badgering at him with a stick and a heavy sack. It was a good courage test for man work.

Dixie's Mountain Shadow of Alan Scott

In the late 70's, Mr. Scott had a special dog, Dixieman, (his full name was Champion Grand Champion Dixieman of A.S. #A002-467) who had more sense than most people. He loved Dixieman and didn't think there could ever be another that was quite the same. When this dog died, Mr. Scott lost interest in large-scale breed-

ing and trimmed down to about three or so dogs by '82. Contrary to popular belief, he did not sell all his dogs to Joe Painter at this time. Over the years Painter may have bought six or seven dogs.

Dixieman of Alan Scott

As far as pit fighting goes, a real tough catch dog may once in a while beat a Pit Bull but it would be an anomaly. Mr. Scott never crossed Pit Bull into his line or used any dogs with this blood. He says that a pure Bulldog is a natural guard and catch dog and has a head full of sense about when and how to do things. They can think their way through a situation. He doesn't want to destroy that ability with over aggressiveness. In fact, he won't even use the word "bull" when talking about Pit Bull Terriers, he just calls them terriers.

Now that he is breeding more dogs and reentering the Bulldog community Mr. Scott looks around and likes much of what he sees. Breeders like Bill Hines have done a good job keeping the Scott line going. However, he doesn't like all the infighting among breeders and feels they should work together the way they did before '81. Because of this Alan Scott, Bill Hines, Don Matthews, Darrin Jones and Rayburn Stover are combining forces to expand the Scott line. They have formed an organization called the Scott Breeders Group. Their efforts have already paid off with a lucky find; one of Dixieman's sons is still alive. He is 14-years old but still going strong, with a thick chest and a huge head. Mr. Scott still has granddaughters of Dixieman in his kennel. A breeding is planned. There is a good chance that the Dixieman strain can be revived.

Bronco Bill of Alan Scott, picture taken in 1971

When he looks beyond his own backyard he is concerned that the breed's popularity with suburbanites could ruin it, as it did the Irish Setter. His biggest fear is that show breeding will take the Bulldog's gameness away. Mr. Scott has bred Bulldogs for physical beauty; his dogs dominated the NKC show circuit. But these show dogs were all real working Bulldogs, every one of them could catch cattle. He thinks a Bulldog should lay around in a relaxed state until called upon to do something, then the dog should turn into a fireball, willing to give his life to complete any mission he undertakes, whether stopping a burglar or throwing a 2000-pound Brahman.
The following is taken from a letter written by Alan Scott in 1978:

"One afternoon last fall I went to check my cows and carried my dog Dixieman of A.S. (Buster to all who know him) with me. Well, the neighbor's bull, a Brangus which would have weighed in excess of 1600 pounds at the time, was in our pasture. I started to run him back across the creek, but he had different plans.

The old devil turned on me. Well needless to say I headed for the nearest tree. As I was approaching it at a very rapid pace of course, Buster heard the commotion and came running. He caught the bull by

the ear. I don't especially like for him to catch the ear, but at the time I didn't give a darn where he caught the S.O.B. (Sweet Old Bull).

Well the battle had started and the bull tried to hook him off his ear, but old Buster just stuck to him. Buster fought him until the bull went down on his knees. I whistled and told him to drop the bull. The bull got up, looked around and headed for the creek with Buster right behind him. When he reached a scope of woods just before the creek, the old devil decided he wanted some more and turned to fight again. You heard about WW I and WW II, well I got to see WW III. Buster whipped him again and the bull headed for home with Buster right behind him again.

When they went into a creek the bull started up a bank that was too steep. When he turned to come back, Buster caught him again. He pulled the bull's head under water and when he came up, he blew water out of his nose and I bet he went six feet back up the same bank again, this time to climb out.

When he went out Buster stopped and came back to me as if to see if I was all right. We finished checking our cows and came home to tell my wife about WW III."

I think this letter helps explain the magic of the Scott line. These dogs would have pleased the Earl of Warren if they could have baited bulls for him in 1209, yet they are calm and sensible enough to see if their master is fine and finish checking cows with him.

Sand Valley Bulldogs

Darrin Jones owns Sand Valley Bulldogs in Attalla, Alabama. His experience with our breed closely parallels Alan Scott's. He acquired his first dog from a local farmer in northern Alabama when he was a teenager in 1979 for cattle catching. For the next seven years he earned money by catching cattle on steep ravines where horses couldn't go and in thick brush where even people couldn't go. Darrin's dogs all had to work for a living. They had to be able to call off a steer once he was caught and know how to take it easy on prize cattle, yet not put up with any guff from bad cattle either.

Like Scott, Darrin noticed that this breed was dying out as a farm utility dog because four wheelers (small all terrain vehicles) and other changes had eliminated the need for catch dogs. Also, like Scott, he loved the dogs for their spirit and thought they should be saved even if modern farming technology was replacing them. He started breeding dogs purchased from locals around Sand Mountain, the same area where Dick the Bruiser originally came from. According to Darrin, basically all the good Bulldogs from the Sand Mountain and Sand Valley area of Alabama were either from or closely related to the kennel of Ashley.

Jones' Preacher

Jones' Sam in 1982, Sam was always there in case he was needed.

His first catch dog was named Sam. He weighed 105-pounds, which is the upper limit for a working cattle catcher. Sam also accompanied Darrin to the rodeo where his master did rope and bullwhip demonstrations similar to the shows put on by Will Rogers in the 30's. Sam was trained to hold a piece of paper steady in his mouth while Darrin bullwhipped it apart. The first time Darrin held an electric wire up with his boot to get at some cows, Sam immediately got on his belly and crawled under the bottom wire.

Old Sam was the main foundation stud in this kennel for years. Sam's direct descendants are the two main brood bitches that Darrin is using today. An important Jones breeding is one of these females to the 14-year old son of Dixieman, King. Besides dogs from Sand Mountain locals this kennel (like most Scott breeders) has gotten foundation dogs from Bill Hines.

Chance, a son of Williamson's Sport

While Darrin has always worked his dogs on cattle and goats, recently he has begun testing them on wild hogs. Not surprisingly, he has found that a good cattle catcher is also a good hog catcher. As an extra measure of trainability he also uses his Bulldogs to herd goats as well as catch them.

Darrin has a talent for spotting valuable specimens, which has made him a key member of the Scott Breeder's Group. I already mentioned King, one of the last living sons of Dixieman. He told me about one other Dixieman son, a brother of King, who at 14-years old is still a working farm dog. Darrin also got a dog from G.L. Williamson's widow named Sport, perhaps the last pure Williamson dog alive.

Darrin's great great uncle was breeding Bulldogs in this area in 1918. A family friend in his mid 80's remembers what Bulldogs were like back then, he recalls seeing a mean cow get loose as a boy of six or seven. An Alabama Bulldog attached himself to this wayward bovine and a titanic battle ensued. The cow whirled the dog around frenetically but he held on to her nose unperturbed. When she finally surrendered the dog's owner whistled him off and Bossy meekly

162

walked back into the barn with a few fearful glances at the Bulldog. This old timer says that the dogs he sees at Sand Valley Bulldogs look and act exactly the way the Bulldogs of his youth did. Darrin says that his dogs are as close to the original north Alabama Bulldog as is possible.

An AB from the 1920's near Lookout Mountain, Alabama

Jones' Chance and Jones' Bulldogger making a catch in deep water

Jack Tate

Jack Tate of Boaz, Alabama, bred a line of Bulldogs from '71 to '90 that has had a profound impact on the current performance lines. His kennel was a fairly small operation consisting of an average of four bitches and one stud dog over the 19-year period. Like the two previous breeders Mr. Tate's dogs also came from northern Alabama. His foundation dogs were related to the Ashley dogs.

Left to right, Jack Tate, Casey Couturier and Darrin Jones

By far the most influential breeding to come from this kennel was the Tuck's Tiger Lady cross to Williamson's Big Joe. This bitch weighed 75-pounds and was 22-inches tall. She had fawn markings and a tight reverse scissors on a snout just short of four-inches. Big Joe weighed 90-pounds, was pure white and similar to Tiger Lady in bite and muzzle length. Over a hundred puppies were raised out of these two dogs. Almost every single one went into Alabama, Arkansas, Mississippi, Tennessee and Florida. Many have been used as foundation dogs for other programs. For instance one, of them was Wright's Rounder, Sergeant Rock's father, and a foundation dog for the Painter line. Though these dogs were proven on hogs by many of their owners, like the other dogs from the Sand Mountain area, they seemed especially able on cattle. Mr. Tate raises Black Angus and didn't usually try to catch cattle with his dogs but when one of them would get loose and tackle a bull on his own recognizance it would prove necessary to choke him down or use breaker bars to get him off the bovine.

One of Mr. Tate's customers used a Tiger Lady/Big Joe offspring to catch cattle on a routine basis. One day the dog was catching a 1700-pound bull and got a hold good enough to hang on with but not painful enough to paralyze the bull. This allowed the big Brangus to get into some trees and bash the dog against branches. There was no way for the dog's owner to stop the bull and the dog was eventually killed, he held his grip till the end.

Big Bull's Budda, inbred Tate Duchess.

While testing a line of dogs this hard is never done on purpose, when it does occur and the dog lasts to the end then we can use this information to ascertain the level of gameness, which in this case was the highest - dead game. These dogs were also proven in guard duty, showing high degrees of territoriality and defensiveness.

In our interview I pointed out to Mr. Tate that some of the original breeders like Alan Scott are getting back into the Bulldog community and reviving their lines. I erroneously thought that the Tate line was not being actively bred. I said it was still fresh enough to separate and keep going. He told me he was tempted but his cattle operation is a full time occupation which he and his wife have kept going for years even though they both taught high school full time up until their recent retirement.

Since then I have learned that Dean Tibbet in Washington state has done wonderful things with the Tate line, producing IWPA

weight pull champions that rival the Mountain Gator dogs. Tibbet's Competition Kennels is an important source of genetic diversity because of his uncompromising policy of X-raying and performance testing his triple bred Tate's Duchess Lady bloodline. Kevin Gibson has also kept the Tate line going. Neither of these breeders relies exclusively on Tate blood, however, so the challenge stands.

Calvin Tuck

Calvin Tuck of Bluntville, Alabama, ended his enlistment in the Marine Corps in 1966 in Rome, Georgia. This is a town very close to Summerville, where John D. Johnson lives. The two men became friends after Calvin bought a pedigreed Black Angus bull from Mr. Johnson around this time. Along with the bull came a gift, a pair of very good Bulldogs. The female weighed 65-pounds and the male weighed roughly 85-pounds. These Old Time Johnson dogs had typical performance builds. This pair caught wild hogs on a large wooded tract next to the Tuck farm in Bluntville and eradicated wild dogs, which were a problem in this area.

Tiger Lady resembled this modern fawn colored AB, a Tiger Lady descendant

Calvin always kept his dogs trained and under control. He told me that there was nothing better than a trained Bulldog and that there was nothing worse than an untrained one. For instance, if a Bulldog was around a herd of cattle and a calf were to break away from the herd real fast, the dog would want to catch it and throw it. Even so, the dog's master should be able to call him off so the calf wouldn't get roughed up.

His first male, Bo Bo, could escort a neighbor's Red-bone hound home that had strayed onto the farm or tear up a pack of wild dogs that were threatening livestock. If a hunter (or anyone) trespassed on Tuck property, Bo Bo would first look at his master before attacking the intruder to make sure he wasn't hurting a friend.

His first female was named Lady. On one occasion she probably saved the Tuck children's lives. A big Angus bull had accidentally been corralled in a pasture without water for several days. Unwittingly the Tuck children crossed the pasture with the mad bull in it. The bull charged them but Lady came streaking to the rescue, got a hold of the bull and threw him flat on his back. He got up again and tried another charge. Lady threw him again and wouldn't let the bull loose till everyone was safe.

Calvin kept Bulldogs for almost 20-years. He only raised about six litters but from just one of his dogs, Tuck's Tiger Lady (sold to Jack Tate as a pup), there are now thousands of descendants. We usually think that all performance blood comes directly from northern Alabama, but we can see in this case there is a strain of Alabama hog dogs where (though some roots may be traced to Sand Valley) Georgia is the actual wellspring. Old Time Johnson dogs were indeed high performance Bulldogs.

Bodyguard Kennels

Mike Harlow owns Bodyguard Kennels in Longwood, Florida. Mr. Harlow brings a special expertise and perspective to the art of breeding guard dogs, he worked for 16-years as a police officer and three years as a K-9 officer. While on the street his dog Nick was directly responsible for 47 arrests. Since retiring from the force he has trained about 15 ABs in protection work. Mr. Harlow is also a Bulldog historian and scholar. He has already published one book on training police and guard dogs entitled K-9 Bodyguards.

The Bodyguard breeding program uses only performance bloodlines, Scott, Painter and Old Time Johnson. These dogs will weigh between 80 and 90-pounds. This is the ideal size

for a police dog or any protector. While Mr. Harlow admires the larger modern Johnson strain they are (on average) too heavy and slow for the uses he puts a dog to. The shortened life span and other health problems are also a concern. He sees the increased size of these big Bulldogs as coming from a St. Bernard out cross and feels that they should rightfully be called Johnson Bulldogs to differentiate them from the more agile performance strains which are closer to the original bull baiting dogs of the 18th century.

125-pound AB doing a chest bite

As to the origin question, Mr. Harlow weighs in on the side of the old English origin and definitely feels that this is not a recent composite breed. He bases this assertion on two things: 1) He has interviewed several old time Bulldog men, such as Ashley, who have been breeding the same dogs in the rural South for over half a century. Mr. Ashley got many of his dogs from a man named A.L. Kittle, whose breeding program stretched back pretty close to the turn of the century. All these old timers tell him this is not a composite breed. 2) The incredible fire and drive that these dogs exhibit towards man work could not have been created from any likely combination of composite breeds.

This fire and toughness makes the American Bulldog the best choice, in Mr. Harlow's opinion, for police or guardian work. He has seen K-9 German Shepherds quit fighting when injured at a riot or in other dangerous situations. In the same situation, receiving the same punishment, a good AB would just wag his tail and keep fighting. Originally the German dog was bred to herd sheep, where the Bulldog was bred for combat. Mr. Harlow has tried to convince police departments to give the AB a chance as a K-9 dog. It is a tough sell, not because a good AB is anything but the best possible dog for this job but the upper levels of most police departments are hide bound, conservative and mired in tradition.

In his own program, Mr. Harlow uses his vast experience to test a potential breeding candidate for combative qualities. However, he not only wants to see that a dog will bite hard and keep fighting in the face of stiff resistance, he wants it to be controllable. Even an untrained Bulldog should be able to be called off by its owner once it has committed itself to an attack and then kept under control once called off and the human assailant has surrendered.

Patch doing the chest bite, John holds arms back to encourage the body bite.

To test a dog's hips he makes it stand on its hind legs for an extended period of time. In his opinion, if it can do this without pain the hips are good. To further test the hips and the dog's overall structure he takes it through the kind of obstacle course that a police dog is trained on. This would include broad jumps and six-foot walls. According to Mr. Harlow, dysplastic dogs can not navigate these obstacles. The three ABs that Mr. Harlow owns are all trained to the level of professional police dogs.

This is a very small kennel and it does not produce a lot of puppies, so you might have to wait a little while to get one, but if you want your next dog to be a bodyguard the wait will be worth it.

As of 1999, one American Bulldog named Wicca has become an actual working police dog in New Jersey. Mr. Harlow was not directly involved in this milestone but his book may have helped set the stage for this dog and others to enter law enforcement. The New Jersey AB police dog is from the Koura bloodline, a line favored by Harlow.

Tar Heel's Oscar

Tar Heel American Bulldogs

David Jackson is a physician in Mount Airy, North Carolina. His kennel is called Tar Heel American Bulldogs. According to Dr. Jackson, he is one of only three breeders who maintain the pure Johnson line. The other two are John D. Johnson and Andrew Robertson. A few years ago, he decided to switch from the breeding of Boxers to ABs and tried to buy some dogs from Johnson. At that time there was a two year waiting list to get a puppy out of Summerville, so Dr. Jackson obtained some of the more common Scott/Johnson Hybrids. A few months later a stroke of good luck allowed him to beat the waiting list and he snagged a few pure Johnson puppies. This has allowed Dr. Jackson to compare the temperaments of the two different kinds of Bulldogs because he has bred and raised both. He says that pure Johnson dogs are bolder, more playful, friendlier and quicker to forgive. On the other hand, even though they have long fuses, once they do get riled they stay worked up longer and can be very stubborn. He finds the Scott/Johnson Hybrids to be more suspicious of strangers and less exuberant.

According to Dr. Jackson, the handful of breeders who maintain this line are doing all AB breeders a service because the dogs Johnson started with in the first half of this century were closer genetically to the old time Bulldogs than the dogs other breeders started with in the 60's and seventies. Johnson himself claims to notice a big difference when he came home from WW II. He found the earlier dogs were heavier, taller and wider, their muzzles were shorter and their jaws were much more undershot, sometimes sticking out a half-inch or more. Whether or not this is what all old time Bulldogs looked like, it does describe Tar Heel Bulldogs, with some males reaching 130-pounds. The conclusion that Dr. Jackson draws is that the modern Johnson strain has less Pit Bull in it.

Bubba weighs 150-pounds, he could lose a pound or two.

Dr. Jackson runs his dogs five-miles a day, three times a week. If he notices anything wrong with their movement he has them X-rayed. Recently his main stud, Buck, came up limping after a run. He was hip X-rayed and informally rated as good. Finally, it was discovered that the constant pounding of his pads on hard pavement was making the toenails bleed. Buck took two weeks off from running and healed right up. He is now pounding the pavement again and has had no further problems. From the photos I've seen, Tar Heel Bulldogs are very imposing, with thick, dense muscles, huge heads and an alert upright stance.

Tar Heel's Buck

Rayburn Stover

Rayburn Stover lives in Horton, Alabama and has been breeding ABs since 1970. As of 1995, he has sold over 2000 puppies and should be considered one of the original breeders. Before the 70's he bred Boxers but switched over to Bulldogs when he realized how smart this breed is.

Stover's Little John, 101-pounds

He got his first dogs from farmers in Alabama. Like many of the Bulldogs of that time and place they were mostly white and extraordinary catch dogs. With little or no training they could catch anything from cattle, pigs and goats to chickens or even bugs. Like Alan Scott, Mr. Stover would use his dogs to catch cattle or other farm animals for his neighbors when their livestock strayed into heavy brush or other places where they couldn't be rousted easily. This still happens every now and then, just the other day a bull got loose in the town of Horton and the only way he could be caught was with Bulldogs.

Stover Bulldogs are usually a 60/40 mix of Scott and Johnson, though he considers himself a Scott breeder because males average 90-pounds and many of his customers use these dogs as catch dogs. Once in a rare while he will see a really big Bulldog that is athletic enough to do catch work. One such dog weighed 135-pounds and was used by a horse trader to catch loose horses and goats. This behemoth would catch horses in an atypical manner, by grabbing them by the flanks and pulling them down. A dog this big and that athletic is a rarity.

Hines' Bossman is the pup in the center, bred by Rayburn Stover.

Another good story about Alabama Bulldogs involves a truck driver who got caught one Friday night in a large storage yard after it had been locked up and the dogs released. The two Bulldogs knocked him down and kept him down till Monday morning. Whenever the man tried to move he would get bitten, if he lay still they would just stand over him. So this poor guy had to lay frozen in one spot for two days.

This is the right level of man aggression for Mr. Stover. He doesn't like a 'man-eater' or a dog that will really maul someone without extensive training. Bulldogs should be capable of anything, however, with the right training. His goal as a breeder is to give trainers the raw material to work with to accomplish anything from

catch work to man work. To this end he wants structural soundness that starts with a big muscular rear, because this is where the driving power comes from. This is so important that his last ad in Dog World had a photograph of his main stud (the 101-pound Little John) with his heavily muscled rear end to the camera. He also wants a short thick neck since this is the second most important place that a dog's power comes from, especially in catch work. The head should be big and square and remember - "Big teeth count when you catch."

Stover's Bitty, niece of Bossman

Dixie and Bruiser, Alabama Bulldogs from the 80's

The hot weather in the South necessitates a four-inch muzzle for proper breathing. One of the hardest things for Mr. Stover to breed out of these dogs is an under bite. He strives to give them all an even bite because when old timers come to buy his dogs for catch work the first thing they do is look at the teeth, if the lower jaw sticks out they won't take it. Finally, he likes Bulldogs to be all white, since this is the original color of the breed. His dogs are known for their athleticism. The smaller ones can jump several feet in the air from a flatfooted stance, making it hard to keep them inside fences. He is also known for supplying top breeders with foundation stock.

Big Bull's Air Draxx

Big Bull Kennels

Big Bull Kennels in Cleveland, Ohio is operated by Kevin Gibson, Ron Smith, Kenneth Smith and Russell White. Kevin started this program in 1978 when he started getting Bulldogs from small farmers in Alabama. These dogs were bred primarily to hunt wild hogs but they were also working farm dogs as well. They did have pedigrees though there wasn't much effort to keep the records straight. Kevin had to rely on the ability of individual dogs, which is probably the best way to judge dog flesh anyway. He would buy entire litters and take them back to Ohio. The people he bought Bulldogs from called this breed Old English White or Great Whites, they weighed 80 or 90-pounds. Some were brindle Bulldogs. Today Big Bull has isolated a strain of ABs with solid colors like brindle and fawn. Kevin has found that his color line Bulldogs mature faster than the more common white strains.

In the 80's Kevin bought dogs from Steve Leclerc and Tate. Many of these dogs had a great deal of blood from Mac the Masher. Since then, Big Bull has tried to isolate that blood and offer dogs from the Masher line. I mention this because many breeders claim to have Masher

blood when they're producing puppies that are only 1/32 of this famous dog. Big Bull uses an actual grandson of Mac the Masher, so their claim of a Masher line is more credible. This kennel does use all major bloodlines but with the original dogs coming from Alabama and the emphasis on Masher you would have to say that they are primarily Scott breeders. They do have one amazing stud dog from Suregrip that is half Painter and half Johnson named Grimlock, known for extreme protectiveness.

Uzi as a puppy

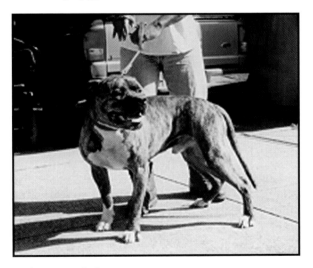

Uzi as an adult

Many Bulldog breeders sell dogs into high crime areas and Cleveland certainly fits this profile. Kevin Gibson is a licensed dog trainer. He can train a dog in anything from basic obedience to guide dog for the blind. His specialty is protection work and this is the main performance test for Big Bull, though they are planning on testing dogs on wild pigs in the near future.

Chuck Voglepouh's King Kong, Fujimo Max x Dixie, treadmill is his favorite toy

Big Bull's Bull

These dogs definitely do well in a country setting though. Ron Smith's father owns a small farm in Ohio and the 128-pound male, Ox, has the run of the place. Despite his size, this dog is fast enough and has enough endurance to play all day with horses. He identifies so strongly with his horses that he won't let anyone ride one, which means Ox has to be tied securely before a horse can be saddled. This dog has a tendency to get into trouble because he has the playfulness of a puppy and the strength of a grizzly bear. He once chased hunters away from a big buck they had shot and then dragged the carcass to his owner's front door just like a cat dropping off a mouse.

For a big dog Ox is nimble. He swims for hours in a small lake and has been known to catch Bluegill with one swift lunge and a snap of his jaws. He has also developed a technique for ambushing and snatching startled crows. This dog has attitude and thinks all of Ohio belongs to Ox.

Ox' father is Grimlock, who is less carefree, he is always on alert for intruders and would send any to the hospital or worse if he perceived a threat. Ron Smith weighs 232-pounds but when he is on the receiving end of a Grimlock attack he feels like a little boy being roughed up by a bully. Grimlock acts like a big baby around the Gibson children and is completely trustworthy with family members.

Air Draxx loves hang time.

Like most performance strains Big Bull males usually weigh somewhere around 90-pounds, females around 80 or less. Their muzzles are broad and of medium length. This kennel strives to give its Bulldogs big muscular rear ends.

Rode Hawg Kennel

Larry Koura and Steve Leclerc have been breeding American Bulldogs in

170

Massachusetts and Illinois since the 80's. Koura's Rode Hawg Kennel is in Capron, Illinois. This line started with foundation stock similar to Screaming Eagle's. This blood was then mixed to Bulldogs related to Kevin Gibson's line.

Griffin's Gypsy is a Koura bred AB with extreme athletic ability. She can jump a 6-foot wall while wearing a 50-pound chain. Her bite work is very good.

The 90-pound, Ring III, Oden goes over 7.2-foot wall while Neal Albert watches

The most important foundation dog for the modern Koura line was Bama Boy. This stud was the equivalent to Woody in the Suregrip line. Like Woody, Bama Boy was man game and his blood has been used to increase guardian capability in the animal game performance strain. The difference is that a Woody/Painter cross was a 'Bandog type' breeding - a big Mastiffy Johnson dog was crossed to a performance (Painter) bitch to get a blend of the two.

While he occasionally threw 100-pound sons with medium/heavy bone, Bama Boy had a pure performance pedigree with no modern Johnson blood and therefore no English Bulldog, which kept the structural integrity of performance bitches but added more biting power for man work.

Oden comes back over the 7.2-foot palisade. Very few dogs this heavy can withstand the pounding necessary to earn a Ring III title.

Oden practices the long jump.

The most famous Koura Bulldog today is Oden - owned, trained and handled by Neal Albert. This 90-pound male not only earned a French Ring III, he won the North American Ring II national championship. This is the greatest protection sport achievement yet by an American Bulldog. Oden has a Canine Good Citizen, one of the lowest Penn-hip scores ever and is the picture of great structure. He better be, to compete in Ring Sport a dog has to go over seven-foot walls and perform 30-foot long jumps.

Oden engages the decoy on the upper thigh while training. This is one of the most effective bites for French Ring or the street.

I am helping to protection train a Koura bred female owned by my buddy Mark Griffin. This dog, Griffin's Gypsy, is OFA good prelim and showing tremendous potential. Her drive is off the scale and she has more raw athleticism than any AB that I've directly worked with. She can literally run most of the bulkier dogs in our club right into the ground. Her temperament is loving, calm, steady and courageous. She can go over a six-foot wall while wearing a 50-pound chain.

Koura blood is being used by California breeders to increase genetic diversity and add structure to the Suregrip/Johnson dogs that dominate the West Coast. With this admixture we should see even better health and longevity.

Tomahawk's Gracie, Dozer x Ruby

Tomahawk Bulldogs

Patrick McAteer and Andrew O'Donell own Tomahawk Bulldogs in Kearny, New Jersey. If you think there is a chance some psychopath might crash your child's slumber party a Tomahawk dog may insure that the only inconvenience this intruder will cause you is mopping up the blood stains afterwards. Tomahawk dogs are bred to be serious man fighters and are not only thoroughly tested in a sport environment they have proven themselves as professional protectors in the real world.

J.R. the Punisher, Penn-hip, OFA, considered one of the toughest Bulldogs.

For example, recently a private investigator was using Tomahawk's Jezzebell during a stake out in a storage facility that was experiencing theft problems. The investigator went out into the yard to check a noise. Jezzebell was 150-feet away in a trailer with a security guard when the investigator encountered three armed men. At the sound of gunshots Jezzebell was released. The investigator took one bullet in the leg and another glanced off his bulletproof vest before Jezzebell hit the three men. The gunmen managed to escape the facility with their lives but just barely. One of them was forced to check into a hospital that night, which should help police track down the other two.

When Mr. McAteer finished recounting this episode to me he mentioned that there was one thing that disappointed him about Jezzebell's performance, she shouldn't have let the gunmen get away. This comment reveals the level of man work expected of these dogs. The training and testing they are put through is unbelievable.

When J.R. (120-pound Woody grandson, OFA and Penn-hip certified) does his bite work, he goes up against a very fit 240-pound man wearing a full body suit. J.R. has to cover an obstacle course to get at this man, which includes six-foot walls and explosive charges set to go off near his feet. He is also fired at with blank guns.

Once he makes his first bite, he is clubbed hard with a stick ball bat. J.R. shakes off these blows as if they were love pats. He is trained not to scatter bite, that is he gets one good grip and hangs on. Though if his first grip is not a good one he must have the intelligence to let go very quickly and get a better one. If his antagonist is not struggling he holds the man steady without inflicting unnecessary damage. If the man is fighting back then the dog must do everything possible to subdue him, which means hanging on once he has a good solid grip, tearing and shaking with his whole body, deepening his grip when possible and absorbing punishment unflinchingly.

If his human opponent is formidable, he also needs to use strategy, such as getting all four feet planted firmly if he has the man down. If the bad guy is standing then J.R. must engulf him with his front legs and use his neck and shoulder muscles to tear him apart. These dogs are bred to do what Bulldogs have done to bears and bulls for a thousand years, but to men. Tomahawk feels that if your family's safety is at stake their canine protector should be a living cyclone of destruction.

The protection training starts at 8-weeks old with potato sacks. Soon the pups graduate to puppy sleeves, then regular sleeves. Adults are sometimes worked with hidden sleeves, which closely simulates real world encounters. When a full body suit is used a hockey mask is added to protect the few inches of exposed flesh not covered by the suit.

Dogs are also temperament tested and must be calm and loving toward their human family. Like all good protection dogs they should out crisply and be easy to control. This program also goes to great lengths to test and screen its breeding stock physically. Adult dogs are run through obstacle courses for athleticism and agility. They are run on treadmills for endurance. They drag pull weights to build up muscle. Their hips are first X-rayed at four months. They are then periodically X-rayed until two years old. Tomahawk uses a veterinarian who is a hip specialist. Together they pour over these X-rays when evaluating a dog. This program has a fanaticism about hips found in few kennels.

Tomahawk's Jezzebell, a real world hero

Like most programs with a heavy emphasis on man fighting, Tomahawk relies extensively on Johnson blood for attitude and performance blood for physical prowess. Mr. McAteer has raised and trained Pit Bulls and knows full well that animal gameness doesn't translate to human gameness, so a big dose of Johnson is key. Their basic formula is 50% Johnson and 50% performance (mainly Painter). Great care is used in selecting all breeding stock but the Johnson component is very carefully screened for soundness.

Bear - Martha's angel

Breeding American Bulldogs

The best American Bulldog breeders follow rigid guidelines before a mating: Breed candidates are board certified free of dysplasia and further screened for all other genetic defects by the breeder over a two year period. These genetically screened dogs must then also have a working/sport title, be structurally sound and pass a temperament test. Part of any successful adult temperament test includes dogs interacting with children in a safe and mellow manner. Breed candidates should therefore be kid tested. Any breed worthy AB should also be able to safely and confidently meet friendly strangers in his or her own backyard after an introduction by the dog's owner/handler. Furthermore, breed worthy Bulldogs should be able to interact with non-alpha dogs away from their own turf in a safe manner. Finally, breedable Bulldogs should be confident and trustworthy with friendly strangers in any public or private setting, after an introduction.

I call the best breeders - first tier. These are the folks that have the experience, knowledge and ethics to earn a title and go through scientific screening processes such as OFA, Pennhip and CERF eye testing. First tier breeders are likely to have kid tested, dog tested and stranger tested all breeding stock. Many use sires and dams that hold formal temperament titles such as the TT, Canine Good Citizen and the WABA OB I, virtually guaranteeing that parent dogs have steady nerves and are trustworthy.

Working/sport titles that ABs have earned so far include Sch, Ring, International Weight pull and the 16 titles issued by WABA, UCDA and ABWPA. In case you've forgotten, these titles are: WST (I & II), BST (I & II), CD/UCD (I, II, III), WPD (I, II, III), WP I, AD and OB I. Only the BST I & II includes a hip evaluation, so a dog that has earned a Sch, Ring Sport, Catch Dog, Weight Pull, Endurance or Obedience title must have a separate hip certification. WABA titles comprise a growing percentage of AB working titles. In America, the WABA is for all practical purposes the place to look for working parents and the resulting working puppy. In Europe, I would investigate the American Bulldog Club of Germany.

Lex of J. Richman, OFA prelim Excellent, 2nd generation Koura/Suregrip

Then there are a host of AB breeders that OFA and scientifically screen their stock as well as temperament test but don't have working titles. I call this group the second tier - breeders that use only mentally and physically sound ABs but don't work them enough to earn titles. Bulldogs from these kennels might have slightly lower working drives than first tier dogs and may therefore be a better choice for the average home owner with a desire for a trouble free backyard Bulldog.

This gives puppy prospects two acceptable groups to choose from. There are more second tier than first tier breeders and this is probably a good thing. Cross-pollination from the two groups will refresh bloodlines and keep the AB strong into the next century.

Then there are third tier breeders that do no scientific screening such as OFA. Third tier breeders range from those who do randomly selected (genetically dangerous) backyard breedings to mass production puppy milling for pet shops. As of 1999 the third tier is bigger than the second tier in the North American AB community. On the other hand, the considerable number of first and second tier ABs are largely genetically walled off from untested/inferior third tier stock. The free interchange seen between tiers one and two does not happen with tier three. As tiers one and two grow the future of the working AB becomes more secure.

Tom Riche's Brindle, BST, CD I, working toward Sch I, Irondog triathlon champion

Mainstream dog people will read these breeding guidelines and wonder where breed type fits into the equation. The American Bulldog community by and large swims outside the mainstream on the question of breed type. Since cookie cutter sameness is the altar that they worship at, many mainstream fanciers do not consider the AB a pure breed.

It is not uncommon for a 130-pound blocky Johnson type AB stud to breed to a 75-pound AB bitch that resembles a slightly lippy, big headed, coarse Pit Bull. The AB community would consider such a combination a fine one if both parents had excellent structure, BSTs and demonstrably superior temperaments. Once full grown, puppies from such a breeding may have great type diversity. Big blocky Johnson dogs can have littermates that are the slender Scott type. If correctly bred, a physically diverse litter will have very uniform temperaments, allowing the breeder to accurately predict the character of each puppy, if not its final appearance.

To the outside world this is heresy. The mainstream believes that one should breed only for the outward physical appearance they call type and produce dogs that are Xeroxes, carbon copies, of a rigid ideal phenotype, often with little concern for temperamental uniformity and

predictability. And worse yet, these blueprints or breed standards are almost always bad designs.

Even German Shepherd Schutzhund breeders have fallen into the breed-for-type trap. They do not breed the best Schutzhund Shepherds to the best and allow type to establish itself naturally. Schutzhund Shepherd breeders strive to follow an artificial standard that describes a short legged, low reared dog better suited to trotting than the sprint work required in their own sport.

Among the Europeans, only Malinois breeders have eschewed show breeding. Because the best working Malinois have been bred to the best, in a few short generations a dog has been created that is better than the German Shepherd for protection sport. Like Malinois aficionados, Bulldog people reject the cookie cutter AKC mentality. Bulldoggers celebrate healthy physical diversity and strive for mental uniformity.

Other breeds with a wide variety of type include the American Pit Bull Terrier, Southern Cur and virtually all true working breeds. Sled dogs lose races if any emphasis is placed on uniform breed type. Cookie cutter AKC Siberian Huskies can't race competitively and aren't even considered by northern sled dog racers.

Matt Green is a first tier breeder with rigid standards. Photo - Michelle LeNoir

There are four or five competing standards within the AB community and as many organizations hosting AB shows. Most AB shows feature a Johnson class and a Scott class. The names vary for the two types but the idea is the same. Any type within the two extremes is permissible. An infinite amount of type exists within these parameters. Yet every Bulldog within these parameters is identifiable as an AB at a glance by an experienced Bulldogger, even though the breed seemingly has the scope of two or three AKC breeds. Someone once remarked sarcastically that it is almost as if Dobermans and Rottweilers were considered a single breed. This wise guy doesn't understand or appreciate the working history of his own breed. The dogs that accompanied Baron Doberman on his tax collection duties, the dogs that weren't afraid of 'even the devil,' were animals of great type diversity. These people don't grasp the essence of the AB and should just leave us alone.

So the question of breed type is left to the individual. Even though in some instances extremes from the two types are mated, most breedings are type to type. Prospective puppy buyers that need to know what their Bull pup will look like as an adult should decide whether they want a performance AB, a Johnson AB or a Suregrip (Hybrid) type and choose a breeder accordingly.

Those who favor a blocky, bulldoggy look would be wise to seriously consider smaller specimens since short muzzled Bulldogs are only athletic if well under 100-pounds. Smaller Johnson dogs will, on average, live longer, healthier lives than the oversized ones.

The debate over line breeding vs. out crossing has at least temporarily swung in favor of the latter since increased genetic diversity will (at this time) produce healthier Bulldogs. First tier pedigrees should contain as many different working titled, hip-certified, dogs as possible. In second tier pedigrees, there should be a genetically diverse group of scientifically screened, temperament tested, Bulldogs. In either case, many of the established lines are too tight and need fresh blood.

The issue of genetic diversity inevitably leads to consideration of the practice of breeding pedigreed ABs to out cross hill Bulldogs. All bloodlines originate in hill country and some recent infusions have proven beneficial. The most recent infusions have been less successful. The hill Bulldog population is shrinking and has been picked over by AB breeders.

There have never been any formal guidelines as to what qualifies as a bona fide Old English White. As time goes on the informal rules that govern introduction of hill Bulldog blood should be strengthened. In my opinion, only Old English Whites from northern Florida should be considered possible crosses to American Bulldogs and only if extensive written pedigrees are available. For example, Don Little's Brittany was a nine generation pedigreed Old English White that has been successfully crossed into Suregrip ABs. Don Little's Brittany represented a long line of proven Florida hog dogs with man working ability. Suregrip to Brittany crosses have produced good working Bulldogs that have bred true.

Since I live in California I pay special attention to West Coast breeders. In the Golden State most bloodlines have derived from Suregrip, Hines and Farnetti in that order. These three are pretty well mixed and ready for out crossing. Hines/Suregrip ABs that are closer to the performance phenotype are being out crossed primarily to the Koura/Bama Boy line.

Hannah, OFA Good, 3rd place in Irondog

Bulldoggy Hines/Suregrip/Farnetti dogs are being crossed to non-Woody (non-Machine) Johnson strains from the East Coast such as the Colette, Sugar Doll, Tuffy and Rebel strains. On the West Coast, in a few years, a Bulldoggy Hines/Suregrip/East Coast Johnson strain will inevitably emerge next to a Hines/Suregrip/Koura performance strain. Eventually line breeding will firm up these nascent strains. Further down the road, breeders will blend the newly emerged performance type with the Bulldoggy strain and unending genetic diversity will continue.

The merging of West Coast and East Coast bloodlines brings up the subject of artificial insemination and the practice of shipping chilled semen across the country. While it is laudable that breeders are expanding the gene pool by using these methods, experience with other dog breeds that have relied on artificial insemination for many generations has proven that over time the ability to reproduce naturally atrophies when artificial methods are substituted for natural methods. By the same token, bitches should deliver naturally and not resort to c-sections.

Manstoppers' Hannah has the ability to earn a BST. Johnson breeders should not shy away from protection sport titles.

The best way to provide a snapshot of the working American Bulldog at the time of this writing is to chronicle the working trials and competitions held by the WABA and the ABA at the 1999 ABA national dog show. The Southland American Bulldog club was the host. Besides 15 dogs taking the BST I, BST II and WST I, there was an Irondog triathlon contest where dogs had to compete in tug of war, agility and a timed foot race. The Irondog competition was stiff so the overall winner had to be a great dog.

The Irondog winner was a double-bred Bama Boy male - Outback's Diesel, fresh blood for the West Coast. The only dog to pass the BST II that day was Rob Boyd's Hammer, a Suregrip/Hines - a proven mix that would add some diversity to pure Suregrip females. From a working viewpoint Diesel, Hammer or one of the many BST I males at that show would be the studs to consider for anyone with a qualified female and a desire to raise a litter of working puppies. The champion of champion standard class featured Boyd's High Jumping Mikie, Karasek's Bear and Sloan's Turbo, a target rich environment for a breeder with the right female. All three of these show champions have BSTs.

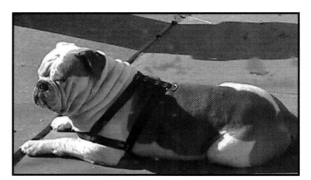

If he lost weight Manstoppers' Tyson could earn a BST. 148-pounds, too heavy

Orthodox show people will examine the type variation within these three standard champions and cry, "there's a second class with even more type variation? Heresy, complete heresy!" Despite shock and indignation from the show crowd, American Bulldog breed clubs and show organizations are flexible enough to accommodate this much variation and maintain a pure breed.

If I were looking for a puppy from one of the many first tier breeders at that show I would consider Tom Riche for a performance AB. Tom has competed in Schutzhund on a national level. Tom is president of the WABA. Tom is the Man. I would want a pup out of his CD I, BST, Irondog champion female - Brindle. She will be bred to Boyd's Mikie. With Tom's training, both Brindle and Mikie will likely earn Sch IIIs. I would also investigate Matt Green, a first tier breeder that adheres to rigid standards.

For a typey Johnson Bulldog I would be forced to choose from second tier breeders. At the 1999 national show Manstoppers kennels was advertising a breeding of Tyson to Hannah, both OFA good. If I wanted a short muzzled, undershot, wrinkly, blocky Johnson puppy, this breeding would spark my interest. I would insist on pick or second pick and try for a smaller female. Though physically and temperamentally sound, neither Tyson nor Hannah has a working title. Hannah does compete in Irondog. Tyson has been crossed to several performance bitches and has thus sired plenty of titled dogs, however none have been anywhere near as typey as their father. Of the 125 or 150 working titled ABs in existence as of 1999, almost none are the extreme Johnson type (there are a few weight pull titled Johnson ABs).

Tyson, OFA Good, has offspring that have earned BST, Sch I and OFA Excellent

Accordingly and unfortunately, Johnson breeders must be held to a lower standard. At minimum, typey Johnson breeders must fall solidly in the upper half of the second tier. I have seen Hannah and Tyson interact with children and strangers in public places. I have seen these dogs do protection work and have done my own temperament testing. They live nearby and I have the luxury of examining these two parent dogs under a variety of circumstances. Second tier breedings force the puppy prospect to do more homework and be more knowledgeable.

Outback's Diesel, OFA Good, double-bred Bama Boy, Irondog triathlon champion. An excellent out cross for California bloodlines

When choosing for working ability among second tier breeders the savvy Bulldog puppy prospect needs to be able to personally examine and test parent dogs. Even a complete novice can tell if parent dogs are overly aggressive or unable to interact safely with friendly strangers. A complete novice can read an OFA certificate and check to make sure it is valid. Whether a novice or an old veteran, it is imperative that a puppy prospect meet the second tier breeder and inspect his kennel in person. If the breeder is local this is obviously easier. Knowledge of American Bulldog genetic defects is key in this endeavor.

Karasek's Bear, BST, CD I, CGC, OFA Good, 1st ABA Grand Champion, Bear matured quickly for an AB, this is a characteristic breeders should select for.

The most common genetic disorders in the American Bulldog are hip dysplasia, shoulder dysplasia, eyelid entropia/ectropia and various skin diseases such as mange. Less common disorders include deafness, internal organ problems and epilepsy. The most common structural defect is a short stifle, which gives the back legs a non-angled appearance. Short-stifled ABs have a greater chance of tearing knee ligaments during vigorous exercise. Cow hocked or sickle hocked ABs also have a tendency to tear knee

179

ligaments. Any Bulldog that has had knee surgery should not be bred whether the dog has a short stifle or crooked back legs or not since there is only a rough correlation between these conformation flaws and the knee injury. Torn knee ligaments rank with hip dysplasia as the leading cause of lameness in ABs. Other common structural defects are a soft palate (which makes the dog snort when he breathes), crossed eyes, extremely small hindquarters, extreme undershot jaw and bowed front legs.

Sloan's Turbo, ABA Champion with titles

A lack of pigmentation around the eyes, lips and testicles is not considered a structural defect but if the dog is exposed to direct sunlight for any length of time he could suffer from sunburn. A kinked tail is also not considered a structural defect but kinked tailed dogs should not be mated to kinked tailed dogs because the tail may disappear in later generations and spine problems could result.

The most common temperamental defects are shyness and nervousness. Shy/nervy ABs are usually the result of inbreeding, so it is possible to have nervy pups from steady parents if they are too closely related. To guard against weak nerves when purchasing a puppy the litter should be temperament tested. First tier breeders usually have the skill to test their own litters and give reliable information to prospects. Second tier breeders often employ professional testers and videotape the test so prospective puppy purchasers can make informed decisions. This technique may be effective but I would like to see the puppy test myself.

American Bulldogs that are bred to the highest standards still have innate flaws. The most fundamental one seems to be a very slow emotional maturity rate. Bulldogs mature quickly physically but not mentally. Ninety percent of body growth usually occurs by one year. The remaining ten percent of growth can last for two more years. The last thing to stop growing is an AB's head at about three years. Around three years emotional maturity finally arrives. It is not unusual for ABs that start protection training at one-year old to show little progress for two years, then turn three or even four and blossom into great sport protection dogs.

ABA Champion Mikie received a perfect 100 in the protection phase of his Schutzhund I.

The moral of the story is not to push your Bulldog in the protection sport arena until he is ready. Often it is best to wait until the dog is three before doing any protection work beyond simple rag games. The first couple years are best spent honing obedience skills. If you intend to do protection training, your early obedience training should employ motivational methods with no corrections or light corrections. A final word on protection sport and personal protection training. Don't do it. If you don't intend to breed your dog, don't do it. Protection sport will not really make any dog a better watchdog. Guarding the ones he loves will either come naturally to any dog or not and sport training will not change this instinct substantially. But protection training without a huge foundation of obedience and a total time commitment from the handler plus a decoy experienced with ABs can ruin what would have otherwise been a fine family guardian. The vast majority of AB owners should train their ABs only in obedience or other non-violent canine sports. Weight pull, agility, endurance and obedience competitions are better avenues for sport training than protection sports or hog hunting for most AB enthusiasts.

A final word on breeding: a physical idiosyncrasy unique to our breed is a great deal of sexual dimorphism. When the male and female of a species look and act differently the species is considered to be highly dimorphic. A male lion is distinguishable at a glance from a lioness. Lions and lionesses act differently as well. This feline species is highly dimorphic. Male and female cheetahs are nearly identical. Cheetahs fall on the opposite end of the spectrum for this trait.

American Bulldogs are sexually dimorphic. Litters that produce males with a Johnson phenotype and females with a performance phenotype are increasingly common. This trait is especially prevalent in the multi-line mixtures or Hybrids. The tradition of using a Johnson type sire and a Scott type dam may be the cause of this evolution. If the trend continues puppy buyers may be able to predict the final appearance of a Hybrid pup based on gender.

Though male ABs may look quite different from females there is little difference in temperament. There is a general belief among protection trainers that males are, on average, harder and tougher. Some people believe that males are easier to put BSTs on. Certainly the majority of BSTs go to males. The actual reason for this is that male American Bulldogs almost always look more impressive than females. It is more fun and cool to train a blocky 100-pound male then his slender 75-pound sister. Consequently, there is a shortage of titled females. This is why the very best breeders such as Tom Riche are now putting time and energy into females.

Bulldogs are natural protectors of women.

Bane and Michelle share Christmas.

Nutrition and Conditioning

Many of the diseases and defects commonly thought to be genetic in today's dogs are actually caused by inferior nutrition. Cheap brands of dog food deliver 50% or more of their protein through vegetable sources, principally grains and soybeans. This is because most commercial dog food manufacturers consider the dog an omnivore. Not only are all dog breeds carnivorous, the Bull breeds are especially dependent on meat since they have for centuries coexisted alongside butchers and farmers that have tended to feed raw meat and raw bones to their four-legged partners. Bulldogs need hefty quantities of raw meat and raw bones as an integral part of their diets.

Besides relying on vegetable protein, cheap commercial dog food is loaded with chemical preservatives and stool hardeners such as beet pulp, builder's clay (sodium bentonite) and wood pulp (cellulose flour). If commercial dog foods were of an acceptable quality they wouldn't produce loose stools and need these chemical hardeners.

Reading the ingredient lists of cheap dog foods can be a real eye opener. Most contain highly processed grain products such as wheat gluten and corn gluten. Your dog does not need to eat glue. A common ingredient is chicken meal, which can be a code word for feathers and beaks. By law the first ingredient listed is suppose to be the most common. When some form of meat is listed first, the shopper is given false hope. Notice how four or five different grain products are typically listed next? Corn gluten, wheat gluten, rice flour, wheat flour, etc...etc... If these grains were all lumped together as a single ingredient it would be apparent that there is much more grain than meat in the common brands of dog food.

Another problem with commercial feed is that certain vital minerals may be present in the mixture but these key nutrients are not in a form readily absorbed into the dog's digestive system. The two most vital minerals are calcium and phosphorous. To metabolize calcium into healthy bone a dog needs both minerals in ratios of 1.2 parts calcium to 1 part phosphorous. Not only do the cheap commercial feeds have ratios of up to 1.8 parts calcium to 1 part phosphorous,

the calcium is usually in the form of bone meal (which is easy to digest) and the phosphorous comes in the form of soybean meal (which is hard to digest). Too much calcium and not enough phosphorous may cause brittle bones and other skeletal problems.

In times past, Bulldogs would eat whatever their masters ate, plus generous helpings of raw meat and bones.

Ask any vet how to feed a large breed puppy and he will tell you to start the pup on adult dog food and keep him as lean as possible. In other words, do whatever you can to get him to grow as slowly as possible so his bones do not get overloaded with calcium and grow faster than the soft tissue, which will distort the bone's shape and cause dysplasia. Veterinarians are trying to compensate for the crummy feed they assume their clients are using, feeds that make the bones grow fast but have inadequate meat protein for soft tissue development.

The fundamental problem with all kibble type dog foods is that whatever miniscule amount of meat they may contain is baked. The normal process actually involves baking the kibble twice, at extremely high temperatures. The industrial blast furnaces they call ovens destroy vital amino acids. Bulldogs need to eat raw meat and raw bones daily to get the right kind of protein and the right balance of calcium and phosphorous.

Watch that raw chicken. Mmm, tasty

There are commercial dog foods that feature freeze-dried raw meat and are preserved with vitamin E. These brands cost more but are more nutrient dense so a dog eats less. Couple this with improved health and lower vet bills and the freeze-dried meat type dog foods are not more expensive in the long run. The downside of these high quality brands is that they are not carried at local pet stores and have to be shipped on special carriers.

My solution to this dilemma is to feed my Bulldogs with the highest quality kibble that I can find at our local pet store and supplement with raw chicken. I feed my dogs 50% naturally preserved kibble and 50% whole raw chicken parts. It is no great chore to buy frozen chicken necks, legs or wings at a very reasonable price and store them in the freezer. I set my chicken parts out in the morning to thaw, feed a kibble breakfast and then a chicken dinner. Other people feed raw chicken to their Bulldogs in frozen form.

Some people believe that it is possible for a dog to get salmonella, a bacteria found on raw chicken. In my research I have not come across anything that says that it is impossible for a dog to contract this disease. On the other hand, I have never heard of a dog actually contracting salmonella poisoning. A dog's stomach acids are something like ten times stronger than a human's. Even the enzymes in a dog's saliva are stronger than human stomach acid. There may be rare dogs that have weak stomach acid. In this instance perhaps it would be prudent to scrub the raw chicken with an antibacterial soap and rinse before feeding. I don't do this with my dogs or know anyone who does but recommend it to strangers who may have unusual dogs with unusual digestive systems.

If you choose to feed a high quality commercial kibble and supplement with raw meat you may use turkey, chicken or beef. If your raw meat supplement does not include small, easy to crunch, raw bones you should also add a dollop of yogurt or cottage cheese to keep the calcium and phosphorous ratio in correct balance. You should not feed your dog cooked bones. When feeding table scraps remember that only meat and vegetables will do a dog any good.

Watch that hand!

The next most important nutrition topic is canine obesity. The vast majority of ABs are overweight. There are many reasons for this. Johnson breeders have fostered a culture where the heavier the dog the better and are constantly bragging about girth and massiveness. Another reason is that Bulldogs can have insanely high food drives and are constantly begging for treats. Feed a Bulldog a huge meal and he will inhale it, look up at his master and beg for more. The natural tendency is to open up the feed bag and pour out a second helping. Most Bulldog owners can't stand to see a look of hunger in their pet's expression. All carnivores are meant to be hungry, virtually all the time. Hunger is a natural condition for a Bulldog. Hunger does not damage a canine's psyche or hurt him in any way. Hunger is a Bulldog's friend. As a responsible owner you must steel yourself to accept hunger as a part of your pet's personality. Your AB will always be hungry if he is healthy. If he is full or being a fussy eater, you are probably doing something wrong, namely over feeding. You should be able to count ribs on the dog's flank as he stands in a relaxed state. You should be able to differentiate one muscle from another at a glance. Obviously, it is possible (though exceedingly rare) for a Bulldog to be too lean. Your Bulldog is underweight if you can, at a glance, count every rib and vertebrae plus clearly see the outline of the hipbones.

Darryl Johnson's Jenny, BST, OFA Good, and in perfect shape for competition.

Just as important as nutrition is conditioning. Even if your Bulldog's diet is the highest quality, he will never be healthy unless he gets enough exercise. Farm dogs that have nearly limitless room to roam and the luxury of chasing rabbits and squirrels every day will keep in good enough condition to maintain natural health and vigor without any human help. Dogs in the cities or suburbs need to go on daily walks of at least one mile.

If you have a reasonably sized backyard you can install a hangtime rope with a tug toy and your Bulldog will leap, grab and swing on this toy every day and to some degree exercise himself. Hangtime ropes are usually connected to a sturdy tree branch roughly eight-feet off the ground. Garage door springs are connected to two lengths of rope. One length is secured to the tree branch; the other is fastened to a very stout tug toy or a tightly sewn rolled burlap rag. Make sure enough rope separates the tug toy and the springs so that your dog can not bite the steel springs. The tug toy should be low enough that your Bulldog can reach it with an easy jump. You should start hang time training with the tug toy low enough that he can reach it without his

back feet leaving the ground. Raise it higher gradually over a period of weeks, never raise it too high.

Hammer keeps fit through hangtime.

Hangtime training can interfere with protection training, especially if you verbally out your dog off the hanging tug toy. If you don't intend to protection train your dog (which most people shouldn't) you may use this conditioning device with impunity. One word of caution - different parts of the country have tried to make any conditioning tool that Pit Bull fighters have ever employed illegal, such as treadmills and hangtime ropes, so check local ordinances before constructing this handy gadget.

Conditioning your Bulldog for the show ring, the many working/sport titles or an Irondog triathlon is a different matter than conditioning merely for health. The first rule of hardcore conditioning is to warm-up your dog before strenuous activities. My ABs are trained to tug against their collars or harnesses when I take them for a walk. We walk two-miles every day. As we walk they tug forward and I resist. Therefore, we both get a resistance workout. Bulldogs will naturally walk this way on leash, tugging to go forward. They must usually be trained to pull lightly if a non-strenuous walk is desired. I do the opposite by encouraging them to pull harder than they normally would by carrying a handful of pebbles and tossing them into bushes directly in front of our path when their tugging weakens. It is important that you have a rock solid stay command to stop them from tugging when you are out on city streets. This is important for avoiding traffic when crossing the street and to keep them from chasing squirrels and cats.

Dave Putnam is tugged two miles daily.

A tug walk is an excellent way to warm a dog up or as a means of conditioning in and of itself. If tugging is used for a warm-up you should go a half-mile, stop and do your primary conditioning. Most of the protection sport activities and some Irondog events involve sprinting, so I grab a bag of food after a short tug walk and do a series of long distance recalls. I put the dog in a down-stay, walk a hundred yards away and give a recall command, rewarding him with food after he's sitting in front of me. I may do five or six recall sprints. After the sprints we observe the next rule of conditioning, the cool-down. This means we go on a second, longer, tug walk. Throughout any conditioning regimen I always have plenty of water handy for the dogs to drink. This is very generalized conditioning. Specific canine sports require specific training. This book has already explored the drag pulling and cart work necessary for successful weight pulling. Hog hunting requires marathon-like endurance and resistance to over heating. The most common method to build wind and a tolerance for heat is long distance running with the handler on a bicycle and the dog trotting alongside. Most hog hunters don't do this because they build endurance for hog hunting by performing that

activity. They simply hunt with their dogs at least three or more times a week. If someone were to hunt only once every week or less he would need to do roadwork with his dog or work him out on a treadmill.

For endurance, roadwork is essential.

Protection training is usually done twice a week. This is not often enough to establish good condition so additional exercise is a must. Progress will come much faster in bite work if your dog is in fantastic shape and doesn't have to overcome exhaustion on top of everything else you're throwing at him. For protection sport conditioning your dog should do sprints and long distance roadwork. He should take it easy on the day of his bite training so he has plenty of drive. Before the bites he should get at least a short warm-up, usually a longish tug walk to the bite field from your car is sufficient.

It is amazing how protection handlers disregard their own physical fitness and focus solely on the dog's condition. When doing sleeve work ABs often need to carry the sleeve longer and further than other guardian breeds. It can be helpful if the dog's handler is running quickly and tirelessly at his side so he can carry and grip with reckless confidence. Human fitness is even more important in hog hunting where exhausted hunters can get so winded they can't throw a hog or get down a steep river bank, endangering man and dog alike. This is why I recommend doing roadwork with your dog rather than relying on a treadmill machine.

In an earlier chapter I recounted how I injured Bully by over conditioning and not allowing her muscles enough time to recover. A handler must be in tune with his dog and learn not to push that hard. All dog training and conditioning works best when gradual steps are taken. Endurance, strength or speed must be built gradually.

An Irondog practicing agility

Other than a CD III level hog hunt, the greatest challenge in conditioning a working American Bulldog is preparing for an Irondog triathlon. This sport has been evolving and growing in importance until it rivals the BST and other working titles in importance to hardcore Bulldoggers. There is no governing body like WABA dictating what constitutes an official Irondog competition, yet there is a great deal of conformity and standardization from one triathlon to another because these things are organized between working Bulldog clubs.

The club hosting the competition usually chooses three of these five events:

1) Hardest hitting dog - Also called Freight Train. The competing ABs are given long bites (Schutzhund courage tests) on a sleeve, driven a few yards and the decoy slips the sleeve. The decoy decides which dog hit the hardest and that dog wins.

2) Sprint race - This is like the race I described between Brody and Belle, except the dogs run one at a time and a second handler is allowed to hold them at the start line.

3) Drag pull race - Like the sprint race except the dogs wear weight pull harnesses and drag weighted sleds. This event is supposed to neutralize the smaller dog's innate advantage of speed.

4) Agility - The dogs race against the clock through an obstacle course that contains hurtles, portable fabric tunnels, teeter-totters and so on.

5) Tug of war - This is the one mandatory event that a hosting club must include if their triathlon is to be taken seriously. Tug of war is an ABA sanctioned sport. If a Bulldog wins three sanctioned tug of wars he is awarded a tug champion title and given a lot of respect. Two dogs compete in any one tug by pulling against bite rags that are snapped to a fifty-foot rope. A wooden barrier separates the dogs and a hole is drilled in this barrier for the rope to slip through. The barrier prevents dogs from seeing each other, letting go of their rags and trying to fight. There are also handlers holding loose lines on the dogs to insure that this doesn't happen.

Riche's Brindle winning her first tug of war. In this sport the leash may be taut only to prevent the dog from wrapping around the barrier and then only for a few seconds.

The three Irondog events are held one after another so there is little opportunity for a dog to rest in between. The most grueling event is the tug of war. There may be up to six or more dogs entered in a given weight class so a round robin elimination system is employed. This means your dog may have to compete in two or thee tugs in any one Irondog. Each individual tug of war can last several minutes if both dogs are somewhat experienced. During the tug, dogs are straining with all their might, tearing at the earth and pulling backwards or being drug forward. The tug battles see-saw back and forth with dogs dragging and being dragged. The desire to give up is intense but a dog's natural gameness urges him to hold on and dig in. The mental and physical exhaustion is intense.

Now imagine how exhausting it must be after surviving two or three grueling tug of wars to be immediately asked to perform a full-scale courage test. Then comes an agility race or one of the other two forms of race. The mental strain is greater for the dog than the physical. The only way to mentally condition for an Irondog triathlon is to stage one yourself and put your dog through this experience several times before the competition. Obviously, you will need other Bulldogs, other handlers and all the gear necessary to host the three events. Unless you want to start your own working Bulldog club from scratch this means you should probably join one of the clubs already in existence.

Riche's Brindle was the winner of the Redwood Irondog Triathlon, June 13, 1999. She didn't just win, she dominated, scoring first or second in every event. If Tom Riche is the Man, then Brindle is the Dog.

Irondog triathlons are designed to test a dog's strength, speed, endurance and courage with as little training as possible. The idea is to see how good the dog is, not how good the handler is at training. The long bite does not require an out or guarding because these are the hardest and most time consuming parts of protection sport training. Any good Bulldog will bang into the sleeve and get a good grip with a few months worth of work. The race is a timed recall but a second handler may hold the dog to enforce a stay. Any good dog with no training will run to his master. Also, any good dog will automatically start tugging on the end of a rope against another dog if proper steps are taken to avoid a fight.

Don't get me wrong, plenty of training and conditioning will be necessary to get your Bulldog through an Irondog, but quite a bit less than the training needed to pass the BST. To actually win an Irondog the level of training is probably comparable to a BST. The level of conditioning needed to win an Irondog, however, is much more than the level needed to pass the BST. The BST is mentally taxing for a dog but only moderately taxing physically. Most of the ABs competing in this sport have BST titles. As of June 1999, the reigning Irondog champion is Tom Riche's Brindle.

So whether you want to win an Irondog, earn a BST or just have a healthy Bulldog it is essential that you have some form of conditioning regimen as well as feed a high quality diet.

Good luck and good Bulldogging.

Work Cited

Historical Documents:

Page 32 - From the letters of R.G. Carter, "Buffalo vs. Bulldog," 1887
Page 33 - Pioneer Women: Voices from the Kansas Frontier, Copyright by Joanna L. Stratton, Simmon & Schuster, 1981
Page 34 - When the Wildwood was in Flower, G. Smith Stanton, J.S. Oglilivie Publishing Company, 1910

Photograph Contributors:

Omar Van Mueller, Lemuel Miller, David Leavitt, Deb Keller, Alan Sloan, Michelle LeNoir, Dr. David Jackson, Gary Fuller, Jose Lopez, Dave Putnam, Al Joye, Al Banuelos, David Thompson, Alan Scott, Kevin Gibson, Mark Oathout, John Blackwell, Mitch Allison, Kyle Symmes, Martha Putnam, Peter Grimm, Mile Harlow, Kevin and Linda White, W. Freely, Tim Phaneuf, Greg Karasek, Matt Green, Mark and Lisa Landers, Darren Owens, Jeff Dailey, A.J. Baldwin, Matt Boyd, Don Matthews, Christina Hinkel, Bob Toye, Mark Griffin, Chris Wells, Tammy Souza, Rachel Hanson, Fred Dutton, J.W. Choi, Peter and Linda Valentino, Dr. Louis De Naples, Dave and Tanja Sanders, Steve Vissuddhidham, Steve Clark, Eva Kadane, Darrin Jones, Rayburn Stover, Neal Albert, Pat McAteer, Denise Bruhn

Historical Images:

Page 9 - Bullbaiting 1 by H. Alken
Page 9 - Bullbaiting 2 by H. Alken
Page 15 - Bearbaiting by H. Alken
Page 17 - Bhotean by Major W. Dougall, 1904
Page 17 - Rosa and Crib by A. Copper, 1817
Page 21 - Belcher by Monday, 1818
Page 29 - Photo of Champion Guido by F.H. Ellis
Page 37 - Photo of Fortune's Frolic by Tom F. Mackness, 1897
Page 37 - Photo of L'Ambassador by C.G. Hopton, Photo of Fortune's Frolic by Tom F. Mackness
Page 38 - Danzig Bear Biter by Johann Elias Riedinger
Page 38 - Drawing the Badger by H. Alken